Quick

THE
DICTIONARY
OF
BIBLE PLACES

THE
DICTIONARY
OF
BIBLE PLACES

PAMELA McQUADE

BARBOUR
PUBLISHING

ISBN 978-1-60260-846-7

Published by Barbour Publishing, Inc., P.O. Box 719, Uhrichsville, Ohio 44683, www.barbourbooks.com

Our mission is to publish and distribute inspirational products offering exceptional value and biblical encouragement to the masses.

 Member of the
Evangelical Christian
Publishers Association

Printed in the United States of America.

The *Dictionary of Bible Places* is designed to help students of the Word understand the places mentioned in scripture, covering everything from cities to landmarks. Most of the places have a definition of what that name meant. Names were very important to the people of these ages, and they often named places to reflect incidents that took place there. Where no meaning of a name is listed, it is unknown or of foreign derivation.

Spellings and names are those used in the King James Version of the Bible, since this work is based on *Strong's Expanded, Exhaustive Concordance of the Bible*. Since many readers use other Bible versions, I have sometimes given alternative translations (for example, the Wilderness of Zin may be referred to as the Desert of Zin).

To assist readers in understanding the geography of the areas referred to in scripture, eight maps have been included begining on page 248. Many places, especially in the Old Testament and where a name is only mentioned once, cannot be accurately identified. On some maps, a question mark indicates that scholars are not certain this is the correct site.

Because the scriptures deal with many people, places, and nations, I have provided a time line that can help readers sort out the differences of empires, rulers, and times. The dates are often approximate, since accurate dating at such a distance and in various cultures is difficult. Scholars often disagree on exact dates for many of these events; and a few dates, such as those of the ministries of the prophets Obadiah and Joel, remain inconclusive. I am deeply indebted to Stephen M. Miller's *The Complete Guide to the Bible* for the lists of the kings of Israel and Judah and the prophets.

Not all the ancient empires and their kings are included, only those that impacted the Jewish people. This span of the empires is provided so that readers can understand the powerful influences that were working throughout the Middle East at the time the scriptures were being written. Keep in mind that under some less powerful rulers, the Mesopotamian empires had little contact with the Jews, while their most powerful kings sought to invade Israel and Judah.

The Babylonian Empire that preceded Assyria's rise to power did not impact Israel as did the Babylonian Empire that followed Assyria's rule. The Greeks called this second Babylonian Empire the Chaldean Empire. Sometimes scripture calls them the Babylonians, but at other times they are the Chaldeans. To be certain readers do not confuse the two empires, throughout the text I have usually referred to this as the Neo-Babylonian (Chaldean) Empire.

My focus in writing has been to give readers an understanding of both the geography of each place and the biblical events that occurred in each place. May this work bring understanding concerning where the Bible events occurred and what happened there.

TIME LINES

2100–1500 B.C.	Age of the patriarchs (Middle Bronze Age)
c. 1950 B.C.	The Amorites conquer Mesopotamia
1500–1200 B.C.	The Exodus and the Promised Land conquest (Late Bronze Age)
c. 1469–c. 1211 B.C.	Possible dates for the Exodus
1200–900 B.C.	Establishment of Israel (Early Iron Age)
c. 1050 B.C.	The Philistines settle in southern Palestine

ANCIENT EMPIRES

Assyrian Empire 1100–609 B.C.

859–824 B.C.	Reign of King Shalmaneser III
855–625 B.C.	Assyrian influence on Palestine
783–773 B.C.	Reign of King Shalmaneser IV
744–727 B.C.	Reign of King Tiglath-pileser III
c. 732–612 B.C.	Israel and Judah subject to Assyria
727–722 B.C.	Fall of Israel to Assyria; Samaria destroyed
722 B.C.	Reign of King Shalmaneser V
705–681 B.C.	Reign of King Sennacherib
612 B.C.	Fall of Nineveh to Neo-Babylonian (Chaldean) Empire
609 B.C.	Chaldeans defeat Assyria

Neo-Babylonian (Chaldean) Empire 605–538 B.C.

c. 626 B.C.	Start of Neo-Babylonian (Chaldean) Empire
586 B.C.	Fall of Jerusalem to the Chaldeans; temple destroyed
539 B.C.	Fall of Neo-Babylonian Empire

Persian Empire 538–331 B.C.

538 B.C.	Cyrus conquers Babylon (Chaldea) and establishes Persian Empire
522–485 B.C.	Reign of King Darius I
486–465 B.C.	Reign of King Ahasuerus (Xerxes) of Persia
c. 479 B.C.	Esther made queen of Persia
465–423 B.C.	Reign of King Artaxerxes I of Persia
333 B.C.	End of Persian control of Palestine
331 B.C.	End of Persian Empire

Macedonian Empire 336–168 B.C.

336–323 B.C.	Rule of Alexander the Great
333 B.C.	Alexander the Great gains control of Palestine
331 B.C.	Alexander the Great conquers Persian Empire

Seleucid rule 312–83 B.C.

175–163 B.C.	Rule of Syrian king Antiochus IV (Epiphanes)

Roman Empire 27 B.C.–A.D. 476

63 B.C.	Roman Empire takes control of Judaea
37–4 B.C	Reign of Herod the Great, king of Judaea

ISRAEL/JUDAH
Prophets

770–750 B.C.	Ministry of the prophet Jonah in Assyria
763–750 B.C.	Ministry of the prophet Amos in Israel
750–722 B.C.	Ministry of the prophet Hosea in Israel
742–687 B.C.	Ministry of the prophet Micah in Judah
740–700 B.C.	Ministry of the prophet Isaiah in Judah
640–621 B.C.	Ministry of the prophet Zephaniah in Judah
627–586 B.C.	Ministry of the prophet Jeremiah in Judah
612–588 B.C.	Ministry of the prophet Habakkuk in Judah
c. 605–536 B.C.	Ministry of the prophet Daniel in Babylon
593–571 B.C.	Ministry of the prophet Ezekiel in Babylon
c. 586 B.C.	Book of Obadiah written to Judah
520 B.C.	Book of Haggai written to Judah
520–518 B.C.	Ministry of the prophet Zechariah in Judah
440–430 B.C.	Ministry of the prophet Malachi in Judah

United Israel

1050–1010 B.C.	Reign of King Saul of Israel
1023 B.C.	Samuel anoints David king of Israel
1010–970 B.C.	Reign of King David of Israel
970–930 B.C.	Reign of King Solomon of Israel
c. 966–959 B.C.	King Solomon builds the temple

Divided Israel

930 B.C.	Start of Divided Kingdom (separate states of Israel and Judah)

Judah

930–913 B.C.	Reign of King Rehoboam
913–910 B.C.	Reign of King Abijam
910–872 B.C.	Reign of King Asa
872–853 B.C.	Reign of King Jehoshaphat
853–841 B.C.	Reign of King Jehoram
841 B.C.	Reign of King Ahaziah
841–835 B.C.	Reign of Queen Athaliah
835–796 B.C.	Reign of King Joash
796–792 B.C.	Reign of King Amaziah
792–750 B.C.	Reign of King Azariah (Uzziah)
750–735 B.C.	Reign of King Jotham
735–715 B.C.	Reign of King Ahaz
715–697 B.C.	Reign of King Hezekiah
697–642 B.C.	Reign of King Manasseh
642–640 B.C.	Reign of King Amon
640–609 B.C.	Reign of King Josiah
609 B.C.	Reign of King Jehoahaz
609–598 B.C.	Reign of King Jehoiakim
598–597 B.C.	Reign of King Jehoiachin
597–586 B.C.	Reign of King Zedekiah

Northern Israel

930–909 B.C.	Reign of King Jeroboam I
909–908 B.C.	Reign of King Nadab
908–886 B.C.	Reign of King Baasha
886–885 B.C.	Reign of King Elah
885–874 B.C.	Reign of King Omri

874–853 B.C.	Reign of King Ahab
853–852 B.C.	Reign of King Ahaziah
852–841 B.C.	Reign of King Joram (Jehoram)
841–814 B.C.	Reign of King Jehu
814–798 B.C.	Reign of King Jehoahaz
798–793 B.C.	Reign of King Jehoash
793–753 B.C.	Reign of King Jeroboam II
753–752 B.C.	Reign of King Zechariah
752 B.C.	Reign of King Shallum
752–742 B.C.	Reign of King Menahem
742–740 B.C.	Reign of King Pekahiah
740–732 B.C.	Reign of King Pekah
732–722 B.C.	Reign of King Hoshea
586 B.C.	Babylonian Empire conquers Judah and destroys Jerusalem and Solomon's temple
538 B.C.	The first exiles return to Jerusalem
c. 516 B.C.	Second temple completed
457 B.C.	Ezra returns to Judah with more exiles
c. 445 B.C.	Nehemiah leads Jews back to Jerusalem
432 B.C.	Nehemiah's second visit to Jerusalem
152–37 B.C.	Rule of the Maccabees

NEW TESTAMENT

c. 6 B.C.	Birth of Jesus
4 B.C.–A.D. 6	Rule of Herod Archelaus, ethnarch of Judaea, Samaria, and Idumea
4 B.C.–A.D. 39	Rule of Herod Antipas, tetrarch of Galilee and Perea
4 B.C.–A.D. 34	Rule of Herod Philip, tetrarch of Iturea and Trachonitis
A.D. 26	Jesus' public ministry begins
A.D. 30	Jesus' death and resurrection
A.D. 47–49	Paul's first missionary journey
A.D. 49	Roman emperor Claudius expels Jews from Rome; church holds Council of Jerusalem
A.D. 50–52	Paul's second missionary journey
c. A.D. 52–56	Paul's third missionary journey

A.D. 59	Paul's first Roman imprisonment begins
A.D. 67–68	Paul's final imprisonment and death in Rome
A.D. 70	Herod's temple destroyed

-A-

ABANA — OT1
Stony

A river of Damascus that the Syrian commander Naaman would have preferred to the Jordan River as a place to wash away his leprosy.

ONLY REFERENCE
2 KINGS 5:12

ABARIM — OT4
Regions beyond

On their way to conquer the Holy Land, Moses and the Israelites pitched their tents in this mountain range east of the Jordan River. From Mount Nebo, which was part of the Abarim range, God allowed Moses a view of the Holy Land just before he died.

FIRST REFERENCE
NUMBERS 27:12
LAST REFERENCE
DEUTERONOMY 32:49

ABDON — OT2
Servitude

One of the forty-eight cities given to the Levites as God had commanded. Abdon was given to them by the tribe of Asher.

FIRST REFERENCE
JOSHUA 21:30
LAST REFERENCE
I CHRONICLES 6:74

ABEL — OT4

1) A stone in Joshua the Beth-shemite's field. After the Philistines stole the ark of the covenant and returned it to Israel on a cart pulled by two milk cows, the ark was set here. When God struck down seventy men for looking upon the ark, the people of Beth-shemesh asked the people of Kirjath-jearim to take it to their city.

ONLY REFERENCE
I SAMUEL 6:18

2) A city in the land of the tribe of Naphtali that David's battle commander Joab besieged in order to capture the rebel Sheba, who had risen up against David's rule.

FIRST REFERENCE
2 SAMUEL 20:14
LAST REFERENCE
2 SAMUEL 20:18

ABEL-BETH-MAACHAH — OT2
Meadow of Beth-maachah

One of three cities in Naphtali that was attacked by the Syrian prince Ben-hadad, at the instigation of King Asa of Judah. During the reign of Pekah, king of Israel, Abel-beth-maachah was conquered by the Assyrian king Tiglath-pileser III, who took its people into captivity in Assyria. Same as Abel-maim.

FIRST REFERENCE
I KINGS 15:20
LAST REFERENCE
2 KINGS 15:29

ABEL-MAIM OT1
Meadow of water

A city in northern Israel that was attacked by the Syrian prince Ben-hadad, at the instigation of King Asa of Judah. Same as Abel-beth-maachah.

ONLY REFERENCE
2 CHRONICLES 16:4

ABEL-MEHOLAH OT3
Meadow of dancing

A city in the Jordan Valley. When Gideon's army routed them, the Midianites fled to Abel-meholah's border. Under King Solomon's governmental organization, Baana was the officer in charge of providing the king with provisions from this place. The prophet Elisha came from Abel-meholah.

FIRST REFERENCE
JUDGES 7:22
LAST REFERENCE
1 KINGS 19:16

ABEL-MIZRAIM OT1
Meadow of Egypt

Joseph brought the body of his father, Jacob, to Abel-mizraim and buried him at this "threshing floor of Atad," east of the Jordan River. When the Canaanites saw Egyptians mourning there, they gave the place this name. Same as Atad.

ONLY REFERENCE
GENESIS 50:11

ABEL-SHITTIM OT1
Meadow of acacias

A spot in the plains of Moab where the Israelites camped before entering the Promised Land.

ONLY REFERENCE
NUMBERS 33:49

ABEZ OT1
To gleam; conspicuous

A city that became part of the inheritance of Issachar when Joshua cast lots in Shiloh to provide territory for the seven tribes that had yet to receive their land.

ONLY REFERENCE
JOSHUA 19:20

ABILENE NT1
Grassy meadow

A Palestinian territory north of Damascus, which was ruled by the tetrarch Lysanias during Tiberius Caesar's reign.

ONLY REFERENCE
LUKE 3:1

ACCAD OT1
A fortress

A city of Shinar that was part of the kingdom of Nimrod.

ONLY REFERENCE
GENESIS 10:10

ACCHO OT1
To hem in

A Canaanite seaport that was part of the inheritance of the tribe of Asher. In the Middle Ages Accho was called Acre. Same as Ptolemais.

ONLY REFERENCE
JUDGES 1:31

ACELDAMA NT1
Field of blood

The name Jerusalem's residents gave to the field Judas bought with the money he got for betraying Jesus. In his sermon in Acts 1, Peter described the unfaithful disciple's gruesome death there: He fell headlong and "burst asunder in the midst, and all his bowels gushed out" (Acts 1:18).

ONLY REFERENCE
ACTS 1:19

ACHAIA NT11

The southern Greek province of the Roman Empire. Here the local Jews made insurrection against Paul and brought him before the proconsul Gallio for judgment. The ruler refused to hear their case and allowed the Jews to beat their synagogue ruler in front of his court.

Epaenetus and the household of Stephanas were some of the first converts in Achaia. Apollos went to Achaia with a recommendation from the Christians at Ephesus; he preached in Achaia, refuting the Jews who denied Christ. Christians of Achaia contributed to the collection of funds for the impoverished Christians in Jerusalem.

Though it bears the name of one church, Paul wrote the book of 2 Corinthians to the Achaians at large. In this epistle he comforted the suffering church of that province and encouraged them in faithfulness.

FIRST REFERENCE
ACTS 18:12
LAST REFERENCE
1 THESSALONIANS 1:8
KEY REFERENCES
ACTS 18:12–17, 27–28;
2 CORINTHIANS 1:1

ACHMETHA OT1

A city in Media. In its palace, the Persian king Darius found a record proving that, as the Jews claimed, King Cyrus had ordered Jerusalem's temple to be rebuilt.

ONLY REFERENCE
EZRA 6:2

ACHOR OT5
Troubled

A valley near Jericho where justice was meted out to the looter Achan, who had disobeyed God's command to destroy everything in Jericho. From the city he had taken a beautiful Babylonian robe, two hundred shekels of silver, and a fifty-shekel-weight wedge of gold. Knowing he was doing wrong, he buried them under his tent.

God had warned that anyone who disobeyed would trouble the camp. The trouble began when the Israelites lost a battle at Ai. Joshua inquired of God what had gone wrong, and the Lord commanded that the people sanctify themselves. Once they had done this, each tribe, then each family in that tribe, was brought before God. Achan was identified as the wrongdoer and stoned in the valley, which was named directly after this incident.

Isaiah prophesied that God would renew Achor, making it "a place for the herds to lie down in, for my people that have sought me" (Isaiah 65:10). Looking ahead, Hosea declared it would be a "door of hope" (Hosea 2:15).

FIRST REFERENCE
JOSHUA 7:24
LAST REFERENCE
HOSEA 2:15

ACHSHAPH OT3
Fascination

A Phoenician city whose king joined Jabin, king of Hazor, and other Canaanite rulers in attacking Joshua and the Israelites after they entered the Promised Land. Later, Achshaph was designated as a border landmark of the land given to the tribe of Asher when Joshua cast lots in Shiloh to provide territory for the seven tribes that had yet to receive an inheritance.

FIRST REFERENCE
JOSHUA 11:1
LAST REFERENCE
JOSHUA 19:25

ACHZIB OT4
Deceitful

1) A city that became part of the inheritance of the tribe of Judah following the conquest of the Promised Land. Micah's prophecy played on the meaning of its name when he predicted that Achzib would be "a lie to the kings of Israel."

FIRST REFERENCE
JOSHUA 15:44
LAST REFERENCE
MICAH 1:14

2) A coastal city that became part of Asher's inheritance when Joshua cast lots in Shiloh to provide territory for the seven tribes that had yet to receive their land. The tribe of Asher did not drive the Canaanites out of Achzib as God had commanded them to do.

FIRST REFERENCE
JOSHUA 19:29
LAST REFERENCE
JUDGES 1:31

ADADAH OT1
Festival

A southern city that became part of the inheritance of the tribe of Judah following the conquest of the Promised Land.

ONLY REFERENCE
JOSHUA 15:22

ADAM OT1
Ruddy

When Joshua led the Israelites across the Jordan River, the river's water rose up in a heap by this city east of the river.

ONLY REFERENCE
JOSHUA 3:16

ADAMAH OT1
Soil (probably red in color)

A fortified or walled city that became part of the inheritance of Naphtali when Joshua cast lots in Shiloh to provide territory for the seven tribes that had yet to receive their land.

ONLY REFERENCE
JOSHUA 19:36

ADAMI OT1
Earthy

A city that became part of the inheritance of Naphtali when Joshua cast lots in Shiloh to provide territory for the seven tribes that had yet to receive their land.

ONLY REFERENCE
JOSHUA 19:33

ADAR OT1
Ample

A city that became part of the inheritance of the tribe of Judah following the conquest of the Promised Land.

ONLY REFERENCE
JOSHUA 15:3

ADDAN OT1
Firm

A Babylonian city where some Jews lived during the Babylonian Exile. At the end of the exile, these people could not prove they were Israelites. Same as Addon.

ONLY REFERENCE
EZRA 2:59

ADDON OT1
Powerful

A Babylonian city where some Jews lived during the Babylonian Exile. At the end of the exile, these people could not prove they were Israelites. Same as Addan.

ONLY REFERENCE
NEHEMIAH 7:61

ADITHAIM OT1
Double prey

A city that became part of the inheritance of the tribe of Judah following the conquest of the Promised Land.

ONLY REFERENCE
JOSHUA 15:36

ADMAH OT5
Earthy

One of five Canaanite "cities of the plain" at the southern end of the Dead Sea. Admah's king, Shinab, took part in a war coalition with Sodom and Gomorrah and the other cities of the plain against Chedorlaomer, king of

Elam, and his Mesopotamian allies. After serving Chedorlaomer for twelve years, the Canaanites rebelled against him. Following their battle against Elam's king and his allies, Abram's nephew, Lot, was captured in Sodom, and Abram had to rescue him. When Sodom and Gomorrah were destroyed by God, Admah also was ruined.

FIRST REFERENCE
GENESIS 10:19
LAST REFERENCE
HOSEA 11:8

ADORAIM OT1
Double mound

A city that King Rehoboam built for Judah's defense.

ONLY REFERENCE
2 CHRONICLES 11:9

ADRAMYTTIUM NT1

An Asian seaport northeast of the island of Lesbos. This was a home port of the ship Paul sailed on when he headed for Rome.

ONLY REFERENCE
ACTS 27:2

ADRIA NT1

Another name for the Adriatic Sea, which lies west of Greece. Before Paul and his companion Luke suffered shipwreck, the Gospel writer records that they were "driven up and down in Adria" by the wind.

ONLY REFERENCE
ACTS 27:27

ADULLAM OT8

1) A city that became part of the inheritance of the tribe of Judah. King Rehoboam fortified Adullam for Judah's defense. It was one of the cities resettled following the Jews' return from the Babylonian exile.

FIRST REFERENCE
JOSHUA 12:15
LAST REFERENCE
MICAH 1:15

2) A cave near the city of Adullam. Here David's family met him after he fled from King Saul. David gathered four hundred discontented men at Adullam and became their captain.

FIRST REFERENCE
1 SAMUEL 22:1
LAST REFERENCE
1 CHRONICLES 11:15

ADUMMIM OT2
Red spots

A pass between Jericho and Jerusalem that formed part of the border of the tribe of Judah's territory. Jesus probably had it in mind as the setting for the parable of the Good Samaritan.

FIRST REFERENCE
JOSHUA 15:7
LAST REFERENCE
JOSHUA 18:17

AENON NT1
Place of springs

A spot near Salim where there was "much water." Here John the Baptist baptized believers shortly before he was imprisoned.

ONLY REFERENCE
JOHN 3:23

AHAVA OT3

Beside this Babylonian river Ezra gathered his people for three days while he sent a messenger to Iddo, the chief of Casiphia, to get some Levites to accompany them to Jerusalem. After they had gathered the Levites, Ezra proclaimed a fast and made preparations for the journey.

FIRST REFERENCE
EZRA 8:15
LAST REFERENCE
EZRA 8:31

AHLAB OT1
Fatness

A city inherited by the tribe of Asher. These Jews did not drive out the Canaanites who lived in Ahlab, as God had commanded.

ONLY REFERENCE
JUDGES 1:31

AHOLAH OT5
Her tent (signifying idolatry)

A name God uses for Samaria in a parable Ezekiel tells about both Israel's and Judah's unholiness.

FIRST REFERENCE
EZEKIEL 23:4
LAST REFERENCE
EZEKIEL 23:44

AHOLIBAH OT6
My tent is in her

A name God uses for Jerusalem and Judah in a parable Ezekiel tells about both Israel's and Samaria's unholiness.

FIRST REFERENCE
EZEKIEL 23:4
LAST REFERENCE
EZEKIEL 23:44

AI OT36

A city east of Bethel that Joshua's spies reported did not have many inhabitants. Joshua sent three thousand men to conquer the city, but his soldiers fled before its warriors. When Joshua prayed about the defeat, God told him Israel had sinned. Once Joshua identified the sinner, Achan, and had him stoned, God commanded the Israelites to again attack the city, which He would give into their hands.

Joshua set a trap for Ai, drawing the people out of the city. Then a smaller unit of soldiers ambushed Ai, took it, and set it on fire. Israel killed all the city's inhabitants and hanged the king. When they heard of the destruction of Ai and the other cities the Israelites had taken, five Amorite kings attacked Gibeon, which had made peace with Israel.

At the time of the captivity, Jews from Ai and its vicinity were transported to Babylon. Same as Aiath, Aija, and Hai.

FIRST REFERENCE
JOSHUA 7:2
LAST REFERENCE
JEREMIAH 49:3
KEY REFERENCES
JOSHUA 7:4–5; 8:1, 16–29

AIATH   OT1

Another form of the name Ai, used by Isaiah in his description of God's removal of the yoke of Assyria from His people. Same as Ai.

ONLY REFERENCE
ISAIAH 10:28

AIJA   OT1

Another form of the name Ai, used by Nehemiah in his description of the Benjaminite resettlement there following the Babylonian exile. Same as Ai.

ONLY REFERENCE
NEHEMIAH 11:31

AIJALON   OT7
Deer field

1) One of the forty-eight cities given to the Levites as God had commanded. Aijalon was given to them by the tribe of Dan. Later Aijalon was taken over by the Amorites.

FIRST REFERENCE
JOSHUA 21:24
LAST REFERENCE
JUDGES 1:35

2) A city belonging to the tribe of Zebulun. Here Elon the Zebulonite, a judge of Israel, was buried.

ONLY REFERENCE
JUDGES 12:12

3) A Benjaminite city whose Israelite inhabitants displaced the people of Gath. During one of Saul's battles with the Philistines, it became part of the battle area. King Rehoboam fortified the city for Judah's defense.

FIRST REFERENCE
I SAMUEL 14:31
LAST REFERENCE
2 CHRONICLES 11:10

4) One of the six cities of refuge established in Israel for those who had committed accidental murder. Aijalon was given to the Levites by the tribe of Judah.

ONLY REFERENCE
I CHRONICLES 6:69

AIN   OT5
Fountain

1) A place that God used to identify the borders of Israel when He first gave the land to His people. Ain lay on the northeast border of Israel, somewhere between Riblah and the Sea of Chinnereth.

ONLY REFERENCE
NUMBERS 34:11

2) A city originally allotted to the tribe of Judah as part of its inheritance following the conquest of the

Promised Land. It became part of the inheritance of Simeon when Joshua cast lots in Shiloh to provide territory for the seven tribes that had yet to receive their land. Later Ain became one of the six Levitical cities of refuge for accidental murderers.

FIRST REFERENCE
JOSHUA 15:32
LAST REFERENCE
I CHRONICLES 4:32

AJALON   OT3
Deer field

1) A valley in which Joshua asked God to make the moon remain still while the Israelites avenged themselves on the Amorites. For a whole day, the sun remained in the heavens so the Israelites could finish their battle. "And there was no day like that before it or after it, that the LORD hearkened unto the voice of a man: for the LORD fought for Israel" (Joshua 10:14).

ONLY REFERENCE
JOSHUA 10:12

2) A city that became part of the inheritance of Dan when Joshua cast lots in Shiloh to provide territory for the seven tribes that had yet to receive their land.

ONLY REFERENCE
JOSHUA 19:42

3) During the reign of King Ahaz, Ajalon was one of the cities of the southern low country of Judah that was invaded and occupied by the Philistines.

ONLY REFERENCE
2 CHRONICLES 28:18

AKRABBIM   OT2
Scorpion or scourge

A hill that God used to identify the southern borders of Israel when he first gave it to His people. In the time of the judges, it was a border with the Amorites.

FIRST REFERENCE
NUMBERS 34:4
LAST REFERENCE
JUDGES 1:36

ALAMMELECH   OT1
Oak of the king

A city that became part of the inheritance of Asher when Joshua cast lots in Shiloh to provide territory for the seven tribes that had yet to receive their land.

ONLY REFERENCE
JOSHUA 19:26

ALEMETH   OT1
A covering

One of the forty-eight cities given to the Levites as God had commanded. Alemeth was given to them by the tribe of Benjamin.

ONLY REFERENCE
I CHRONICLES 6:60

ALEXANDRIA   NT3

This Egyptian city on the western edge of the Nile Delta was the birthplace of the preacher Apollos.

He came to Ephesus and was taught the complete gospel message by Priscilla and Aquila. When Paul sailed to Rome, he did so in two ships that identified Alexandria as their home port.

FIRST REFERENCE
ACTS 18:24
LAST REFERENCE
ACTS 28:11

ALLON OT1

A city that became part of the inheritance of Naphtali when Joshua cast lots in Shiloh to provide territory for the seven tribes that had yet to receive their land.

ONLY REFERENCE
JOSHUA 19:33

ALLON-BACHUTH OT1
Oak of weeping

The place where Deborah, Rebekah's nurse, was buried.

ONLY REFERENCE
GENESIS 35:8

ALMON OT1
Hidden

One of the forty-eight cities given to the Levites as God had commanded. Almon was given to them by the tribe of Benjamin.

ONLY REFERENCE
JOSHUA 21:18

ALMON-DIBLATHAIM OT2
Almon toward Diblathaim

A place where the Israelites camped on their way to the Promised Land.

FIRST REFERENCE
NUMBERS 33:46
LAST REFERENCE
NUMBERS 33:47

ALOTH OT1
Mistresses

Under King Solomon's governmental organization, a region responsible for supplying provisions for the king.

ONLY REFERENCE
1 KINGS 4:16

ALUSH OT2

A place on the Exodus route where the Israelites camped after they left Egypt.

FIRST REFERENCE
NUMBERS 33:13
LAST REFERENCE
NUMBERS 33:14

AMAD OT1
People of time

A city that became part of the inheritance of Asher when Joshua cast lots in Shiloh to provide territory for the seven tribes that had yet to receive their land.

ONLY REFERENCE
JOSHUA 19:26

AMAM　　　OT1
Gathering spot

A city that became part of the inheritance of the tribe of Judah following the conquest of the Promised Land. It lay between Hazor and Shema.

ONLY REFERENCE
JOSHUA 15:26

AMANA　　　OT1
Something fixed (like a covenant or allowance)

A mountain of Lebanon that may have been near the source of the Abana River. Solomon uses it poetically in his wooing of the Shulammite.

ONLY REFERENCE
SONG OF SOLOMON 4:8

AMMAH　　　OT1
A unit of measure

A hill to which David's commander Joab and Joab's brother Abishai pursued Abner, the commander of Saul's army, after Abner killed their brother. The Benjaminites supported Abner, and Joab backed down.

ONLY REFERENCE
2 SAMUEL 2:24

AMMON　　　OT91
Tribal (meaning inbred)

The land of the people of Ben-Ammi, who was the son of Lot born of his incest with his younger daughter. When Israel invaded the Promised Land, God told His people they would not be given the land of Ammon, which was northeast of the Dead Sea, for it belonged to Lot's children. But Israel did take some land that had once belonged to the Ammonites and had subsequently been conquered by the Amorites.

The Ammonites did not follow the ways of the Lord and varied between rising up against Israel and paying homage to Israel's greater power. The Israelite captain Jephthah first led the people of Gilead in battle against Ammon and subdued it.

An attack of the Ammonites caused Israel to fear and beg Samuel for a king. Saul proved his leadership abilities when King Nahash of Ammon besieged Jabesh-gilead and would not make peace with that city. Saul rallied the people of Israel and Judah against Ammon and led them to victory in battle. King David had a peaceful relationship with Nahash of Ammon, but Nahash's son Hanun offended David's friendly overtures. Aware of his offense and David's contempt for him, King Hanun renewed warfare with Israel, hiring Syrian warriors to fight alongside his own troops. Together Joab and David defeated the joined armies, and David dedicated the silver and gold he captured from that nation to God.

In the spring, Joab besieged Ammon's capital, Rabbah, but David stayed behind in Jerusalem and became involved with Bathsheba. Bathsheba's husband, Uriah, died in battle against Rabbah.

But these victories did not end warfare between the countries. The Ammonites attacked Judah during King Jehoshaphat's reign. King Jotham fought and prevailed against Ammon, which paid tribute to him. Later, Ammon joined Judah's king Jehoiakim in his rebellion against the Babylonian king Nebuchadnezzar.

Nehemiah took the Jews to task for intermarrying with the Ammonites, for their children could not even speak Hebrew. The last mention of Ammon in scripture is in Zephaniah, where the prophet foretells the nation's destruction.

FIRST REFERENCE
GENESIS 19:38
LAST REFERENCE
ZEPHANIAH 2:9
KEY REFERENCES
DEUTERONOMY 2:19; JUDGES 11:32–33;
I SAMUEL 12:12; 2 CHRONICLES 27:5

AMPHIPOLIS NT1
A city surrounded by a river

A northeastern Macedonian city that Paul and Silas passed through on their way to Thessalonica.

ONLY REFERENCE
ACTS 17:1

ANAB OT2
Fruit

A Canaanite city in what became part of Judah's hill country following the conquest of the Promised Land. Joshua conquered Anab and its inhabitants, the Anakim.

FIRST REFERENCE
JOSHUA 11:21
LAST REFERENCE
JOSHUA 15:50

ANAHARATH OT1
A gorge

A city that became part of the inheritance of Issachar when Joshua cast lots in Shiloh to provide territory for the seven tribes that had yet to receive their land.

ONLY REFERENCE
JOSHUA 19:19

ANANIAH OT1
God has covered

A Benjaminite city resettled by the Jews after the Babylonian exile.

ONLY REFERENCE
NEHEMIAH 11:32

ANATHOTH OT14
Answers

One of the forty-eight cities given to the Levites as God had commanded. Anathoth was given to them by the tribe of Benjamin. King Solomon banished Abiathar the priest to Anathoth after he supported Adonijah as heir to David's throne. Jeremiah was a priest of Anathoth, but men of that city sought his life, and God promised to punish them for their wickedness. When Babylon besieged Jerusalem, as a sign of hope for the future, God commanded Jeremiah to buy his cousin's field in his hometown of Anathoth. When Nebuchadnezzar captured Judah, 128 men from Anathoth were carried off to Babylon. Following the exile, the Benjaminites resettled the city.

FIRST REFERENCE
JOSHUA 21:18
LAST REFERENCE
JEREMIAH 32:9
KEY REFERENCES
1 KINGS 2:26; JEREMIAH 11:21–23; 32:7–9

ANEM   OT1

Two fountains

One of the forty-eight cities given to the Levites as God had commanded. Anem was given to them by the tribe of Issachar.

ONLY REFERENCE
1 CHRONICLES 6:73

ANER   OT1

One of the forty-eight cities given to the Levites as God had commanded. Aner was given to them by the tribe of Manasseh.

ONLY REFERENCE
1 CHRONICLES 6:70

ANIM   OT1

Fountains

A city that became part of the inheritance of the tribe of Judah following the conquest of the Promised Land.

ONLY REFERENCE
JOSHUA 15:50

ANTIOCH   NT19

1) The capital of Syria, where Stephen preached to the Jews. Cypriot Jews who had heard the message had shared it with Greeks. The church in Jerusalem sent Barnabas to Antioch when they heard that Gentiles were hearing the Word. Barnabas went to Tarsus to get Saul's assistance in his mission. They joined Stephen in Antioch. In this city, believers first received the name Christians.

Paul and Barnabas received their missionary calling in Antioch. Later in this city, Paul confronted Peter with his refusal to eat with Gentiles. Following the Council of Jerusalem, Paul, Barnabas, Judas Barsabas, and Silas returned to Antioch to declare the council's decision about circumcision, the law, and Gentiles.

FIRST REFERENCE
ACTS 6:5
LAST REFERENCE
GALATIANS 2:11
KEY REFERENCES
ACTS 11:19, 26; 13:1; GALATIANS 2:11

2) Called Antioch in Pisidia, this city in the Roman province of Phrygia, in Asia Minor, received the Good News through Paul's ministry. Angered, some Jews of the city stoned Paul, who returned to the city then left the next day.

FIRST REFERENCE
ACTS 13:14
LAST REFERENCE
2 TIMOTHY 3:11

ANTIPATRIS NT1

A city between Caesarea and Lydda. Here Claudius Lysias's soldiers protected Paul after the Jews of Jerusalem threatened his life.

ONLY REFERENCE
ACTS 23:31

APHEK OT8
Fortress (implying strength)

1) A Canaanite city in which the Philistines camped before the battle in which they captured the ark of the covenant. The Philistines again gathered here under King Achish to fight King Saul. But Achish's troops refused to fight as long as David and his warriors were on their side, because David had been their enemy when he served Saul.

FIRST REFERENCE
JOSHUA 12:18
LAST REFERENCE
1 SAMUEL 29:1

2) A city that had not yet fully fallen under Israel's sway when Joshua was old. It became part of the inheritance of Asher when Joshua cast lots in Shiloh to provide territory for the seven tribes that had yet to receive their land. Same as Aphik.

FIRST REFERENCE
JOSHUA 13:4
LAST REFERENCE
JOSHUA 19:30

3) A city where King Ahab of Israel and King Ben-hadad of Syria fought. Israel routed its enemies and captured the king.

FIRST REFERENCE
1 KINGS 20:26
LAST REFERENCE
2 KINGS 13:17

APHEKAH OT1
Fortress

A city that became part of the inheritance of the tribe of Judah following the conquest of the Promised Land.

ONLY REFERENCE
JOSHUA 15:53

APHIK OT1
Fortress (implying strength)

A city that became part of the inheritance of the tribe of Asher. The tribe of Asher did not drive the Canaanites out of Aphik as God had commanded them to do. Same as Aphek 2.

ONLY REFERENCE
JUDGES 1:31

APHRAH OT1

A Philistine city cited by the prophet Micah as rolling in the dust in mourning at the judgment of the Lord.

ONLY REFERENCE
MICAH 1:10

APOLLONIA NT1
Named for the Greek god Apollo

A Macedonian city that Paul and his companions passed through on their way to Thessalonica.

ONLY REFERENCE
ACTS 17:1

APPII NT1
Appius (Appii is its possessive case)

A town outside of Rome. Here some Roman Christians met Paul as he headed toward that city.

ONLY REFERENCE
ACTS 28:15

AR OT6

A city of Moab that God gave to Lot's heirs. God would not let the Israelites fight Ar when they returned to the wilderness following their refusal to enter the Promised Land. The prophet Isaiah foretold that Ar would be destroyed.

FIRST REFERENCE
NUMBERS 21:15
LAST REFERENCE
ISAIAH 15:1

ARAB OT1
Ambush

A city that became part of the inheritance of the tribe of Judah following the conquest of the Promised Land.

ONLY REFERENCE
JOSHUA 15:52

ARABAH OT1
A desert (in the sense of sterility)

Another name for the Jordan Valley, in which the Jordan River lies. It was part of the inheritance of the tribe of Benjamin.

ONLY REFERENCE
JOSHUA 18:18

ARABIA OT6/NT2
Sterile

A large peninsula in southwest Asia where many nomadic people lived. The children of Abraham and Keturah largely settled the northern part of Arabia, while Ishmael's descendants settled the northwestern part of the peninsula. Ishmaelites bought Joseph from his brothers (Genesis 37:25). The kings of Arabia brought gold and silver to King Solomon. Ophir, which traded gold, almug trees, and precious stones with King Solomon, may have been in Arabia. Jeremiah prophesied God's judgment of Arabia, along with many other peoples. Ezekiel described Arabia as selling "lambs, and rams, and goats" to Tyre (Ezekiel 27:21).

Following his conversion, Paul visited Arabia. He described it as the site of Mount Sinai and compared Arabia to Hagar ["Agar" in the KJV].

FIRST REFERENCE
1 KINGS 10:15
LAST REFERENCE
GALATIANS 4:25

ARAD · OT2

Fugitive

A Canaanite kingdom west of the Jordan River. King Arad fought the Israelites when they came to the Promised Land. He captured some Israelites, and so the nation vowed to destroy the king's cities. Joshua and his army conquered Arad. The descendants of Moses' father-in-law, Jethro, moved into the "wilderness of Judah, which lieth in the south of Arad" (Judges 1:16).

FIRST REFERENCE
JOSHUA 12:14
LAST REFERENCE
JUDGES 1:16

ARAM · OT2

The highland

1) An early name for Syria, used during the time of Balaam. Aram covered more territory than modern Syria, extending to the Euphrates River. Balaam came from Aram to curse Israel. See also Syria.

ONLY REFERENCE
NUMBERS 23:7

2) A city taken by Jair, a descendant of Judah.

ONLY REFERENCE
1 CHRONICLES 2:23

ARAM-NAHARAIM · OT1

Aram of the two rivers

A name for northwest Mesopotamia. King David fought this nation and Aram-zobah.

ONLY REFERENCE
TITLE OF PSALM 60

ARAM-ZOBAH · OT1

Aram of Tsoba

A name for central Syria. King David fought this nation, killing twenty-two thousand men (2 Samuel 8:5).

ONLY REFERENCE
TITLE OF PSALM 60

ARARAT · OT2

A name for the Assyrian province of Uratu. Noah's ark rested on its mountains when the flood subsided. Jeremiah foretold that this nation would rise up against Babylon. See also Armenia.

FIRST REFERENCE
GENESIS 8:4
LAST REFERENCE
JEREMIAH 51:27

ARBAH · OT1

Another name for Hebron. Abraham and Isaac lived here, and Jacob visited his father in Arbah.

ONLY REFERENCE
GENESIS 35:27

ARCHI · OT1

Part of the inheritance of Joseph's descendants through his son Ephraim.

ONLY REFERENCE
JOSHUA 16:2

AREOPAGUS NT1
Rock of Ares (a Greek god)

At this hill Athens's original court and council had met. In Paul's day the council was in charge of religious matters in the city. The philosophers of the city, who had been debating with him, brought Paul to a meeting of the council and asked him about his teaching. The apostle took the opportunity to speak to them about Christ, and a few people came to the Lord as a result of his message. Others mocked his message of the resurrection of the dead. Same as Mars' Hill.

ONLY REFERENCE
ACTS 17:19

ARGOB OT4
Stony

A region of Og that the Israelites conquered after they turned back from entering the Promised Land. This territory became part of the inheritance of the tribe of Manasseh. Jair, Manasseh's son, named it Bashan-havoth-jair.

FIRST REFERENCE
DEUTERONOMY 3:4
LAST REFERENCE
1 KINGS 4:13

ARIEL OT4
Lion of God; heroic

A name Isaiah used to describe the city of Jerusalem. He foresaw sorrow in the city, as it would be besieged by enemies. But when the Lord returns, it "shall be as a dream of a night vision."

FIRST REFERENCE
ISAIAH 29:1
LAST REFERENCE
ISAIAH 29:7

ARIMATHAEA NT4

Home of Joseph, a rich man and member of the ruling Jewish council called the Sanhedrin. Secretly Jesus' disciple, Joseph claimed the body of Jesus after His death and placed it in his own tomb.

FIRST REFERENCE
MATTHEW 27:57
LAST REFERENCE
JOHN 19:38

ARMAGEDDON NT1

A symbolic name for the place of the last great battle on earth, fought between the Antichrist and Jesus, as revealed to the apostle John in the Revelation.

ONLY REFERENCE
REVELATION 16:16

ARMENIA OT2

A name translated "Ararat" in some Bible versions. This country between the Caspian Sea and the Black Sea included the province of Ararat. Here two sons of the Assyrian king Sennacherib fled after they murdered their father. See also Ararat.

FIRST REFERENCE
2 KINGS 19:37
LAST REFERENCE
ISAIAH 37:38

ARNON OT25
A brawling stream

A river that formed the boundary between the lands of the Amorites and the Moabites. The territory was taken by the Israelites under Moses' leadership. Reuben's tribe inherited the land near the city of Aroer, on the bank of the Arnon.

The Ammonites asked Israel's captain Jephthah to return their land, but he refused. See also Aroer 2.

FIRST REFERENCE
NUMBERS 21:13
LAST REFERENCE
JEREMIAH 48:20
KEY REFERENCES
DEUTERONOMY 3:8; JOSHUA 13:16

AROER OT16
Nudity

1) A city built by the tribe of Gad. Joab and his captains camped here when they went to number the Israelites for King David. Isaiah foretold that Aroer would be forsaken and only flocks would live there.

FIRST REFERENCE
NUMBERS 32:34
LAST REFERENCE
ISAIAH 17:2

2) An Amorite city near the Arnon River that was the capital city under King Sihon. Following Israel's conquest of the Promised Land, Aroer became part of the Reubenite inheritance. This city was part of the land the Ammonites asked Israel's captain Jephthah to return to them. He refused and fought them at Aroer instead. King Hazael of Syria conquered this city during the rule of King Jehu of Israel.

FIRST REFERENCE
DEUTERONOMY 2:36
LAST REFERENCE
JEREMIAH 48:19

3) A city of Judah to which David sent some of the spoils from his warfare with the Amalekites.

ONLY REFERENCE
I SAMUEL 30:28

ARPAD OT4
Spread out

A Syrian city, always mentioned with Hamath, that was conquered by Assyria. To intimidate Judah, Sennacherib's messengers to Jerusalem used it as an example of a city that could not stand before their king's might. Isaiah referred to Arpad and Hamath as he spoke of God's punishment of Assyria. Jeremiah also spoke of Syria's destruction. Same as Arphad.

FIRST REFERENCE
2 KINGS 18:34
LAST REFERENCE
JEREMIAH 49:23

ARPHAD OT2
Spread out

A name that Isaiah used for a Syrian city conquered by King Sennacherib. The Assyrian ruler's messengers used

Arphad as an example of a city that could not stand before their king's might. Same as Arpad.

FIRST REFERENCE
ISAIAH 36:19
LAST REFERENCE
ISAIAH 37:13

ARUBOTH OT1
Lattices, windows, dove cots, chimneys, or sluices

Under King Solomon's governmental organization, a district responsible for supplying provisions for the king.

ONLY REFERENCE
1 KINGS 4:10

ARUMAH OT1
Height

Hometown of Abimelech, Gideon's son by his concubine.

ONLY REFERENCE
JUDGES 9:41

ARVAD OT2
A refuge for the roving

An island off the coast of Phoenicia, north of Sidon. Its mariners rowed and piloted Tyre's ships, and its warriors manned Tyre's walls.

FIRST REFERENCE
EZEKIEL 27:8
LAST REFERENCE
EZEKIEL 27:11

ASHAN OT4
Smoke; vapor; dust; anger

A city that became part of the inheritance of the tribe of Judah following the conquest of the Promised Land. Later it became a Levitical city. When Joshua further divided the land, it became part of the land given to the tribe of Simeon.

FIRST REFERENCE
JOSHUA 15:42
LAST REFERENCE
1 CHRONICLES 6:59

ASHCHENAZ OT1

A kingdom, along with Ararat and Minni, in Armenia. The prophet Jeremiah spoke of these nations being called into battle against Babylon during God's judgment of the Chaldeans.

ONLY REFERENCE
JEREMIAH 51:27

ASHDOD OT21
Ravager

One of the few cities in which the Anakims were left after the Israelites conquered the Promised Land. Though it theoretically became part of the inheritance of the tribe of Judah, that tribe never conquered it. Instead Ashdod became one of the five most important Philistine cities. When the Philistines captured the ark of the covenant, they brought it to Ashdod. The people of the city suffered under God's judgment for taking the ark, so they asked that it be removed to Gath.

Judah's king Uzziah broke down Ashdod's walls and built cities around it. Nehemiah confronted the Jews who had married the people of this pagan city. During Isaiah's ministry, Ashdod was taken by the Assyrians. Various prophets speak of the punishment God meted out to Ashdod.

FIRST REFERENCE
JOSHUA 11:22
LAST REFERENCE
ZECHARIAH 9:6
KEY REFERENCES
I SAMUEL 5:1–7; NEHEMIAH 13:23–24

ASHDOTH-PISGAH   OT3
Ravines of the Pisgah (elsewhere translated "the slopes of Pisgah")

Mount Pisgah's eastern slope, which belonged to the Amorite king Sihon until Israel conquered the Promised Land. The land became part of the inheritance of the tribe of Reuben.

FIRST REFERENCE
DEUTERONOMY 3:17
LAST REFERENCE
JOSHUA 13:20

ASHER   OT4
Happy

Under King Solomon's governmental organization, a district responsible for supplying provisions for the king.

FIRST REFERENCE
JOSHUA 17:7
LAST REFERENCE
I KINGS 4:16

ASHKELON   OT9
Weighing place

An ancient city north of Gaza, Ashkelon was one of five major Philistine cities. Here Samson killed thirty men after his wife gave them the solution to a riddle he had posed to them. The prophets condemned this pagan city. Jeremiah spoke of its punishment by God; Amos prophesied the destruction of its ruler; and Zephaniah and Zechariah foretold that Ashkelon would be desolated. Same as Askelon.

FIRST REFERENCE
JUDGES 14:19
LAST REFERENCE
ZECHARIAH 9:5

ASHNAH   OT2

1) A city that became part of the inheritance of the tribe of Judah following the conquest of the Promised Land.

ONLY REFERENCE
JOSHUA 15:33

2) Another city that became part of the inheritance of the tribe of Judah following the conquest of the Promised Land.

ONLY REFERENCE
JOSHUA 15:43

ASHTAROTH   OT5
Name of a Sidonian god

1) A city of Bashan on the eastern shore of the Jordan River. King Og

reigned in Ashtaroth, and the book of Joshua reports that giants lived there. Manasseh's son Machir inherited the city. Same as Astaroth.

FIRST REFERENCE
JOSHUA 9:10
LAST REFERENCE
JOSHUA 13:31

2) One of the forty-eight cities given to the Levites as God had commanded. Ashtaroth was given to them by the tribe of Manasseh.

ONLY REFERENCE
1 CHRONICLES 6:71

ASHTEROTH KARNAIM OT1
Ashteroth of the double horns

A city of the Rephaims that was attacked by King Chedorlaomer of Elam.

ONLY REFERENCE
GENESIS 14:5

ASIA NT21

A Roman province in the western part of the peninsula of Asia Minor, whose capital was Ephesus. For a time, the Holy Spirit prohibited Paul from preaching in Asia, but Paul came to Ephesus on his second missionary journey and remained there two years, spreading the Gospel to the whole province. When Demetrius the silversmith started a riot over Paul's preaching, the apostle moved on to Macedonia.

Though the apostle left, Asia was not forgotten. Paul lamented to Timothy, "All they which are in Asia be turned away from me" (2 Timothy 1:15). Peter wrote his first epistle in part to the believers of Asia, and John addressed his Revelation to "the seven churches which are in Asia" (Revelation 1:4): Ephesus, Smyrna, Pergamos, Thyatira, Sardis, Philadelphia, and Laodicea.

FIRST REFERENCE
ACTS 2:9
LAST REFERENCE
REVELATION 1:11
KEY REFERENCES
ACTS 16:6–8; 19:10, 22, 26, 27, 31; 1 PETER 1:1

ASKELON OT3
Weighing place

The book of Judges reports that Judah conquered Askelon, taking it from the Canaanites, but the tribe did not maintain control of the city, which later became an important Philistine city. After the Philistines captured the ark of the covenant, it caused trouble in whatever city it was sent to. So the Philistines returned the troublesome object to Israel, along with a guilt offering of five golden tumors ("emerods") and five golden mice, one for each of the major cities of that nation, including Askelon.

When David lamented Saul and Jonathan's deaths, he warned that the news of their demise should not be published in Askelon, because its people would rejoice. Same as Ashkelon.

FIRST REFERENCE
JUDGES 1:18
LAST REFERENCE
2 SAMUEL 1:20

ASSHUR — OT5

To be straight (in the sense of being successful)

Another term for Assyria, Asshur was named for the grandson of Noah, who built the Assyrian cities of Nineveh, Rehoboth, and Calah. Balaam prophesied that Asshur would carry away the Kenites but be afflicted by ships from the coast of Chittim. Ezekiel spoke of Asshur as merchants for Tyre ("Tyrus" in the KJV) and used it as an example of a fallen nation, testified to only by graves. The prophet Hosea pointed out the inability of this nation to save Israel. Same as Assur. See also Assyria.

FIRST REFERENCE
NUMBERS 24:22
LAST REFERENCE
HOSEA 14:3

ASSOS — NT2

A port city in Asia Minor. Paul's companions met him here after they left Troas. Paul traveled on foot from Troas to Assos, while his companions went by ship.

FIRST REFERENCE
ACTS 20:13
LAST REFERENCE
ACTS 20:14

ASSUR — OT2

To be straight (in the sense of being successful)

Another name for Assyria. When Israel's enemies wanted to help rebuild Jerusalem's temple, they claimed they had sacrificed to the Lord since the time of Esar-haddon, king of Assur. Psalm 83 speaks of Assur as an enemy joined with the children of Lot. Same as Asshur.

FIRST REFERENCE
EZRA 4:2
LAST REFERENCE
PSALM 83:8

ASSYRIA — OT118

To be straight (in the sense of being successful)

An empire that spread from its original nation in the upper plain of Mesopotamia to incorporate a wide arc of land that swept from Egypt north through Syria and Palestine to eastern Asia Minor, and east to Babylonia and the Persian Gulf.

For a thousand talents of silver, King Pul (Tiglath-pileser III) of Assyria supported Israel's wicked king Menahem's claim to the throne. During the reign of King Pekah of Israel, Tiglath-pileser attacked the nation and transported captives back to his homeland.

Shalmaneser, king of Assyria, attacked Hoshea, king of Israel, who became his vassal and gave him gifts, but when Shalmaneser discovered Israel's king had conspired against him with Egypt, he besieged Hoshea's land for three years. Assyria conquered the nation, and Israel's people went into captivity. Then Assyria's king repopulated the land with pagan peoples and commanded that a priest teach these new Samaritans about the Lord.

King Ahaz of Judah called on the Assyrian king Tiglath-pileser to save him from Syria, at the price of the silver and gold in the Lord's house and his own palace. Though Tiglath-pileser did not attack Judah, neither did he provide Ahaz with the help Judah's king had hoped for. Ahaz's successor, King Hezekiah of Judah, rebelled against the Assyrians, and in the fourteenth year of his reign, Sennacherib took the fortified cities of Judah. Hezekiah submitted and paid tribute to rid his land of the Assyrians, and the temple gold and silver were given to Assyria.

Sennacherib sent messengers to Judah to undermine Hezekiah and encourage his nation's warriors to fight for Assyria. When the warriors of Judah refused, the messengers threatened them with conquest. Through the prophet Isaiah, God described Assyria as "the rod of mine anger, and the staff in their hand is mine indignation" (Isaiah 10:5), and Assyria brought God's punishment to a hypocritical nation. But the prophet also foretold the fall of Sennacherib (Isaiah 37:21–29) and Assyria (2 Kings 19:20–28). God promised the faithful Hezekiah that Assyria would not enter Jerusalem (Isaiah 37:33). In the night, the angel of the Lord killed 185,000 Assyrian soldiers in their camp. Those who were not killed arose to find the bodies around them. Sennacherib left Judah and returned to his capital at Nineveh, where he was killed by two of his sons (Isaiah 37:36–38).

During the reign of Hezekiah's son, Manasseh, Assyria again attacked Judah, captured the king, and carried him to Babylon, along with many of his people. When Manasseh humbled himself before God, he was returned to his position in Jerusalem.

Through Isaiah, God promised that Assyria would be punished and a remnant of Judah would return to the Lord (Isaiah 10:12, 21). Hosea repeatedly uses Assyria as an example of unfaithfulness. Micah uses this nation's name as a symbol for Israel's enemies. Even out of Assyria, Zechariah prophesies, God will gather His people in the time of the latter rain. See also Asshur and Assur.

FIRST REFERENCE
GENESIS 2:14
LAST REFERENCE
ZECHARIAH 10:11
KEY REFERENCES
2 KINGS 15:29; 18:13–14; 19:36;
2 CHRONICLES 33:11; ISAIAH 37:37

ASTAROTH   OT1
Name of a Sidonian god

A city of Bashan where King Og lived. Same as Ashtaroth 1.

ONLY REFERENCE
DEUTERONOMY 1:4

ATAD   OT2
To pierce or to make fast

A threshing floor beyond the Jordan River where Joseph and his family mourned the death of Jacob. Same as Abel-mizraim.

FIRST REFERENCE
GENESIS 50:10
LAST REFERENCE
GENESIS 50:11

ATAROTH   OT5
Crowns

1) A city with good lands for cattle that the tribe of Gad requested Moses to give them as they came to the Promised Land.

FIRST REFERENCE
NUMBERS 32:3
LAST REFERENCE
NUMBERS 32:34

2) A city that was part of the inheritance of Ephraim after Israel conquered the Promised Land.

FIRST REFERENCE
JOSHUA 16:2
LAST REFERENCE
JOSHUA 16:7

3) A place in Judah where the family of Joab lived.

ONLY REFERENCE
I CHRONICLES 2:54

ATAROTH-ADAR
OT1
Crowns of Addar

A city on the border of the territory of the tribes of Benjamin and Ephraim. Same as Ataroth-addar.

ONLY REFERENCE
JOSHUA 18:13

ATAROTH-ADDAR   OT1
Crowns of Addar

A city on the border of the territory of the tribes of Benjamin and Ephraim. Same as Ataroth-adar.

ONLY REFERENCE
JOSHUA 16:5

ATHACH   OT1
To sojourn; lodging

A city of Judah to which David sent some of the spoils from his warfare with the Amalekites.

ONLY REFERENCE
I SAMUEL 30:30

ATHENS   NT7
Named after the Greek goddess Athena

An influential Greek city on the peninsula of Attica, Athens was famed for its culture and philosophy. Paul traveled there from Berea, after the Jews of Thessalonica had stirred up trouble for him. Distressed by Athens's idolatry, which he would have seen at every turn at the Acropolis, which held many temples, the apostle preached the Gospel in the synagogue. Then at the invitation of the Athenian philosophers, who had disputed with him about the message he had been preaching in the marketplace, he spoke at Mars' Hill (the Areopagus) to those philosophers and the members of the council of the Areopagus, who were responsible for the religious life of the city. Paul pointed out their altar to an unknown god and sought to tell them about the God they did not know. A few Athenians came to faith in Christ.

FIRST REFERENCE
ACTS 17:15
LAST REFERENCE
I THESSALONIANS 3:1

ATROTH OT1
Crowns

A fortified city built up by the children of Gad, who kept their flocks there.

ONLY REFERENCE
NUMBERS 32:35

ATTALIA NT1

A city of Pamphylia, on the southern coast of Asia Minor, that Paul visited on his first missionary journey, between his visits to Perga and Antioch.

ONLY REFERENCE
ACTS 14:25

AVA OT1

A city in the Assyrian Empire from which King Shalmaneser repopulated Judah after he took the Jews captive and carried them to Babylon.

ONLY REFERENCE
2 KINGS 17:24

AVEN OT3
Idolatry

1) A name for the Egyptian city of Heliopolis. The Jewish prophets foretold its destruction. Same as On.

ONLY REFERENCE
EZEKIEL 30:17

2) A shortened form of the name Beth-aven, which means "house of vanity." This name for Bethel emphasized the religious failings of the city. Same as Beth-aven.

ONLY REFERENCE
HOSEA 10:8

3) A plain (translated "valley" in some versions) in Syria, near Damascus, which was probably a pagan place of worship.

ONLY REFERENCE
AMOS 1:5

AVIM OT1

A city that became part of the inheritance of Benjamin when Joshua cast lots in Shiloh to provide territory for the seven tribes that had yet to receive their land.

ONLY REFERENCE
JOSHUA 18:23

AVITH OT2
Ruin

A city of Edom that was ruled by Hadad, son of Bedad, before Israel had any kings.

FIRST REFERENCE
GENESIS 36:35
LAST REFERENCE
I CHRONICLES 1:46

AZAL OT1
Noble

The prophet Zechariah predicted that in the day of the Lord the Mount of Olives will split, creating a great valley that will reach to this place near Jerusalem.

ONLY REFERENCE
ZECHARIAH 14:5

AZEKAH OT7
Tilled

When Joshua fought the five Amorite kings who attacked Gibeon, he fought their army up to this town. During the battle, the Lord cast down hailstones on the Amorites. Azekah became part of the inheritance of Judah. During King Saul's reign, when the Philistines attacked Israel and wanted a man to fight Goliath, they camped near Azekah. King Rehoboam fortified the city. Azekah was one of the last fortified cities to fall when the Chaldeans (Babylonians) attacked Israel. After the Babylonian exile, members of the tribe of Judah resettled here.

FIRST REFERENCE
JOSHUA 10:10
LAST REFERENCE
JEREMIAH 34:7

AZEM OT2
Bone

A city that became part of the inheritance of the tribe of Judah following the conquest of the Promised Land. It was given to Simeon when Joshua cast lots in Shiloh to provide territory for the seven tribes that had yet to receive their land.

FIRST REFERENCE
JOSHUA 15:29
LAST REFERENCE
JOSHUA 19:3

AZMAVETH OT2
Strong one of death

A city in Judah to which captives returned after the Babylonian exile.

FIRST REFERENCE
EZRA 2:24
LAST REFERENCE
NEHEMIAH 12:29

AZMON OT3
Bonelike

A spot in southern Canaan that God gave Moses as a marker of the boundary of Israel. Azmon also formed part of the border of the tribe of Judah's territory.

FIRST REFERENCE
NUMBERS 34:4
LAST REFERENCE
JOSHUA 15:4

AZNOTH-TABOR OT1
Flats (or tops) of Tabor

These hills marked the western border of the inheritance of Naphtali when Joshua cast lots in Shiloh to provide territory for the seven tribes that had yet to receive their land.

ONLY REFERENCE
JOSHUA 19:34

AZOTUS NT1
Greek form of Ashdod

To this city the apostle Philip was caught away by the Holy Spirit after he baptized the Ethiopian eunuch near the road between Jerusalem and Gaza.

ONLY REFERENCE
ACTS 8:40

AZZAH OT3
Strong

A city of the Avim tribe, it later became the Philistine city of Gaza. King Solomon had dominion over Azzah and its king.

FIRST REFERENCE
DEUTERONOMY 2:23
LAST REFERENCE
JEREMIAH 25:20

-B-

BAAL OT1
Name of a Phoenician god

A city that became part of the inheritance of the tribe of Simeon.

ONLY REFERENCE
1 CHRONICLES 4:33

BAALAH OT5
A mistress

1) A city that formed part of the border of the tribe of Judah's territory. Here the ark of the covenant rested from the time the Philistines returned it to Judah until King David brought it to Jerusalem. Same as Baale of Judah and Kirjath-jearim.

FIRST REFERENCE
JOSHUA 15:9
LAST REFERENCE
1 CHRONICLES 13:6

2) A mountain that formed part of the border of the tribe of Judah's territory.

ONLY REFERENCE
JOSHUA 15:11

BAALATH OT3
Mistresship

A border city that became part of the inheritance of Dan when Joshua cast lots in Shiloh to provide territory for the seven tribes that had yet to receive their land. King Solomon fortified Baalath.

BAALATH-BEER OT1

Mistress of a well

A city that became part of the inheritance of Simeon when Joshua cast lots in Shiloh to provide territory for the seven tribes that had yet to receive their land.

ONLY REFERENCE
JOSHUA 19:8

BAALE OF JUDAH OT1

Masters of Judah

A place where the ark of the covenant was placed after the Philistines stole it then returned it to Judah. David went there to bring the ark into Jerusalem. Same as Baalah 1, Kirjath-baal, and Kirjath-jearim.

ONLY REFERENCE
2 SAMUEL 6:2

BAAL-GAD OT3

Baal of fortune

A Canaanite city in the valley of Lebanon that was conquered by Joshua, who killed its king. When Joshua was old, the Israelites had not subdued Baal-gad.

FIRST REFERENCE
JOSHUA 11:17
LAST REFERENCE
JOSHUA 13:5

BAAL-HAMON OT1

Possessor of a multitude

A place where King Solomon owned a profitable vineyard. Its exact location is unknown.

ONLY REFERENCE
SONG OF SOLOMON 8:11

BAAL-HAZOR OT1

Possessor of a village

A place near Ephraim where King David's son Absalom had sheepshearers.

ONLY REFERENCE
2 SAMUEL 13:23

BAAL-HERMON OT2

Possessor of Hermon

A Philistine city that became part of the land of the half-tribe of Manasseh. It lay near Mount Hermon.

FIRST REFERENCE
JUDGES 3:3
LAST REFERENCE
1 CHRONICLES 5:23

BAAL-MEON OT3

Baal of the habitation

A town in the Transjordan area that the tribe of Reuben rebuilt after the conquest of the Promised Land. Though the Reubenites occupied the lane to Nebo and Baal-meon, they evidently did not hold on to it. Ezekiel spoke of it as being

Moabite in his prophecy against Moab and Seir. The prophet called Baal-meon "the glory of that land" (NIV) but spoke of its punishment by God, because Moab believed the house of Judah was just like other nations.

FIRST REFERENCE
NUMBERS 32:38
LAST REFERENCE
EZEKIEL 25:9

BAAL-PERAZIM
OT4

Possessor of breaches

A place where David attacked the Philistines after they heard that he had been anointed king over Israel. The Lord broke forth "as the breach of waters" (2 Samuel 5:20), giving David victory.

FIRST REFERENCE
2 SAMUEL 5:20
LAST REFERENCE
I CHRONICLES 14:11

BAAL-SHALISHA
OT1

Baal of Shalisha

Hometown of a man who brought Elisha bread as a firstfruits offering. Elisha gave it to the men whose deadly stew he had purified.

ONLY REFERENCE
2 KINGS 4:42

BAAL-TAMAR OT1
Possessor of the palm tree

Site of a battle between Israel and the tribe of Benjamin. After members of the tribe of Benjamin abused a Levite's concubine until she died, Israel took up arms against the tribe to punish this evil act.

ONLY REFERENCE
JUDGES 20:33

BAAL-ZEPHON
OT3

Baal of winter (in the sense of cold)

A place by the Red Sea where the Israelites camped at the beginning of the Exodus.

FIRST REFERENCE
EXODUS 14:2
LAST REFERENCE
NUMBERS 33:7

BABEL OT2
Confusion

Nimrod's kingdom, in Mesopotamia, where the Lord confused the language of the people and scattered them across the earth.

FIRST REFERENCE
GENESIS 10:10
LAST REFERENCE
GENESIS 11:9

Confusion

An ancient Mesopotamian city on the Euphrates River. Babylon's location made it an important city of trade. Genesis 10:10 describes Babel (some versions translate this "Babylon") as the start of Nimrod's kingdom. During the Old Babylonian Empire and King Hammurabi's reign, the city reached a peak it would not match until the Neo-Babylonian Empire. The Kassite Nebuchadnezzar I made it his capital. Under the Assyrians Babylon was destroyed by Sennacherib then rebuilt by Ashurbanipal.

After conquering Israel during the reign of King Hoshea, Shalmaneser V, king of Assyria, took people from this, his capital city, and moved them to the cities of Samaria to replace the Israelites his conquering army had captured and carried to Babylon. Through the Babylonian settlers, pagan worship combined with Jewish religious practices became standard in Samaria, causing New Testament–era Jews to despise the people who lived there.

When King Hezekiah of Judah showed his precious objects to the emissaries of the Assyrian king, Isaiah prophesied that all these goods and the children of Judah would be carried to Babylon. The next king of Judah, Hezekiah's son Manasseh, was captured by the Assyrians and carried to Babylon. He remained there until he humbled himself before God.

The Chaldean King Nebuchadnezzar II fulfilled Isaiah's prophecy of goods and people being carried off to Babylon when he attacked Jerusalem and captured King Jehoiachin, his people, and his valuables. Nebuchadnezzar conquered the last three kings of Judah: Jehoiakim, his son Jehoiachin, and Jehoiachin's uncle Zedekiah. He took them all to Babylon. Along with Zedekiah, the people of Judah went into exile in 586 B.C.

The Chaldean (Babylonian) Empire fell to Persia in 539 B.C. In the same year, King Cyrus of Persia declared that Jerusalem's temple should be rebuilt. From Babylon, Ezra led the first Israelites back to Judah to carry out this command.

Repeatedly, scripture speaks of the destruction of Babylon. Isaiah compares its fall to Lucifer's and castigates Babylon as an oppressor. Jeremiah predicted the fall of Zedekiah and the destruction of Jerusalem, but through him God also promised the exile would last only seventy years. Even before Jerusalem fell to Nebuchadnezzar, the prophet promised that another nation would come from the north and vanquish Babylon, destroying it completely.

The prophet Ezekiel spoke of the empire of Babylon almost as a weapon in God's hand as it fought against Tyre ("Tyrus" in the KJV) and Egypt.

When Judah fell to Nebuchadnezzar, the prophet Daniel was carried to Babylon, along with other young men from his nation. Daniel became one of Babylon's wise men and served Nebuchadnezzar and his son Belshazzar. When Darius the

Mede ("Median" in the KJV) took the throne, Daniel became a high official of the nation.

In the New Testament, Peter refers to a church at Babylon, which may be a reference to the congregation at Rome. In the book of Revelation, Babylon takes on a symbolic meaning as a fallen, sinful city. Numerous scholars have also equated this with Rome.

FIRST REFERENCE
2 KINGS 17:24
LAST REFERENCE
REVELATION 18:21
KEY REFERENCES
2 KINGS 20:17; 24:10–12; 2 CHRONICLES 36:10; REVELATION 14:8; 17:5

BACA   OT 1
Weeping

A valley poetically described by the sons of Korah as becoming a place of springs when believers go through it.

ONLY REFERENCE
PSALM 84:6

BAHURIM   OT 5
Young men

After King David insisted that his wife Michal be returned to him, Abner carried her back to Jerusalem. When they reached this village outside Jerusalem, Abner ordered Michal's grieving second husband, Paltiel, to turn back from following her. Here Shimei cursed King David as he fled from Absalom, then changed his mind and supported David with a thousand men. David's messengers, Jonathan and Ahimaaz, hid from Absalom in a well at Bahurim.

FIRST REFERENCE
2 SAMUEL 3:16
LAST REFERENCE
1 KINGS 2:8

BAJITH   OT 1
A house; family

One of Moab's "high places" where pagan worship occurred. Here Isaiah prophesied the Moabites would grieve after their nation was destroyed.

ONLY REFERENCE
ISAIAH 15:2

BALAH   OT 1
Failure

A city that became part of the inheritance of Simeon when Joshua cast lots in Shiloh to provide territory for the seven tribes that had yet to receive their land.

ONLY REFERENCE
JOSHUA 19:3

BAMAH   OT 1
High place

A high place where idols were worshipped in Israel. Through the prophet Ezekiel, God confronted the nation about its idolatry here and called them to return to Him.

ONLY REFERENCE
EZEKIEL 20:29

BAMOTH OT2
Heights

A place in Moab where the Israelites camped on their way to the Promised Land. Perhaps the same as Bamoth-baal.

FIRST REFERENCE
NUMBERS 21:19
LAST REFERENCE
NUMBERS 21:20

BAMOTH-BAAL OT1
Heights of Baal

A city east of the Jordan River that became part of the inheritance of the tribe of Reuben. Perhaps the same as Bamoth.

ONLY REFERENCE
JOSHUA 13:17

BASHAN OT59

The nation of the Amorite king Og and home of the remnant of the giants that area was famous for. Bashan lay to the east and north of the Sea of Galilee, above Gilead. Israel fought Og at Edrei and conquered Bashan. Later it became part of the inheritance of the tribe of Manasseh. Machir, Manasseh's son, a man of war, inherited Bashan. King Hazael of Syria attacked and conquered this land. The prophets speak of the oaks of Bashan, which will be subdued by the Lord.

FIRST REFERENCE
NUMBERS 21:33
LAST REFERENCE
ZECHARIAH 11:2
KEY REFERENCES
DEUTERONOMY 3:1, 13

BASHAN-HAVOTH-JAIR OT1
Bashan hamlets of Jair

A region of Og that the Israelites conquered after they refused to enter the Promised Land. Moses gave this territory to the tribe of Manasseh. Jair, Manasseh's son, inherited and named it. Same as Argob.

ONLY REFERENCE
DEUTERONOMY 3:14

BATH-RABBIM OT1
The daughter (or city) of Rabbah

A gate in Heshbon that Solomon used to describe the beauty of his beloved.

ONLY REFERENCE
SONG OF SOLOMON 7:4

BEALOTH OT1
Mistresses

A city that became part of the inheritance of the tribe of Judah following the conquest of the Promised Land.

ONLY REFERENCE
JOSHUA 15:24

BEER OT2

1) The site of a well to which God brought Moses and the Israelites when they needed water as they wandered in the wilderness. Probably the same as Beer-elim

ONLY REFERENCE
NUMBERS 21:16

2) A town Jotham fled to when his brother Abimelech became king of Shechem.

ONLY REFERENCE
JUDGES 9:21

BEER-ELIM OT1
Well of heroes

A well in Moab. Isaiah uses it to describe the grief of Moab at her destruction. Probably the same as Beer 1.

ONLY REFERENCE
ISAIAH 15:8

BEER-LAHAI-ROI OT1
Well of a Living (One), my seer

A wilderness well situated between Kadesh and Bered. The angel of the Lord met the pregnant Hagar here after she fled from Sarai, who treated her harshly after she conceived. Same as Lahai-roi.

ONLY REFERENCE
GENESIS 16:14

BEEROTH OT6
Wells

1) An Israel campsite around the time Moses received the Ten Commandments. From here God's nation traveled to Moserah.

ONLY REFERENCE
DEUTERONOMY 10:6

2) A city of the Gibeonites, who tricked Joshua into making peace with them. Beeroth became part of the inheritance of the tribe of Benjamin and was the hometown of Rechab, captain over the men of Saul's son Ish-bosheth. When Judah returned from the Babylonian captivity, Beeroth was resettled.

FIRST REFERENCE
JOSHUA 9:17
LAST REFERENCE
NEHEMIAH 7:29

BEER-SHEBA OT34
Well of an oath

A wilderness in which Hagar and Ishmael wandered after they were sent out of Abraham's camp. Beersheba was the site of a covenant between Abraham and Abimelech, king of Gerar. Subsequently Abraham planted a grove and worshipped the Lord there. After Abraham pleased God by his willingness to sacrifice his son Isaac, he lived in Beer-sheba. Here God promised to bless Abraham and renewed His covenant with Isaac.

Initially Beer-sheba was part of the inheritance of the tribe of Judah. But it became part of the inheritance of Simeon when Joshua cast lots in Shiloh to provide territory for the seven tribes that had yet to receive their land.

When scripture says "from Dan even to Beer-sheba," it indicates everything from the northernmost to the southernmost part of Israel.

FIRST REFERENCE
GENESIS 21:14
LAST REFERENCE
AMOS 8:14
KEY REFERENCES
GENESIS 21:31–33; 26:23–24; JOSHUA 19:2

BEESH-TERAH OT1
With Ashteroth

One of the forty-eight cities given to the Levites as God had commanded. Beesh-terah was given to them by the tribe of Manasseh.

ONLY REFERENCE
JOSHUA 21:27

BELA OT2
A gulp (implying destruction)

A Canaanite city of the plain that joined in the Canaanite war against King Chedorlaomer of Elam and his Mesopotamian allies. Same as Zoar.

FIRST REFERENCE
GENESIS 14:2
LAST REFERENCE
GENESIS 14:8

BENE-BERAK OT1
Sons of lightning

A city that became part of the inheritance of Dan when Joshua cast lots in Shiloh to provide territory for the seven tribes that had yet to receive their land.

ONLY REFERENCE
JOSHUA 19:45

BENE-JAAKAN OT2
Sons of Yaakan

An encampment of the Israelites during the Exodus.

FIRST REFERENCE
NUMBERS 33:31
LAST REFERENCE
NUMBERS 33:32

BENJAMIN OT3
Son of the right hand

A gate in Jerusalem that was near the temple. Here Irijah accused the prophet Jeremiah of traitorously going over to the Chaldeans.

FIRST REFERENCE
JEREMIAH 20:2
LAST REFERENCE
ZECHARIAH 14:10

BEON OT1

A place east of the Jordan River that the children of Gad and Reuben requested to have as their inheritance before Israel had finished conquering the Promised Land.

Moses made them agree to aid in the conquest of the land before they would gain their inheritance.

ONLY REFERENCE
NUMBERS 32:3

BERACHAH OT2
Benediction

A valley where King Jehoshaphat of Judah and his people praised God for saving them from the Moabites and Amonites.

ONLY REFERENCE
2 CHRONICLES 20:26

BEREA NT3
Region beyond the coastline

Paul and Silas fled to this Macedonian city after the Jews of Thessalonica caused them trouble. The Bereans accepted the two men's message, checking it against scripture, until the Thessalonians again stirred up trouble.

FIRST REFERENCE
ACTS 17:10
LAST REFERENCE
ACTS 20:4

BERED OT1
Hail

A southern Palestinian town near Beer-lahai-roi.

ONLY REFERENCE
GENESIS 16:14

BEROTHAH OT1
Cypress or cypresslike

In a prophetic view of the restoration of Jerusalem, Ezekiel saw this city, lying between Damascus and Hamath, as a northern boundary of the land of the tribes of Israel.

ONLY REFERENCE
EZEKIEL 47:16

BEROTHAI OT1
Cypress or cypresslike

A city of Hadadezer, king of Zobah, which King David conquered and plundered of its brass.

ONLY REFERENCE
2 SAMUEL 8:8

BESOR OT3
Cheerful

A brook where David left his tired troops as the rest of his army followed the Amalekites who had invaded his city of Ziklag and taken its women and children captive.

FIRST REFERENCE
1 SAMUEL 30:9
LAST REFERENCE
1 SAMUEL 30:21

BETAH OT1
A place of refuge; safety

A city of Hadadezer, king of Zobah. King David conquered the city as he reestablished his border at the Euphrates River. He took large quantities of brass from Betah and Berothai. Betah appears as "Tebah" in the NIV.

ONLY REFERENCE
2 SAMUEL 8:8

BETEN OT1
To babble (implying to vociferate loudly)

A border town that became part of the inheritance of Issachar when Joshua cast lots in Shiloh to provide territory for the seven tribes that had yet to receive their land.

ONLY REFERENCE
JOSHUA 19:25

BETHABARA NT1
Ferry house

A place east of the Jordan River where John the Baptist baptized believers.

ONLY REFERENCE
JOHN 1:28

BETH-ANATH OT3
House of replies

A fortified or walled city that became part of the inheritance of Naphtali when Joshua cast lots in Shiloh to provide territory for the seven tribes that had yet to receive their land. Naphtali did not drive the Canaanites from this city.

FIRST REFERENCE
JOSHUA 19:38
LAST REFERENCE
JUDGES 1:33

BETH-ANOTH OT1
House of replies

A city that became part of the inheritance of the tribe of Judah following the conquest of the Promised Land.

ONLY REFERENCE
JOSHUA 15:59

BETHANY NT11
Date house

A village about two miles outside of Jerusalem. Bethany is best known as the home of Jesus' friends Lazarus, Martha, and Mary. When Lazarus became ill, Jesus did not come to the village until he had died. When He did arrive, Martha and Mary mourned that He had not been there to prevent their brother's death. Jesus brought his friend back to life, causing trouble with the chief priests, who wanted to kill Him. For a time Jesus went to the town of Ephraim. Six days before the Last Supper, He returned and went to dinner at the home of Simon the Leper, in Bethany. There Mary of Bethany anointed him with oil. When the disciples objected to her wasting it, Jesus told them she was preparing Him for burial and that she would be remembered for her deed wherever the Gospel was told.

Near Bethany Jesus had the disciples get a donkey for him to ride into Jerusalem. After His triumphal entry into Jerusalem, He stayed at Bethany. He cursed a fig tree near this village. From Bethany after His resurrection, He ascended into heaven.

FIRST REFERENCE
MATTHEW 21:17
LAST REFERENCE
JOHN 12:1

BETH-ARABAH
OT3
House of the desert

A border city of the tribe of Judah's territory, Beth-arabah became part of the inheritance of Benjamin when Joshua cast lots in Shiloh to provide territory for the seven tribes that had yet to receive their land.

FIRST REFERENCE
JOSHUA 15:6
LAST REFERENCE
JOSHUA 18:22

BETH-ARAM OT1
House of the height

A city that was part of the inheritance of Gad when Moses gave the first inheritances to Israel.

ONLY REFERENCE
JOSHUA 13:27

BETH-ARBEL OT1
House of God's ambush

Hosea used the destruction of this fortress as a warning to sinful Israel.

ONLY REFERENCE
HOSEA 10:14

BETH-AVEN OT7
House of vanity

A place near Ai and west of Michmash. The book of Joshua speaks of "the wilderness of Beth-aven" (Joshua 18:12). In a running battle with the Philistines, Saul's troops went as far as Beth-aven. Hosea uses this name for the city of Bethel, a place of worship that had been turned into a place of idolatry. Same as Aven 2.

FIRST REFERENCE
JOSHUA 7:2
LAST REFERENCE
HOSEA 10:5

BETH-AZMAVETH
OT1
House of Azmaveth

A town of Judah to which Jews returned after the Babylonian exile.

ONLY REFERENCE
NEHEMIAH 7:28

BETH-BAAL-MEON OT1
House or habitation of Baal

A Moabite town that Moses gave to the tribe of Reuben as part of its inheritance. Same as Beth-meon.

ONLY REFERENCE
JOSHUA 13:17

BETH-BARAH OT1

House of the ford

A place near the Jordan River. Gideon called the people of Mount Ephraim to fight the Midianites up to this place.

ONLY REFERENCE
JUDGES 7:24

BETH-BIREI OT1

House of a creative one

A city of the tribe of Simeon.

ONLY REFERENCE
I CHRONICLES 4:31

BETH-CAR OT1

House of pasture

When the Philistines attacked Israel at Mizpeh, the Israelites pursued them to this spot.

ONLY REFERENCE
I SAMUEL 7:11

BETH-DAGON OT2

House of Dagon

1) A city that became part of the inheritance of the tribe of Judah following the conquest of the Promised Land.

ONLY REFERENCE
JOSHUA 15:41

2) A city that became part of the inheritance of Asher when Joshua cast lots in Shiloh to provide territory for the seven tribes that had yet to receive their land.

ONLY REFERENCE
JOSHUA 19:27

BETH-DIBLATHAIM OT1

House of the two fig cakes

A town in Moab that the prophet Jeremiah foresaw would be spoiled when God sent wanderers who would destroy Moab and make it wander, too.

ONLY REFERENCE
JEREMIAH 48:22

BETHEL OT66

House of God

A Canaanite town, originally called Luz, where Abram and Jacob built altars and worshipped God. Here God renewed His covenant with Jacob, who renamed the town "Bethel." Deborah, Rebekah's nurse, was buried here under an oak tree, at a site named Allon-bachuth.

Joshua fought the king of Bethel as Israel took control of the Promised Land. Following the conquest, the city became part of the inheritance of the tribe of Benjamin. In the time of the judges, the ark of the covenant was housed at Bethel, and people came there to inquire of God. The Israelites did this before they fought the tribe of Benjamin and when they had to make a decision about finding wives for the remaining men of the tribe.

The prophet Samuel regularly held his circuit court in Bethel.

Mount Bethel (or "the hill country of Bethel" [NIV]), a hilly area near the city, is mentioned in Joshua 16:1, when Joseph's sons inherited it, and in 1 Samuel 13:2, in connection with Saul's army.

Following the division of the kingdom, King Jeroboam of Israel made two calf idols and placed one in Bethel to encourage the people to fall away from the Lord. Amos prophesied the destruction of Bethel's altars and used the city as a picture of idolatry. After Israel fell to Assyria, the Assyrian king ordered that a captured priest of Israel direct the foreigners who had been moved to Israel in worship of the Lord. The priest who was chosen lived in Bethel.

Abijah, king of Judah, warred with King Jeroboam and won Bethel and other cities from him (2 Chronicles 13:19).

Elijah and Elisha visited Bethel just before Elijah was taken up into heaven in a fiery chariot. There "the company of the prophets" (2 Kings 2:5 NIV) asked Elisha if he knew God would take his master that day.

An unnamed prophet came to Bethel to foretell King Josiah's birth and his destruction of idolatry in the land. When he took power, Josiah destroyed the altar and high places of idolatry in Israel.

Benjaminites from Geba resettled Bethel following their return from Babylon. Same as El-bethel and Luz 1.

FIRST REFERENCE
GENESIS 12:8
LAST REFERENCE
AMOS 7:13
KEY REFERENCES
GENESIS 28:19; 35:1; 2 KINGS 23:15

BETH-EMEK OT I
House of the valley

A city that became part of the inheritance of Asher when Joshua cast lots in Shiloh to provide territory for the seven tribes that had yet to receive their land.

ONLY REFERENCE
JOSHUA 19:27

BETHER OT I
A section

Mountains that King Solomon used as part of his description comparing his beloved to a deer on the heights.

ONLY REFERENCE
SONG OF SOLOMON 2:17

BETHESDA NT I
House of kindness

This pool near Jerusalem's sheep market was surrounded by five porches where those who were blind, ill, or paralyzed waited. They believed that after an angel moved the water of the pool, the first person in the water would be healed of disease. Here Jesus came to a man who had been an invalid for thirty-eight years and asked if he wanted to get well. After the man explained his inability to reach the pool, Jesus told him to pick up his mat and walk, and the man was immediately cured.

ONLY REFERENCE
JOHN 5:2

BETH-EZEL OT1
House of the side

A city of Judah that Micah mentions as he prophetically mourns over Judah's unfaithfulness.

ONLY REFERENCE
MICAH 1:11

BETH-GAMUL OT1
House of the weaned

A Moabite city, in that nation's plain country, that the prophet Jeremiah foretold would be judged by God.

ONLY REFERENCE
JEREMIAH 48:23

BETH-HACCEREM OT2
House of the vineyard

A town of Judah that was ruled in part by Malchiah during Nehemiah's era. Jeremiah referred to it as a place from which a warning signal should be given as disaster fell on Judah.

FIRST REFERENCE
NEHEMIAH 3:14
LAST REFERENCE
JEREMIAH 6:1

BETH-HARAN OT1

A fortified or walled city that became part of the inheritance of the tribe of Gad.

ONLY REFERENCE
NUMBERS 32:36

BETH-HOGLA OT1
House of a partridge

A place that formed part of the tribe of Judah's northern border. Same as Beth-hoglah.

ONLY REFERENCE
JOSHUA 15:6

BETH-HOGLAH OT2
House of a partridge

A city that became part of the inheritance of Benjamin when Joshua cast lots in Shiloh to provide territory for the seven tribes that had yet to receive their land. Same as Beth-hogla.

FIRST REFERENCE
JOSHUA 18:19
LAST REFERENCE
JOSHUA 18:21

BETH-HORON OT14
House of hollowness

After five Amorite kings fought Joshua and his troops at Gibeon, Joshua chased these rulers and their men as far as the city of Beth-horon. Then the Lord cast great hailstones on them, defeating the army.

Beth-horon became part of the inheritance of the children of Joseph (the tribes of Manasseh and Ephraim). It became part of the inheritance of Benjamin when Joshua cast lots in Shiloh to provide territory for the seven tribes that had yet to receive their land. Later it became a Levitical city.

During Saul's kingdom, Beth-horon was attacked by the Philistines. King Solomon fortified its upper and lower cities. King Amaziah of Judah hired an army of Ephraimites to fight in his battle with the children of Seir. But when the Lord declared they should not fight, he sent them home. Instead they attacked Beth-horon and ransacked the city.

FIRST REFERENCE
JOSHUA 10:10
LAST REFERENCE
2 CHRONICLES 25:13
KEY REFERENCES
JOSHUA 10:11; 2 CHRONICLES 8:5

BETH-JESHIMOTH
OT3
House of the deserts

This frontier town of Moab, at the northeastern corner of the Dead Sea, was ruled by King Sihon before Joshua and his army conquered the Promised Land. Following the conquest, Beth-jeshimoth became part of the inheritance of the tribe of Reuben. When Ezekiel spoke of the judgment of Moab, he called this city "the glory of the country" (Ezekiel 25:9). Same as Beth-jesimoth.

FIRST REFERENCE
JOSHUA 12:3
LAST REFERENCE
EZEKIEL 25:9

BETH-JESIMOTH
OT1
House of the deserts

A campsite for the Israelites before the conquest of Canaan. Same as Beth-jeshimoth.

ONLY REFERENCE
NUMBERS 33:49

BETH-LEBAOTH
OT1
House of lionesses

A city that became part of the inheritance of Simeon when Joshua cast lots in Shiloh to provide territory for the seven tribes that had yet to receive their land.

ONLY REFERENCE
JOSHUA 19:6

BETH-LEHEM
OT24
House of bread

1) Near this ancient town, also called Ephrath, Rachel was buried. Later it was the home of Naomi and Ruth, following the deaths of their husbands and their return to Naomi's homeland. In Beth-lehem's town gate, Boaz redeemed the land of Naomi's husband, Elimelech, along with the responsibility to care for Naomi and Ruth. Most of the book of Ruth takes place here.

David and his family lived in Beth-lehem, and there Samuel anointed him king after seeing and rejecting all his brothers. When a garrison of Philistines held Bethlehem, at his glancing mention of his desire for water from its well, three of King David's mighty men broke into the city to get him a drink. David's grandson King Rehoboam fortified the city. Micah called the city Beth-lehem Ephratah and prophesied that though she was small, the Messiah would come from her. Same as Bethlehem, Beth-lehem-judah, Ephratah, and probably Ephrath.

FIRST REFERENCE
GENESIS 35:19
LAST REFERENCE
MICAH 5:2
KEY REFERENCES
I SAMUEL 16:4; I CHRONICLES 11:16–18;
MICAH 5:2

2) A city that became part of the inheritance of Zebulun when Joshua cast lots in Shiloh to provide territory for the seven tribes that had yet to receive their land.

ONLY REFERENCE
JOSHUA 19:15

3) Home of Ibzan, who judged Israel for seven years and was buried here.

FIRST REFERENCE
JUDGES 12:8
LAST REFERENCE
JUDGES 12:10

BETHLEHEM NT8
House of bread

Also called Bethlehem of Judaea, to distinguish it from another Bethlehem northwest of Nazareth, this town south of Jerusalem was the birthplace of Jesus, as foretold by the prophet Micah, who called it Bethlehem Ephratah. The wise men visited the baby Jesus here and offered Him gifts of gold, frankincense, and myrrh. God warned them in a dream not to report back to Herod, who had told them where to find the child. Then God warned Joseph to take his family into Egypt to avoid Herod's anger. The wrathful king killed all the children under age two who lived in Bethlehem. Same as Beth-lehem 1, Beth-lehem-judah, Ephratah, and probably Ephrath.

FIRST REFERENCE
MATTHEW 2:1
LAST REFERENCE
JOHN 7:42

BETH-LEHEM-JUDAH OT10
House of bread

Hometown of a Levite who became a priest for Micah of Mount Ephraim. It was also the home of a Levite's unnamed concubine whom the men of Gibeah abused. The next day her "husband" cut up her body and "sent her into all the coasts of Israel" (Judges 19:29). Elimelech, Naomi's husband, also came from Beth-lehem-judah, as did King David's father, Jesse. Same as Beth-lehem, Bethlehem, Ephratah, and probably Ephrath.

FIRST REFERENCE
JUDGES 17:7
LAST REFERENCE
I SAMUEL 17:12

BETH-MAACHAH
OT2

House of Maachah

Sheba, the son of Bichri, fled to this city east of Tyre when King David's battle commander Joab put down the rebellion Sheba had started. Joab followed him there and demanded that the city hand him over. The people of Beth-maachah cut off the rebel's head and threw it over the wall to Joab.

FIRST REFERENCE
2 SAMUEL 20:14
LAST REFERENCE
2 SAMUEL 20:15

BETH-MARCABOTH OT2

Place of the chariots

A city that became part of the inheritance of Simeon when Joshua cast lots in Shiloh to provide territory for the seven tribes that had yet to receive their land.

FIRST REFERENCE
JOSHUA 19:5
LAST REFERENCE
1 CHRONICLES 4:31

BETH-MEON OT1
House or habitation of [Baal]

A city of Moab that Jeremiah foresaw would be judged by God. Same as Beth-baal-meon.

ONLY REFERENCE
JEREMIAH 48:23

BETH-NIMRAH
OT2

House of the leopard

A fortified or walled city built up by the tribe of Gad.

FIRST REFERENCE
NUMBERS 32:36
LAST REFERENCE
JOSHUA 13:27

BETH-PALET OT1
House of escape

A city that became part of the inheritance of the tribe of Judah following the conquest of the Promised Land. Same as Beth-phelet.

ONLY REFERENCE
JOSHUA 15:27

BETH-PAZZEZ OT1
House of dispersion

A city that became part of the inheritance of Issachar when Joshua cast lots in Shiloh to provide territory for the seven tribes that had yet to receive their land.

ONLY REFERENCE
JOSHUA 19:21

BETH-PEOR OT4
House of Peor

In a valley near this place in Moab, Moses and the Israelites encamped while God had Moses review His laws. God buried Moses near Beth-peor, though no one knew exactly where. When Joshua was old, this land east of the Jordan River was given to the tribe of Reuben.

FIRST REFERENCE
DEUTERONOMY 3:29
LAST REFERENCE
JOSHUA 13:20

BETHPHAGE   NT3
Fig house

A village close to Jerusalem and Bethany, on the Mount of Olives. Here Jesus asked the disciples to bring Him a colt on which He would ride into Jerusalem on Palm Sunday.

FIRST REFERENCE
MATTHEW 21:1
LAST REFERENCE
LUKE 19:29

BETH-PHELET   OT1
House of escape

A city of Judah resettled by the Jews after the Babylonian exile. Same as Beth-palet.

ONLY REFERENCE
NEHEMIAH 11:26

BETH-REHOB   OT2
House of the street

A city near Dan. The Ammonites hired Syrian soldiers from Beth-rehob when they planned to attack Israel. They made these plans after their new king, Hanun, insulted the men David had sent to comfort him following his father's death.

FIRST REFERENCE
JUDGES 18:28
LAST REFERENCE
2 SAMUEL 10:6

BETHSAIDA   NT7
Fishing house

1) A city in Galilee. Jesus did many "mighty works" here and reproached its people for their lack of repentance, telling them that if the Gentile cities of Tyre and Sidon had heard His message, they would have repented. Philip, Andrew, and Peter came from Bethsaida. Perhaps the same as Bethsaida 2.

FIRST REFERENCE
MATTHEW 11:21
LAST REFERENCE
JOHN 12:21

2) A town northeast of the sea of Galilee where Jesus healed a blind man. In a desert place belonging to the city, Jesus preached to a crowd then fed a crowd of five thousand from the loaves and fish of a boy's lunch. After feeding the people, Jesus sent His disciples on to Bethsaida in a boat then came to them on the water.

Some scholars believe that Bethsaida may have been at the spot where the Jordan River flows into the Sea of Galilee, and portions of the town may have been on each side of the river. If that is true, this is the same as Bethsaida 1.

FIRST REFERENCE
MARK 8:22
LAST REFERENCE
LUKE 9:10

BETH-SHAN OT3
House of ease

Though it was within the territory of Issachar, the tribe of Manasseh inherited this city. Manasseh could not drive the Canaanites out of the city, but at the height of their power turned them into forced labor.

The Philistines fastened the bodies of King Saul and his sons to the wall of this city after they died in battle. The men of Jabesh-gilead recovered the bodies and buried them in their town. Same as Beth-shean.

FIRST REFERENCE
I SAMUEL 31:10
LAST REFERENCE
2 SAMUEL 21:12

BETH-SHEAN OT6
House of ease

A city that became part of the inheritance of Manasseh. The tribe never drove out the Canaanites. Under King Solomon's governmental organization, Beth-shean was responsible for supplying provisions for the king. Same as Bethshan.

FIRST REFERENCE
JOSHUA 17:11
LAST REFERENCE
I CHRONICLES 7:29

BETH-SHEMESH
OT21
House of the sun

1) A town that formed part of the border of the territory inherited by the tribe of Judah. The tribe gave Beth-shemesh to the Levites as God had commanded.

When their cities were afflicted by the Lord because they had stolen the ark of the covenant, the Philistines put it on a cart pulled by two milk cows. If the cart headed toward Beth-shemesh, they would know the Lord had sent their afflictions. As they returned the ark to Israel, the oxen that bore it went straight to Beth-shemesh, to the field of Joshua of Beth-shemesh, and stopped by a large rock. Here the people chopped up the cart and sacrificed the cows as a burnt offering to God. But because seventy men of Beth-shemesh looked into the ark, God killed them. So the grieving people of the town sent the ark to Kirjath-jearim, where it remained for twenty years.

Kings Jehoash of Israel and Amaziah of Judah met in battle at Beth-shemesh. Judah's army fled, and Jehoash captured Amaziah and attacked Jerusalem, breaking down six hundred feet of its wall and plundering the city.

During the reign of King Ahaz of Judah, Beth-shemesh was one of the cities of the southern low country of Judah invaded by the Philistines. Scripture states that God used this method to punish Ahaz for his sin.

FIRST REFERENCE
JOSHUA 15:10
LAST REFERENCE
2 CHRONICLES 28:18
KEY REFERENCES
I SAMUEL 6; 2 KINGS 14:8–14

2) A city that became part of the inheritance of Issachar when Joshua cast lots in Shiloh to provide territory for the seven tribes that had yet to receive their land.

ONLY REFERENCE
JOSHUA 19:22

3) A fortified or walled city that became part of the inheritance of Naphtali when Joshua cast lots in Shiloh to provide territory for the seven tribes that had yet to receive their land. The tribe never drove the Canaanites out of this city.

FIRST REFERENCE
JOSHUA 19:38
LAST REFERENCE
JUDGES 1:33

4) A place of idolatry, perhaps a temple, in Egypt. The prophet Jeremiah spoke of the images of Beth-shemesh being destroyed.

ONLY REFERENCE
JEREMIAH 43:13

BETH-SHITTAH
OT I
House of the acacia

When Gideon went to fight against the Midianites with the three hundred men God had chosen for him by the way they drank water, the Midianite army fled to Beth-shittah.

ONLY REFERENCE
JUDGES 7:22

BETH-TAPPUAH
OT I
House of the apple

A city that became part of the inheritance of the tribe of Judah following the conquest of the Promised Land.

ONLY REFERENCE
JOSHUA 15:53

BETHUEL
OT I
Destroyed of God

Shimei, a man of the tribe of Simeon, who had sixteen sons and six daughters, lived with his family in this town. Same as Bethul.

ONLY REFERENCE
I CHRONICLES 4:30

BETHUL
OT I
Destroyed of God

A city that became part of the inheritance of Simeon when Joshua cast lots in Shiloh to provide territory for the seven tribes that had yet to receive their land. Same as Bethuel.

ONLY REFERENCE
JOSHUA 19:4

BETH-ZUR
OT3
House of the rock

A city that became part of the inheritance of the tribe of Judah following the conquest of the Promised Land. King Rehoboam of Judah fortified Beth-zur. Following the return from the Babylonian exile, Nehemiah the son of Azbuk ruled half of the city.

FIRST REFERENCE
JOSHUA 15:58
LAST REFERENCE
NEHEMIAH 3:16

BETONIM OT1
Hollows

A city east of the Jordan River that Moses made part of the inheritance of Gad.

ONLY REFERENCE
JOSHUA 13:26

BEULAH OT1
To marry

A prophetic name for the land of Israel, picturing its restoration to God's favor.

ONLY REFERENCE
ISAIAH 62:4

BEZEK OT3
Lightning

A place where Judah fought and defeated the Canaanites and Perizzites after Joshua died. At Bezek Saul also gathered and numbered his three hundred thousand men of Israel and thirty thousand of Judah before he set out to rescue the city of Jabesh.

FIRST REFERENCE
JUDGES 1:4
LAST REFERENCE
I SAMUEL 11:8

BEZER OT4
An inaccessible spot

One of the six cities of refuge established in Israel for those who had committed accidental murder. Bezer was given to the Levites by the tribe of Reuben.

FIRST REFERENCE
DEUTERONOMY 4:43
LAST REFERENCE
I CHRONICLES 6:78

BILEAM OT1
Not of the people; foreigner

One of the forty-eight cities given to the Levites as God had commanded. Bileam was given to them by the tribe of Manasseh.

ONLY REFERENCE
I CHRONICLES 6:70

BILHAH OT1
Timid

A city that became part of the inheritance of the tribe of Simeon.

ONLY REFERENCE
I CHRONICLES 4:29

BITHRON OT1
The craggy spot

An area of the eastern part of the Jordan River valley. Saul's battle commander Abner and his men escaped from David's commander Joab by walking all night and passing through Bithron.

ONLY REFERENCE
2 SAMUEL 2:29

BITHYNIA NT2

A Roman province in northern Asia Minor that Paul and his companions sought to visit, but were kept from doing so by the Holy Spirit. Peter wrote his first epistle to the Bithynians and other people of this area. Chalcedon and Nicea were in this province.

FIRST REFERENCE
ACTS 16:7
LAST REFERENCE
I PETER 1:1

BIZJOTHJAH OT1
Contempts of God

A city that became part of the inheritance of the tribe of Judah following the conquest of the Promised Land.

ONLY REFERENCE
JOSHUA 15:28

BOAZ OT2

The left pillar on the porch of Jerusalem's temple.

FIRST REFERENCE
I KINGS 7:21
LAST REFERENCE
2 CHRONICLES 3:17

BOCHIM OT2
The weepers

A place near Gilgal. Here, before the Israelite tribes went to their newly inherited lands, the angel of the Lord spoke to them, reminding them of God's covenant with them.

FIRST REFERENCE
JUDGES 2:1
LAST REFERENCE
JUDGES 2:5

BOHAN OT2
Thumb

A stone that formed part of the border of the tribe of Judah's territory. Bohan was named after one of Reuben's sons.

FIRST REFERENCE
JOSHUA 15:6
LAST REFERENCE
JOSHUA 18:17

BOSCATH OT1
A swell of ground

Hometown of Jedidah, mother of King Josiah of Judah.

ONLY REFERENCE
2 KINGS 22:1

BOZEZ OT1
Shining

A cliff on one side of a pass that Jonathan and his armor bearer had to cross to get to the Philistines' garrison before their heated battle at Michmash.

ONLY REFERENCE
I SAMUEL 14:4

BOZKATH OT1
A swell of ground

A city that became part of the inheritance of the tribe of Judah following the conquest of the Promised Land.

ONLY REFERENCE
JOSHUA 15:39

BOZRAH OT9

1) A city of Edom and hometown of King Jobab, son of Zerah. Isaiah refers to a sacrifice (probably meaning a battle) in this city. The prophet Jeremiah foresaw its destruction, and Amos foretold the destruction of Bozrah's palaces.

FIRST REFERENCE
GENESIS 36:33
LAST REFERENCE
MICAH 2:12

2) A Moabite city that Jeremiah foretold would be destroyed.

ONLY REFERENCE
JEREMIAH 48:24

-C-

CABBON OT1
To heap up; hilly

A city that became part of the inheritance of the tribe of Judah following the conquest of the Promised Land.

ONLY REFERENCE
JOSHUA 15:40

CABUL OT2
Limitation; sterile

1) A city that became part of the inheritance of Asher when Joshua cast lots in Shiloh to provide territory for the seven tribes that had yet to receive their land.

ONLY REFERENCE
JOSHUA 19:27

2) An area in northern Israel with twenty towns that King Solomon gave to King Hiram of Tyre, who had helped build Jerusalem's temple and Solomon's palace. Unimpressed by the gift, Hiram named it appropriately. Same as Galilee.

ONLY REFERENCE
I KINGS 9:13

CAESAREA NT17

1) Known as Caesarea Philippi, to differentiate it from the Caesarea built by Herod the Great. Here Jesus asked His disciples, "Whom do men say that I the Son of man am?" (Matthew 16:13). Same as Philippi 1.

2) Hometown of Philip the evangelist, this seaport of Judea was built by Herod the Great, who lived there. When Herod Agrippa delivered a speech from his throne in Caesarea, the people acclaimed him as a god. Herod did not correct them, so an angel of the Lord struck him down and he died. The God-fearing centurion Cornelius was stationed in Caesarea when God gave both him and Peter visions that indicated that God accepted faithful Gentiles. Here Claudius Lysias and Festus judged the Jews' case against the apostle Paul. This Caesarea was also called Caesarea Maritima or Caesarea Augusta.

FIRST REFERENCE
ACTS 8:40
LAST REFERENCE
ACTS 25:13
KEY REFERENCES
ACTS 10:1; 21:8; 23:33; 25:6

CAIN OT1

Fixity; a lance (as in striking fast)

A city that became part of the inheritance of the tribe of Judah following the conquest of the Promised Land.

ONLY REFERENCE
JOSHUA 15:57

CALAH OT2

To be complete; maturity

An Assyrian city built by Asshur.

FIRST REFERENCE
GENESIS 10:11
LAST REFERENCE
GENESIS 10:12

CALEB-EPHRATAH OT1

Forceable fruitfulness

The place where Heron, a descendant of Judah, died before his son Ashur was born.

ONLY REFERENCE
1 CHRONICLES 2:24

CALNEH OT2

Part of the early kingdom of Nimrod, in Shinar. Amos mentions a city by this name in connection with the Syrian city of Hamath and the Philistine city of Gath, so it is possible that these two references speak of two different cities. Same as Calno and Canneh.

FIRST REFERENCE
GENESIS 10:10
LAST REFERENCE
AMOS 6:2

CALNO OT1

A city of Assyria. Same as Calneh and Canneh.

ONLY REFERENCE
ISAIAH 10:9

CALVARY NT1

Skull (a translation of the Greek word kranion)

The place lying not far outside of Jerusalem where Jesus was crucified. The Latin word *Calvary* is used a single time in scripture, in the book of Luke, and is often simply translated as "the Skull" (NIV). This place was also called by the Aramaic name Golgotha, the term used by the other Gospel writers. Same as Golgotha.

ONLY REFERENCE
LUKE 23:33

CAMON OT1

An elevation

The burial place of the judge Jair. Camon may have been in Gilead.

ONLY REFERENCE
JUDGES 10:5

CANA NT4

A Galilean village where Jesus and His disciples attended a wedding and the Lord performed His first miracle, turning water into wine. The family who was holding the wedding ran out of wine, so Mary, Jesus' mother, came to Him with the news. He told the servants to fill six large water jars with twenty to thirty gallons of water. When they drew the liquid out again, it was a good wine. In Cana, a royal official from Capernaum came to Jesus, asking Him to heal his dying son.

Before the wonder-seeking Galileans, Jesus simply told the man his son would live. On his way home, the official's servants met him with the news that his son was alive.

Jesus' disciple Nathanael came from Cana.

FIRST REFERENCE
JOHN 2:1
LAST REFERENCE
JOHN 21:2

CANAAN OT81/NT1

Humiliated

The land east of the Mediterranean Sea as far as the Jordan River, and from the Taurus Mountains, going south beyond Gaza. Canaan included the areas later called Phoenicia, Palestine, and Syria. Its inhabitants were the descendants of Noah's grandson Canaan, including his firstborn child, Sidon, the Hittites, Jebusites, Amorites, Girgasites, Hivites, Arkites, Sinites, Arvadites, Zemarites, and Hamathites (Genesis 10:15–18).

God brought Abram and his family from Ur of the Chaldees to the land of Canaan. Promising they would become a great nation there, the Lord covenanted with Abram that his descendants would own the land and that He would be their God.

Though Abram's grandson Isaac fled from Canaan, he returned and continued the covenant. As famine covered the land, Isaac's son Jacob sent his sons to Egypt to buy food. They discovered that Joseph, the brother they had sold into slavery, was now prime minister of that land. Jacob moved to Egypt with his entire family. But when Jacob died, Joseph buried him in Canaan.

Before Israel's return to the Promised Land, Moses sent twelve spies into Canaan to see what they were up against. The men described the people and their territory: "The Canaanites dwell by the sea, and by the coast of Jordan" (Numbers 13:29). All but two of the spies decided these people were too powerful for Israel to attack. For this faithlessness, God caused the Israelites to wander in the wilderness for forty years. Before they finally entered the Promised Land, God commanded Moses to climb Mount Nebo and look out toward Canaan. Moses and all those of his generation, who had accepted the report of the ten spies, died before Israel claimed the land.

When the Israelites returned to Canaan, those pagan inhabitants would become their enemies. God commanded His people not to follow in the Canaanites' ways. Before Israel entered the land, God renewed His promise to give them Canaan.

Following the Promised Land's conquest, at God's command, Israel's leaders cast lots to divide the property among the tribes. However, scripture often states that the tribes did not fully eradicate the Canaanites. Where they were too powerful, Israel coexisted with its enemies. So the pagan peoples, whose gods were brutal and connected with cult prostitution, influenced the Israelites to fall into pagan worship practices. It took many years for Israel to subdue the Canaanites. Yet when Joshua was very old, God promised that He would enable His people to complete the unfinished task.

During the rule of the prophet Deborah, the Israelites contended with the Canaanites, who ruled over them. God commanded Barak to lead Israel to victory against Jabin, king of Canaan, and his battle commander Sisera. Because Barak would not go into battle without Deborah, God gave Sisera's death to a woman, Jael, wife of Heber the Kenite. But all Sisera's troops were killed by Barak's soldiers. Jabin was subdued, and eventually, as its power expanded, Israel destroyed him.

David fought the Philistine giant Goliath and later, as king of Israel, conquered Philistia. After bringing the ark of the covenant to Jerusalem, King David rejoiced in God's promise, "Unto thee will I give the land of Canaan, the lot of your inheritance" (Psalm 105:11). But the Israelites slipped ever more deeply into sin, worshipping the gods of the land they conquered. Ezekiel used the land of Canaan as a picture of Jerusalem's unfaithfulness (Ezekiel 16:3). And Zephaniah spoke of the destruction of Canaan, land of the Philistines (Zephaniah 2:5).

The only New Testament

reference to Canaan is in Matthew 15:22, in the story of the woman of Canaan whose daughter was demon-possessed. Same as Chanaan.

FIRST REFERENCE
GENESIS 11:31
LAST REFERENCE
MATTHEW 15:22
KEY REFERENCES
GENESIS 12:5; 17:8; LEVITICUS 18:3

CANNEH — OT1

An Assyrian city that the prophet Ezekiel called "the merchants of Sheba." Same as Calneh and Calno.

ONLY REFERENCE
EZEKIEL 27:23

CAPERNAUM — NT16

Comfortable village

A village on the Sea of Galilee's north shore, Capernaum was chosen by Jesus as His ministry headquarters. He left Nazareth for Capernaum when Herod imprisoned John the Baptist. Thus He fulfilled the prophecy of Isaiah that Zebulun (which was the tribe of Nazareth) and Naphtali (which was the tribe of Capernaum) would see a great light. Jesus taught in Capernaum's synagogue. From here, He called several disciples—fishermen Peter, Andrew, James, and John, and the tax collector Matthew—and He performed many miracles. While He ministered in Cana, Jesus healed a royal official's son who was ill in Capernaum. On the way back home, the official met his servants, who gave him the news that his son lived.

Before a crowd of people, Jesus healed a man sick with palsy who had been lowered through the roof to Him because his bearers could not get through the crowd that surrounded the place. Jesus forgave the man's sin, and when the people around him became offended, He commanded him to walk. A Roman centurion came to Capernaum asking Jesus to heal his servant. When the Lord prepared to visit his home, the man asked that He simply say the words to heal the servant, since he was a man accustomed to such authority. Jesus publicly commended his faith.

Yet despite the miracles they viewed and their astonishment at Jesus' doctrine, the people of this city did not believe in Him. Jesus took them to task for their desire for miracles and lack of faith, warning: "Thou, Capernaum, which art exalted unto heaven, shalt be brought down to hell: for if the mighty works, which have been done in thee, had been done in Sodom, it would have remained until this day. But I say unto you, That it shall be more tolerable for the land of Sodom in the day of judgment, than for thee" (Matthew 11:23–24).

In Capernaum Peter rashly promised the tax collectors that Jesus would pay the temple tax. Therefore Jesus ordered Peter to catch a fish. The fish had money in its mouth to pay the tax for both of them.

FIRST REFERENCE
MATTHEW 4:13
LAST REFERENCE
JOHN 6:59
KEY REFERENCES
MATTHEW 4:12–17; 8:5–13; 17:24–27; MARK
2:1–12; JOHN 6:16–24

CAPHTOR   OT3
A wreath-shaped island

The original Philistine homeland, before the Philistines conquered Palestine. Some scholars believe it was Crete, but a certain identification of Caphtor cannot be made.

FIRST REFERENCE
DEUTERONOMY 2:23
LAST REFERENCE
AMOS 9:7

CAPPADOCIA   NT2

A Roman province in Asia Minor, north of Cilicia and east of Galatia. People from this area were in Jerusalem and heard their language spoken at Pentecost. Peter wrote his first epistle to the Christians of Cappadocia, as well as others in central and northern Asia Minor.

FIRST REFERENCE
ACTS 2:9
LAST REFERENCE
I PETER 1:1

CARCHEMISH   OT2

A city on the upper Euphrates River where Egypt's pharaoh Necho met Nebuchadrezzar (also called Nebuchadnezzar), king of Babylon, in battle. Though Necho warned the king of Judah not to take part in the battle, Josiah disguised himself and went to the plain of Megiddo to fight. Josiah was shot by archers. His men brought him to Jerusalem, where he died of his wounds.

Nebuchadrezzar captured Carchemish and established his nation as rulers of the Near East. Same as Charchemish.

FIRST REFERENCE
ISAIAH 10:9
LAST REFERENCE
JEREMIAH 46:2

CARMEL   OT26
A planted field

1) A Palestinian mountain range that became part of the inheritance of the tribe of Asher. On Mount Carmel, Elijah confronted Ahab, king of Israel, and the priests of Baal. He suggested that both he and the Baal's priests prepare a sacrifice. Both would call on their gods, and Israel would worship the one who lit the sacrifice with fire. Though the 450 prophets of Baal called on Baal for half the day, there was no response. Elijah mocked them, and they continued their efforts until evening with no response.

Then Elijah called the people to him and repaired the altar of the Lord. Three times he had them pour four large jars of water on the altar and the sacrifice. The prophet stepped forward and prayed. God sent down fire that consumed the altar, the water, and the wood beneath the sacrifice. At this dramatic event, Israel's faith turned to the Lord. Elijah ordered that the prophets of Baal be killed, so the people of Israel captured them, brought them to the Kishon Valley, and executed them there.

A Shunammite woman whom Elisha had promised a child came to him at Carmel when her son died. Under King Uzziah of Judah, vineyards flourished on Carmel.

Isaiah prophesied that Carmel would "see the glory of the LORD" (Isaiah 35:2); Amos predicted that when the Lord roars from Zion, "the top of Carmel shall wither" (Amos 1:2), and those who hide there He will "take. . .out thence" (Amos 9:3).

FIRST REFERENCE
JOSHUA 12:22
LAST REFERENCE
NAHUM 1:4
KEY REFERENCE
I KINGS 18:19–42

2) A town that became part of the inheritance of the tribe of Judah following the conquest of the Promised Land. Nabal held property in Carmel. Though David protected the wealthy Nabal's property, at sheepshearing time the foolish man refused to share his bounty with David and his men. David was about to attack Nabal when his wife, Abigail, heard what her husband had done and stepped in, bringing David bread, wine, sheep, grain, and fruit. On her way to David, she met him and his men as they were ready to attack. She fell before David, apologized for her husband, and gave him the food. After Abigail stepped in to help David, her husband died, and David sent to Carmel to ask her to marry him.

FIRST REFERENCE
JOSHUA 15:55
LAST REFERENCE
I SAMUEL 25:40

CASIPHIA OT1
Silvery

Home of the chief Iddo, Casiphia lay somewhere near the route that Ezra and the returning Babylonian exiles traveled on their way home to Jerusalem. While he and the exiles waited at the Ahava canal, Ezra sent messengers to Casiphia, asking Iddo to send him ministers for the house of the Lord. Three days later the Levites and temple servants whom Iddo sent Ezra arrived at the canal.

ONLY REFERENCE
EZRA 8:17

CEDRON NT1

A brook near Jerusalem. Jesus crossed the Cedron Valley on His way to the Garden of Gethsemane, where He prayed before Judas betrayed Him. Same as Kidron.

ONLY REFERENCE
JOHN 18:1

CENCHREA NT3

Probably from the Greek word meaning millet

Corinth's port city, where Paul shaved his head for a vow. Paul described Phoebe, who carried his letter to the Romans from Greece, as a "servant of the church which is at Cenchrea" (Romans 16:1).

FIRST REFERENCE
ACTS 18:18
LAST REFERENCE
ROMANS 16:1

CHALDEA OT 7

Though in its early use, Chaldea meant the southern part of Babylonia, near the Persian Gulf, in scripture this name is also sometimes used to describe the Neo-Babylonian (or Chaldean) Empire.

Abraham originally came from the Chaldean city of Ur (Genesis 11:28).

Twice the Chaldeans attempted to take power from Assyria, conquering Babylon, but their conquests were not successful for long. One of these rebels, Merodach-Baladan, took over Babylon for a time and sent to King Hezekiah, seeking his support against Assyria. Hezekiah showed Merodach-Baladan's representatives his treasures—his storehouses, armory, and palace. The prophet Isaiah foretold that everything the men had seen and some of Hezekiah's descendants would be carried off to Babylon (2 Kings 20:12–19).

Around 626 B.C. Nabopolassar rebelled, conquered the Assyrian capital, Nineveh, and successfully established the Neo-Babylonian (or Chaldean) Empire. Scripture uses "Babylonians" to describe this nation, not the Old Babylonian Empire that had preceded Assyria in power.

God prospered Chaldea for a while as He brought Nabopolassar's son Nebuchadnezzar and his troops against the land of Judah. Under King Nebuchadnezzar's power, King Jehoiakim of Judah became a Chaldean vassal and then rebelled against his overlord. His son Jehoiachin surrendered to the Chaldeans within three months, and Zedekiah was made king. But Zedekiah also rebelled, and Jerusalem was taken by Chaldea. Many of Judah's people were taken into exile.

Jeremiah promised that God would destroy this nation that opposed Judah and repay the evil that had been done against His people. The prophet Ezekiel told a parable in which Jerusalem played the harlot with the Chaldeans. For her involvement with these pagan nations, God promised to bring His wrath against Jerusalem.

FIRST REFERENCE
JEREMIAH 50:10
LAST REFERENCE
EZEKIEL 23:16

CHANAAN NT2
Greek form of Canaan

This is the Greek word Paul and Stephen used to describe the land of Canaan and its history. Same as Canaan.

FIRST REFERENCE
ACTS 7:11
LAST REFERENCE
ACTS 13:19

CHARASHIM OT1
Mechanics

A valley settled by a descendant of Judah, a craftsman named Joab.

ONLY REFERENCE
1 CHRONICLES 4:14

CHARCHEMISH OT1

A city on the west bank of the Euphrates River that became the site of a battle between Necho, pharaoh of Egypt, and King Nebuchadnezzar of Babylon. Same as Carchemish.

ONLY REFERENCE
2 CHRONICLES 35:20

CHARRAN NT2
Greek form of Haran

A Greek form of the name Haran that Stephen used when he preached in the synagogue before he was stoned to death. Same as Haran.

FIRST REFERENCE
ACTS 7:2
LAST REFERENCE
ACTS 7:4

CHEBAR OT8
Length

The prophet Ezekiel was near this Mesopotamian river, with other exiles to Babylon, when he saw a prophetic vision of God and His cherubim. Some of the captives from Judah lived near this river, which was probably a canal south of Babylon and near the city of Nippur. Chebar may have been a place of prayer for the Jews.

FIRST REFERENCE
EZEKIEL 1:1
LAST REFERENCE
EZEKIEL 43:3

CHEPHAR-HAAMMONAI OT1
Village of the Ammonite

A city that became part of the inheritance of Benjamin when Joshua cast lots in Shiloh to provide territory for the seven tribes that had yet to receive their land.

ONLY REFERENCE
JOSHUA 18:24

CHEPHIRAH OT4
The village

A city of the Gibeonites that became part of the inheritance of Benjamin when Joshua cast lots in Shiloh to provide territory for the seven tribes that had yet to receive their land. It was resettled by the Jews after the Babylonian exile.

FIRST REFERENCE
JOSHUA 9:17
LAST REFERENCE
NEHEMIAH 7:29

CHERITH OT2
A cut

A ravine east of the Jordan River, in Gilead. After the prophet Elijah foretold a drought that would last for a few years, God sent him to Cherith, where he could hide from King Ahab of Israel. Here Elijah was fed by ravens and drank from the brook in the ravine.

FIRST REFERENCE
I KINGS 17:3
LAST REFERENCE
I KINGS 17:5

CHESALON OT1
Fertile

A mountain that formed part of the northern border of the tribe of Judah's territory. In some translations it is spelled "Kesalon." Same as Jearim.

ONLY REFERENCE
JOSHUA 15:10

CHESIL OT1

A city that became part of the inheritance of the tribe of Judah following the conquest of the Promised Land.

ONLY REFERENCE
JOSHUA 15:30

CHESULLOTH OT1
Fattened

A city that became part of the inheritance of Issachar when Joshua cast lots in Shiloh to provide territory for the seven tribes that had yet to receive their land.

ONLY REFERENCE
JOSHUA 19:18

CHEZIB OT1

The village where Judah's son Shelah was born.

ONLY REFERENCE
GENESIS 38:5

CHIDON OT1
Probably related to striking with a dart

A threshing floor where Uzza died because he put out his hand to keep the ark of the covenant from falling as the oxen that drew it stumbled. God killed him for disrespecting His holiness, which was symbolized by the ark.

ONLY REFERENCE
I CHRONICLES 13:9

CHILMAD OT1

An unknown place that, along with Sheba and Asshur, traded with Tyre.

ONLY REFERENCE
EZEKIEL 27:23

CHINNERETH OT4
Harp-shaped

An Old Testament name for the Sea of Galilee and the area around it. Joshua 19:35 mentions a fortified or walled city by this name that became part of the inheritance of Naphtali when Joshua cast lots in Shiloh to provide territory for the seven tribes that had yet to receive their land. Same as Chinneroth and Cinneroth.

FIRST REFERENCE
NUMBERS 34:11
LAST REFERENCE
JOSHUA 19:35

CHINNEROTH OT2
Harp-shaped

A variant spelling of Chinnereth. Same as Chinnereth and Cinneroth.

FIRST REFERENCE
JOSHUA 11:2
LAST REFERENCE
JOSHUA 12:3

CHIOS NT1

An island in the Aegean Sea, west of Smyrna. Paul sailed near Chios on his voyage from Troas to Jerusalem.

ONLY REFERENCE
ACTS 20:15

CHISLOTH-TABOR OT1
Flanks of Tabor

A city that became part of the inheritance of Zebulun when Joshua cast lots in Shiloh to provide territory for the seven tribes that had yet to receive their land.

ONLY REFERENCE
JOSHUA 19:12

CHOR-ASHAN OT1
Furnace of smoke

A city of Judah to which David sent some of the spoils from his warfare with the Amalekites.

ONLY REFERENCE
1 SAMUEL 30:30

CHORAZIN NT2

A city in which Jesus did many "mighty works." When the people did not repent, He reproved them, remarking that the Syrian cities of Tyre and Sidon would have repented had they seen these works.

FIRST REFERENCE
MATTHEW 11:21
LAST REFERENCE
LUKE 10:13

CHOZEBA OT1
Fallacious

A city of Judah that was settled by the sons of Shelah.

ONLY REFERENCE
1 CHRONICLES 4:22

CHUN OT1
Established

A city ruled by King Hadarezer of Zobah, whom Israel's king David conquered. Following the conquest, David brought much brass from Chun, which his son Solomon used to create some of the temple implements. In some Bible versions it is spelled "Cun."

ONLY REFERENCE
I CHRONICLES 18:8

CILICIA NT8

A Roman province in southeastern Asia Minor that included Paul's hometown, Tarsus. The Council of Jerusalem wrote to the Gentile Christians of Cilicia, encouraging them in their faith and not requiring them to be circumcised. Paul and Silas ministered to the churches there. On Paul's way to Rome, he sailed along the coast of this province.

FIRST REFERENCE
ACTS 6:9
LAST REFERENCE
GALATIANS 1:21

CINNEROTH OT1
Harp-shaped

An Old Testament name for the Sea of Galilee and the area around it. Here Ben-hadad fought in support of King Asa of Judah against Baasha, king of Israel, conquering the area. Same as Chinnereth and Chinneroth.

ONLY REFERENCE
I KINGS 15:20

CLAUDA NT1

An island near Crete. A ship that Paul took to Rome met with a storm and was driven past Clauda.

ONLY REFERENCE
ACTS 27:16

CNIDUS NT1

A city of southwest Asia Minor that Paul's ship sailed past on its way to Rome.

ONLY REFERENCE
ACTS 27:7

COLOSSE NT1
Colossal

A city in the Roman province of Phrygia, in Asia Minor. The apostle Paul wrote the book of Colossians to the Christians in Colosse. He probably ministered in Colosse when he visited Phrygia.

ONLY REFERENCE
COLOSSIANS 1:2

COOS NT1

An island where Paul stopped on his voyage to Jerusalem. He visited here after he sailed from Ephesus and before he reached Rhodes.

ONLY REFERENCE
ACTS 21:1

CORINTH　　NT6

A Greek city, a trading center, and capital of the Roman province of Achaia. Paul visited Corinth during his second missionary journey, after he ministered in Athens. In Corinth Paul met fellow tentmakers Aquila and Priscilla, who became friends and co-laborers with him. Paul preached in the Corinthian synagogue until the Jews there strongly opposed him. But Crispus, the chief ruler of the synagogue, and his household were converted and baptized. Paul stayed for a year and a half, teaching among the Gentiles, until the Jews brought him up on charges before Gallio, deputy of Achaia. Gallio refused to hear the case and allowed Crispus to be beaten before his court. Shortly thereafter Paul left the city.

Paul wrote two epistles (1 and 2 Corinthians) to the troubled church at Corinth. A letter of rebuke, written between the two letters that appear in scripture, seems to have been lost.

FIRST REFERENCE
ACTS 18:1
LAST REFERENCE
2 TIMOTHY 4:20

CRETE　　NT5

An island south of Greece that Paul passed on his way to Rome. Though Paul advised the centurion in whose care he was traveling that they should stop at Crete, his advice was not heeded and their ship was wrecked. Paul's student Titus ministered on Crete, appointing elders for the church.

FIRST REFERENCE
ACTS 27:7
LAST REFERENCE
TITUS 1:5

CUSH　　OT1

The exact location of Cush is unclear in scripture, and scholars have varying opinions of its location. Ezekiel 29:10 seems to indicate that it was south of Egypt, but other verses seem to imply that it also included Arabia (Isaiah 11:11; 45:14). The word translated "Cush" in modern versions often appears as "Ethiopia" in the King James Version of the Bible. Isaiah prophesied that God would recover a remnant of his people from Cush. See Ethiopia.

ONLY REFERENCE
ISAIAH 11:11

CUTH　　OT1

A city northeast of Babylon from which people were brought to resettle Samaria after its people were taken away as captives by the Assyrians. The people of Cuth worshipped a pagan god named Nergal. Same as Cuthah.

ONLY REFERENCE
2 KINGS 17:30

CUTHAH · OT1

A city northeast of Babylon from which people were brought to resettle Samaria after its people were taken away as captives by the Assyrians. Same as Cuth.

ONLY REFERENCE
2 KINGS 17:24

CYPRUS · NT8

An island south of Asia Minor's Roman province of Cilicia and west of Syria that was the disciple Barnabas's homeland. During the persecution following Stephen's death, Jewish believers traveled to Cyprus and preached only to the Jews. But the believers of Cyprus passed the Good News on to Antioch, preaching to the Greeks there. Barnabas and Saul visited Cyprus early in their missionary efforts. After they went their separate ways, Barnabas returned with Mark. Paul only passed by Cyprus on his way to Jerusalem and again on his way to Rome.

FIRST REFERENCE
ACTS 4:36
LAST REFERENCE
ACTS 27:4

CYRENE · NT4

A Greek city of Libya and hometown of Simon, the man whom the Romans chose to bear Jesus' cross. People from Cyrene were present at Pentecost. Jews from Cyrene argued with Stephen and persuaded others to charge him with blasphemy. With the Cypriots, some men of Cyrene helped spread the Gospel to the Greeks in Antioch.

FIRST REFERENCE
MATTHEW 27:32
LAST REFERENCE
ACTS 13:1

-D-

DABAREH OT1
A word

A Levitical city of the tribe of Issachar. Same as Daberath.

ONLY REFERENCE
JOSHUA 21:28

DABBASHETH OT1
Sticky mass (meaning the hump of a camel)

A city that became part of the inheritance of Zebulun when Joshua cast lots in Shiloh to provide territory for the seven tribes that had yet to receive their land.

ONLY REFERENCE
JOSHUA 19:11

DABERATH OT2
A word

A city that became part of the inheritance of Issachar when Joshua cast lots in Shiloh to provide territory for the seven tribes that had yet to receive their land. Same as Dabareh.

FIRST REFERENCE
JOSHUA 19:12
LAST REFERENCE
1 CHRONICLES 6:72

DALMANUTHA NT1

A place on the western shore of the Sea of Galilee. Jesus and His disciples left for Dalmanutha after the feeding of the four thousand.

ONLY REFERENCE
MARK 8:10

DALMATIA NT1

An area on the eastern coast of the Adriatic Sea. Paul sent Titus to minister here.

ONLY REFERENCE
2 TIMOTHY 4:10

DAMASCUS OT45/NT15

An ancient Syrian city, northeast of Tyre, that King David conquered when the Syrians supported Hadadezer, king of Zobah, in battle. Following David's conquest, Damascus paid Israel tribute. But by the time of King Asa, Judah was paying tribute to King Ben-hadad of Damascus and attempting to gain the support of the city against Baasha, king of Israel.

After he lost a battle and was captured, the Syrian king Ben-hadad II promised King Ahab of Israel that he would return the cities his father had taken from Israel and allow Israel to trade in Damascus's lucrative markets, if Ahab would spare his life.

When King Ahaz of Judah met Assyria's king Tiglath-pileser in Damascus, he saw a pagan altar there and had it copied so he could use it in pagan worship in the temple in Jerusalem.

The prophets Isaiah, Jeremiah, and Amos foretold the destruction of Damascus by the Assyrians.

Near Damascus Saul was confronted by Christ. Temporarily blinded, he had to be led into the city, where he was healed when Ananias laid hands on him. Converted, Saul quickly began preaching Christ in the synagogues of Damascus. Same as Syria-Damascus.

FIRST REFERENCE
GENESIS 14:15
LAST REFERENCE
GALATIANS 1:17
KEY REFERENCES
2 SAMUEL 8:6; 1 KINGS 20:26–34; 2 KINGS 16:10–14; ISAIAH 17:1; ACTS 9:3

DAN OT23
Judge

The name of both a city and the area inherited by the tribe of Dan.

The city of Dan was originally named Laish (or Leshem). Before the tribe received its inheritance in the west, they attacked this city and renamed it after their forefather. The city lay in the northernmost part of Israel, leading to the expression "from Dan even to Beer-sheba," which indicated the two farthest points of the nation (Judges 20:1).

After Jeroboam became king of Israel, he feared his people would return to the rule of David's descendants. So he drew them into idolatry by setting up a golden calf god in the city of Dan.

The tribal area of Dan lay in the west, between Ephraim and Judah. When Ezekiel prophesied about the coming Messiah and the division of the land, Dan was given land in the northernmost part of Israel. He also foresaw that there would be a gate of Dan in the New Jerusalem.

FIRST REFERENCE
GENESIS 14:14
LAST REFERENCE
AMOS 8:14
KEY REFERENCES
JUDGES 18:29; 2 KINGS 10:29; EZEKIEL 48:1

DAN-JAAN OT1
Judge of purpose

A place where Joab, the commander of David's army, brought the captains of his host when they counted the people of Israel.

ONLY REFERENCE
2 SAMUEL 24:6

DANNAH OT1

A city that became part of the inheritance of the tribe of Judah following the conquest of the Promised Land.

ONLY REFERENCE
JOSHUA 15:49

DEBIR — OT13
Shrine or oracle

1) A city of the Anakim that Joshua and his troops attacked, captured, and destroyed. Debir became part of the inheritance of the tribe of Judah following the conquest of the Promised Land and later became a Levitical city. Same as Kirjath-sannah and Kirjath-sepher.

FIRST REFERENCE
JOSHUA 10:38
LAST REFERENCE
I CHRONICLES 6:58
KEY REFERENCES
JOSHUA 10:38–39; 15:15; JUDGES 1:11

2) Part of the border of the territory given to the tribe of Gad.

ONLY REFERENCE
JOSHUA 13:26

DECAPOLIS — NT3
Ten-city region

A territory defined by a confederation of ten cities settled by the Greeks, Decapolis was largely southeast of the Sea of Galilee, with an area west of the Jordan River around Scythopolis (Bethshan). People from this area were among the crowd that followed Jesus early in His ministry. Around the Decapolis, a Gadarene whom Jesus released from a legion of evil spirits testified to his healing.

FIRST REFERENCE
MATTHEW 4:25
LAST REFERENCE
MARK 7:31

DEDAN — OT6

An area near Edom that the prophet Jeremiah described as drinking of God's wrath. When the prophet Ezekiel prophesied against Edom, he foretold its desolation to Dedan. He also spoke multiple times of Dedan's people as being merchants to Tyre.

FIRST REFERENCE
JEREMIAH 25:23
LAST REFERENCE
EZEKIEL 38:13

DERBE — NT4

A city of Asia Minor's Roman province of Lycaonia. Paul and Barnabas fled to Derbe after Paul was stoned at Lystra. Paul's companion Gaius was from Derbe.

FIRST REFERENCE
ACTS 14:6
LAST REFERENCE
ACTS 20:4

DIBLATH — OT1

The prophet Ezekiel described Diblath, a place in northern Canaan, as being desolate. Same as Riblah.

ONLY REFERENCE
EZEKIEL 6:14

DIBON — OT9
Pining

1) A Moabite city that the tribe of Gad asked to have as their

inheritance and turned into a fortified city. But Joshua 13:17 counts it as part of the inheritance of Reuben. The prophet Isaiah saw Moab weeping in Dibon, and the prophet Jeremiah foresaw the city's judgment by God. Same as Dimon and Dimonah.

FIRST REFERENCE
NUMBERS 21:30
LAST REFERENCE
JEREMIAH 48:22

2) A city of Judah resettled by the Jews after the Babylonian exile.

ONLY REFERENCE
NEHEMIAH 11:25

DIBON-GAD   OT2
Pining Gad

A campsite of the Israelites on their way to the Promised Land.

FIRST REFERENCE
NUMBERS 33:45
LAST REFERENCE
NUMBERS 33:46

DILEAN   OT1

A city that became part of the inheritance of the tribe of Judah following the conquest of the Promised Land.

ONLY REFERENCE
JOSHUA 15:38

DIMNAH   OT1
A dung heap

A Levitical city of the tribe of Zebulun.

ONLY REFERENCE
JOSHUA 21:35

DIMON   OT1
Pining

A Moabite city. The prophet Isaiah described its waters as being full of blood. Same as Dibon 1 and Dimonah.

ONLY REFERENCE
ISAIAH 15:9

DIMONAH   OT1
Pining

A city that became part of the inheritance of the tribe of Judah following the conquest of the Promised Land. Same as Dibon 1 and Dimon.

ONLY REFERENCE
JOSHUA 15:22

DINHABAH   OT2

The capital city of King Bela of Edom.

FIRST REFERENCE
GENESIS 36:32
LAST REFERENCE
1 CHRONICLES 1:43

DIZAHAB   OT1
Of gold

A spot in the Sinai Desert near which Moses spoke to the Israelites. His speeches are preserved in the book of Deuteronomy.

ONLY REFERENCE
DEUTERONOMY 1:1

DOPHKAH OT2
A knock

A campsite of the Israelites on their way to the Promised Land.

FIRST REFERENCE
NUMBERS 33:12
LAST REFERENCE
NUMBERS 33:13

DOR OT6
Dwelling

A Canaanite city and its surrounding area that Joshua and his troops conquered. It became part of the inheritance of Manasseh, but the tribe did not drive out the original inhabitants of the area.

Under King Solomon's governmental organization, Dor was responsible for supplying provisions for the king.

FIRST REFERENCE
JOSHUA 11:2
LAST REFERENCE
1 CHRONICLES 7:29

DOTHAN OT3

A place where Joseph's brothers pastured their sheep and sold him into slavery. Later Dothan became the prophet Elisha's home.

FIRST REFERENCE
GENESIS 37:17
LAST REFERENCE
2 KINGS 6:13

DUMAH OT2
To be dumb; silence; death (figuratively)

1) A city that became part of the inheritance of the tribe of Judah following the conquest of the Promised Land.

ONLY REFERENCE
JOSHUA 15:52

2) An oasis in Edom. In the prophet Isaiah's oracle about Dumah, a watchman is asked, "What is left of the night?" (NIV) as Edom seeks to hope for the morning.

ONLY REFERENCE
ISAIAH 21:11

DURA OT1
Circle or dwelling

A plain in Babylon where King Nebuchadnezzar set up a golden statue and demanded that his subjects bow before it. Shadrach, Meshach, and Abednego refused and were thrown into the fiery furnace.

ONLY REFERENCE
DANIEL 3:1

-E-

EBEN-EZER OT3
Stone of the help

1) The site of Israel's camp when, during the time of the judge Samuel, they went into battle against the Philistines encamped at Aphek. Israel brought the ark of the covenant from Shiloh to their campsite at Eben-ezer, hoping the ark would save them. Instead Israel fled before the Philistines, who captured the ark, and the priest Eli's sons were slain.

FIRST REFERENCE
I SAMUEL 4:1
LAST REFERENCE
I SAMUEL 5:1

2) A stone that Samuel set up between Mizpeh and Shen that commemorated Israel's victory over the Philistines at Mizpeh.

ONLY REFERENCE
I SAMUEL 7:12

EBRONAH OT2
Transitional

A campsite of the Israelites on their way to the Promised Land.

FIRST REFERENCE
NUMBERS 33:34
LAST REFERENCE
NUMBERS 33:35

ED OT1

The name of an altar built by the Reubenites and Gadites as a witness that, though they lived across the Jordan River, they shared in the western tribes' worship of the Lord.

ONLY REFERENCE
JOSHUA 22:34

EDAR OT1
An arrangement (that is, a muster of animals)

A tower that Israel camped by after Rachel died and was buried near Beth-lehem.

ONLY REFERENCE
GENESIS 35:21

EDEN OT18
Pleasure

1) A garden that God planted for Adam and Eve to live in just after their creation. Eden was filled with pleasant trees and plants for food. God made the animals and had Adam name them. The couple were to care for Eden but were commanded not to eat of "the tree of the knowledge of good and evil." When they listened to the serpent and disobeyed God's command, God sent the couple out of the garden so they could not eat of the tree of life and live forever in their sin.

The prophets Isaiah and Ezekiel promised that if God's people sought righteousness, God would make their desolate land like the Garden of Eden.

FIRST REFERENCE
GENESIS 2:8
LAST REFERENCE
JOEL 2:3
KEY REFERENCES
GENESIS 2:8–3:24; ISAIAH 51:3; EZEKIEL 36:35

2) The Assyrians conquered this area that traded with Tyre. According to the book of Amos, its people went into exile in Kir.

FIRST REFERENCE
2 KINGS 19:12
LAST REFERENCE
AMOS 1:5

EDER   OT1

An arrangement (that is, a muster of animals)

A city that became part of the inheritance of the tribe of Judah following the conquest of the Promised Land.

ONLY REFERENCE
JOSHUA 15:21

EDOM   OT7

Red

The land of Esau (who was also called Edom), which was inhabited by his descendants and lay south of Moab and southeast of the Dead Sea, south of Zered Brook. The prophet Jeremiah described the inhabitants of this mountainous nation as living "in the clefts of the rock, that holdest the height of the hill" (Jeremiah 49:16). Edom was ruled by kings well before Israel established a kingly line. Refused permission to cross Edom on the King's Highway, the Israelites traveled just beyond the edge of that nation on their way to the Promised Land.

King Saul fought Edom, along with the other nations that surrounded Israel. When David conquered the nation, putting garrisons throughout it, he fulfilled Balaam's prophecy that Israel would possess it, including its highest point, Mount Seir (2 Samuel 8:14; Numbers 24:18). For six months after this conquest, David's battle commander Joab remained in Edom "until he had cut off every male in Edom" (1 Kings 11:16).

Solomon used the Edomite ports of Elath and Ezion-geber for the ships sent to him by Hiram of Tyre. During King Jehoram of Judah's reign, Edom successfully rebelled, freeing itself from Jewish rule (2 Kings 8:22). King Amaziah of Judah went to war with Edom, killed ten thousand of its warriors, and took its capital, Selah. Amaziah's son, King Azariah, regained Elath for Judah, but the nation did not hold it. Under King Ahaz, it was taken by Rezin, king of Syria.

Edom did not forget its history of warfare with Judah. When Jerusalem was attacked by the Chaldeans, the Edomites delighted in its destruction (Psalm 137:7). But Jeremiah continued his prophecy with the promise that though the nation made its nest "as high as the eagle," God would bring it down (Jeremiah 49:16). The prophet Ezekiel foretold that because Edom took vengeance on Israel, its land would be made desolate by God (Ezekiel 25:13–14).

Eventually, under the Maccabees, the Edomites were incorporated into the Jewish people. Same as Idumaea and Idumea.

FIRST REFERENCE
GENESIS 36:21
LAST REFERENCE
2 CHRONICLES 8:17

EDREI   OT8
Mighty

1) A city of Bashan and site of a battle between Og, king of Bashan, and the Israelites. It became part of the inheritance of the tribe of Manasseh following Israel's conquest of the Promised Land.

FIRST REFERENCE
NUMBERS 21:33
LAST REFERENCE
JOSHUA 13:31

2) A fortified or walled city that became part of the inheritance of Naphtali when Joshua cast lots in Shiloh to provide territory for the seven tribes that had yet to receive their land.

ONLY REFERENCE
JOSHUA 19:37

EGLAIM   OT1
A double pond

A Moabite city that Isaiah prophesied would grieve at the destruction of its nation.

ONLY REFERENCE
ISAIAH 15:8

EGLON   OT8
Vituline (having to do with calves or veal)

An Amorite city, ruled by King Debir, that opposed Joshua and the Israelites when they invaded the Promised Land. Joshua killed Debir and his battle allies. Then Israel besieged Eglon, conquered it, and killed all its people. The city became part of the inheritance of the tribe of Judah following the conquest of the Promised Land.

FIRST REFERENCE
JOSHUA 10:3
LAST REFERENCE
JOSHUA 15:39

EGYPT   OT587/NT24

An often-powerful nation southwest of Israel, in the northeastern corner of Africa, Egypt first appears in scripture when famine affected Canaan and Abram and Sarai attempted to find sanctuary in that country. Because of her beauty, Pharaoh took Sarai into his household and gave her brother Abram many gifts. When Pharaoh discovered that Abram was also her husband, he sent the couple out of his country.

God promised in His covenant with Abram that his ancestors would own the land "from the river of Egypt," a stream marking Judah's southwestern border, to the Euphrates (Genesis 15:18).

Sold into slavery by his jealous brothers, Jacob's son Joseph ended up ruling Egypt, second in power only to Pharaoh. As the famine Joseph foretold spread to Canaan, his brothers traveled to Egypt for some of the food their brother had stockpiled to provide for the lean years. After Joseph revealed himself to them, Jacob and his family moved to Egypt, to the land of Goshen, where they prospered and multiplied.

A new king ruled Egypt and, fearing the Israelites, made them slaves. Attempting to limit their numbers, he ordered the midwives to kill all male newborns. So when Moses was born, his mother hid him then set him adrift in a small basket. An Egyptian princess found and raised the infant. As an adult, Moses attempted to defend his fellow Israelites, killed an Egyptian, and fled to Midian. But God returned him to Egypt with a message of judgment for Pharaoh and one of hope for Israel.

When Pharaoh refused to let Israel leave his country, God poured out increasing judgments, in the form of plagues, on the ruler and his nation. Though God turned the Nile to blood; overwhelmed the land with frogs, gnats, and flies; struck the cattle with a plague and the people with boils; sent hail and locusts down on the land; and darkened the sun, Pharaoh remained adamant. Only after all the firstborn of both humans and animals died did he let Israel go.

Still unable to give them up, the ruler gathered his soldiers and followed God's people. Therefore God destroyed Egypt's troops in the Red Sea as He led His people to safety on dry ground. This salvation of His people became an ongoing theme in scripture, and there are numerous references to this event in the Bible.

King Solomon married one of Pharaoh's daughters and traded with that land. But his son Rehoboam, king of Judah, saw Jerusalem attacked and plundered by Shishak, king of Egypt. Hoshea, king of Israel, conspired with So, king of Egypt, and brought down on himself the wrath of the king of Assyria. As a result, the northern kingdom was made captive by the Assyrians. When Egypt's pharaoh Necho opposed the king of Assyria, King Josiah of Judah supported Assyria and was killed in battle. Josiah's son Jehoahaz was captured by Necho, who made Jehoiakim king in his place.

After Nebuchadnezzar conquered Judah, the remaining leaders of Judah did not believe Jeremiah's prophecy when he told them to remain in that land. Instead they led all the Jews who had not been deported to Babylon, including Jeremiah and his scribe Baruch, to Egypt. As the prophet had warned, Nebuchadnezzar attacked Egypt, so the people of Judah did not avoid the empire they so feared. In the Prophets, Egypt is commonly associated with paganism and the Jews' unfaithfulness to God.

Following the birth of Jesus, God commanded Joseph to take Mary and Jesus into Egypt to escape Herod the Great's rage. After Herod's death, God called the family back to Israel.

FIRST REFERENCE
GENESIS 12:10
LAST REFERENCE
REVELATION 11:8
KEY REFERENCES
GENESIS 41:41; EXODUS 6:11; 20:2;
2 KINGS 25:26; MATTHEW 2:14

EKRON   OT22
Eradication

One of the five major Philistine cities, Ekron remained unconquered when Joshua was old. Originally part of the inheritance of the tribe of Judah, it became part of the inheritance of Dan when Joshua cast lots in Shiloh to provide territory for the seven tribes that had yet to receive their land. Judges 1:18 tells of Judah's capture of Ekron and its territory, but obviously the land fell back into Philistine hands, since Ekron again belonged to the Philistines when the ark of the covenant was captured. After the Philistines captured the ark, the people of Ekron refused to have it in their city because they had heard of the destruction it caused in Ashdod and Gath.

King Ahaziah of Israel looked to Baal-zebub, the god of Ekron, when he wanted to know if he would recover from a fall. God sent Elijah to confront the king with his faithlessness. The prophets foretold the destruction of this pagan city. Jeremiah described it as one of the places upon which God's wrath will be poured, and Zephaniah foresaw that it will be uprooted (Jeremiah 25:20; Zephaniah 2:4).

FIRST REFERENCE
JOSHUA 13:3
LAST REFERENCE

ZECHARIAH 9:7
KEY REFERENCES
I SAMUEL 5:10; 2 KINGS 1:2

ELAH   OT3
An oak (or other strong tree)

The valley where King Saul and his men camped when they confronted Goliath and the Philistines. None of the soldiers in Saul's army was willing to fight the giant. David came to visit his brothers, fought with the Philistine champion, and killed Goliath here.

FIRST REFERENCE
I SAMUEL 17:2
LAST REFERENCE
I SAMUEL 21:9

ELAM   OT15
Hidden (that is, distant)

A nation east of Babylonia, north of the Persian Gulf. Elam's king Chedorlaomer led the force that attacked Sodom and captured Abram's nephew Lot.

The prophet Isaiah foretold a time when God would recall His people from Elam, a nation that had allied itself with Assyria and attacked Jerusalem. Jeremiah prophesied that the Lord would judge Elam, and Ezekiel foresaw a slain multitude of its soldiers.

FIRST REFERENCE
GENESIS 14:1
LAST REFERENCE
DANIEL 8:2
KEY REFERENCES
JEREMIAH 49:34; EZEKIEL 32:24

ELATH OT 5
Trees or a grove of palms

A port on the Gulf of Aqabah that is mentioned as Israel bypassed Edom during the Exodus. Azariah (also called Uzziah), king of Judah, rebuilt Elath. During King Ahaz of Judah's reign, Rezin, king of Syria, recovered the city. Same as Eloth.

FIRST REFERENCE
DEUTERONOMY 2:8
LAST REFERENCE
2 KINGS 16:6

EL-BETHEL OT 1
The God of Bethel

A place where Jacob built an altar because God had appeared there before him as he fled from his brother, Esau. Same as Bethel and Luz 1.

ONLY REFERENCE
GENESIS 35:7

ELEALEH OT 5
God is going up

A town the tribe of Reuben requested as part of its inheritance before Israel crossed the Jordan River. In his oracle about the destruction of Moab, Isaiah saw Elealeh crying out and weeping in grief.

FIRST REFERENCE
NUMBERS 32:3
LAST REFERENCE
JEREMIAH 48:34

EL-ELOHE-ISRAEL OT 1
The mighty God of Israel

An altar that Jacob erected at Shalem after his reconciliation with his brother, Esau.

ONLY REFERENCE
GENESIS 33:20

ELEPH OT 1
A family (as in yoking or taming an ox or cow)

A city that became part of the inheritance of Benjamin when Joshua cast lots in Shiloh to provide territory for the seven tribes that had yet to receive their land.

ONLY REFERENCE
JOSHUA 18:28

ELIM OT 6
Palm trees

An encampment of the Israelites during the Exodus. Elim had twelve wells and seventy palm trees.

FIRST REFERENCE
EXODUS 15:27
LAST REFERENCE
NUMBERS 33:10

ELLASAR OT 2

A nation that joined King Chedorlaomer of Elam in an attack on Sodom, during which Abram's nephew Lot was captured. Ellasar's king was named Arioch.

FIRST REFERENCE
GENESIS 14:1
LAST REFERENCE
GENESIS 14:9

ELON OT1
Oak grove

A city that became part of the inheritance of Dan when Joshua cast lots in Shiloh to provide territory for the seven tribes that had yet to receive their land.

ONLY REFERENCE
JOSHUA 19:43

ELON-BETH-HANAN OT1
Oak grove of the house of favor

Under King Solomon's governmental organization, a town responsible for supplying provisions for the king.

ONLY REFERENCE
1 KINGS 4:9

ELOTH OT3
Trees or a grove (of palms)

An Edomite port on the Red Sea where King Solomon started a navy. King Uzziah (also called Azariah) of Judah built up the port and regained it as part of Judah's territory. Same as Elath.

FIRST REFERENCE
1 KINGS 9:26
LAST REFERENCE
2 CHRONICLES 26:2

EL-PARAN OT1
Oak of Paran

A place near Canaan's wilderness. King Chedorlaomer of Elam and the other kings who rose up against Sodom fought a battle up to this place.

ONLY REFERENCE
GENESIS 14:6

ELTEKEH OT2

A city that became part of the inheritance of Dan when Joshua cast lots in Shiloh to provide territory for the seven tribes that had yet to receive their land. Eltekeh became one of the six cities of refuge established in Israel for those who had committed accidental murder.

FIRST REFERENCE
JOSHUA 19:44
LAST REFERENCE
JOSHUA 21:23

ELTEKON OT1
God is straight

A city that became part of the inheritance of the tribe of Judah following the conquest of the Promised Land.

ONLY REFERENCE
JOSHUA 15:59

ELTOLAD OT2
God is generator

A city that became part of the inheritance of the tribe of Judah following the conquest of the Promised Land. Later Eltolad became part of the inheritance of Simeon when Joshua cast lots in Shiloh to provide territory for the seven tribes that had yet to receive their land.

FIRST REFERENCE
JOSHUA 15:30
LAST REFERENCE
JOSHUA 19:4

EMMAUS NT1

A village about seven miles from Jerusalem. As Cleopas and another disciple were traveling to Emmaus after the Crucifixion, they met the resurrected Jesus but did not recognize Him. They discussed the events surrounding His crucifixion, and Jesus interpreted the scriptures about Himself. The two disciples recognized Him as He broke bread with them in Emmaus.

ONLY REFERENCE
LUKE 24:13

ENAM OT1
Double fountain

A city that became part of the inheritance of the tribe of Judah following the conquest of the Promised Land.

ONLY REFERENCE
JOSHUA 15:34

ENDOR OT3
Fountain of dwelling

A town that became part of the inheritance of Manasseh, though it fell within Issachar's boundaries. When God did not respond to Saul's inquiry about the threat of the Philistine troops at Gilboa, Saul went to Endor to consult a medium. Saul asked the medium to bring up Samuel for him. The spirit told Saul that both Israel and Saul would be given into the hands of the Philistines. When Saul went into battle, Israel lost, and Saul and his sons were killed.

FIRST REFERENCE
JOSHUA 17:11
LAST REFERENCE
PSALM 83:10

EN-EGLAIM OT1
Fountain of two calves

A place in the Red Sea that Ezekiel foretold would be filled with fish when Jerusalem is finally restored.

ONLY REFERENCE
EZEKIEL 47:10

EN-GANNIM OT3
Fountain of gardens

1) A city that became part of the inheritance of the tribe of Judah following the conquest of the Promised Land.

ONLY REFERENCE
JOSHUA 15:34

2) A city that became part of the inheritance of Issachar when Joshua cast lots in Shiloh to provide territory for the seven tribes that had yet to receive their land. Later it became a Levitical city.

FIRST REFERENCE
JOSHUA 19:21
LAST REFERENCE
JOSHUA 21:29

EN-GEDI OT6
Fountain of a kid

A city on the Dead Sea that became part of the inheritance of the tribe of Judah following the conquest of the Promised Land. David lived here for a time when Saul sought his life. Ezekiel foresaw it as a place whose waters would be teeming with fish when Jerusalem is finally restored. Same as Hazazon-tamar and Hazezon-tamar.

FIRST REFERENCE
JOSHUA 15:62
LAST REFERENCE
EZEKIEL 47:10

EN-HADDAH OT1
Fountain of sharpness

A city that became part of the inheritance of Issachar when Joshua cast lots in Shiloh to provide territory for the seven tribes that had yet to receive their land.

ONLY REFERENCE
JOSHUA 19:21

EN-HAKKORE OT1

A spring in Lehi that God created for the thirsty Samson after he killed a thousand men with the jawbone of a donkey.

ONLY REFERENCE
JUDGES 15:19

EN-HAZOR OT1
Fountain of a village

A fortified or walled city that became part of the inheritance of Naphtali when Joshua cast lots in Shiloh to provide territory for the seven tribes that had yet to receive their land.

ONLY REFERENCE
JOSHUA 19:37

EN-MISHPAT OT1
Fountain of judgment

A city or its surrounding area that King Chedorlaomer of Elam and his Mesopotamian allies attacked as they battled against the Amalekites and the Amorites. Same as Kadesh, Kadesh-barnea, and Kedesh 4.

ONLY REFERENCE
GENESIS 14:7

ENOCH OT1
Initiated

A city that Cain built and named after his son.

ONLY REFERENCE
GENESIS 4:17

EN-RIMMON OT1
Fountain of a pomegranate

A place in Judah resettled by the Jews after the Babylonian exile.

ONLY REFERENCE
NEHEMIAH 11:29

EN-ROGEL OT4
Fountain of a traveler

A spring that identified part of the border between the tribes of Judah and Benjamin. When King David's son Adonijah attempted to take the throne, he held a feast here.

FIRST REFERENCE
JOSHUA 15:7
LAST REFERENCE
1 KINGS 1:9

EN-SHEMESH OT2
Fountain of the sun

A spring that identified part of the border between the tribes of Judah and Benjamin.

FIRST REFERENCE
JOSHUA 15:7
LAST REFERENCE
JOSHUA 18:17

EN-TAPPUAH OT1
Fountain of an apple tree

A town that identified part of the border of the tribe of Manasseh.

ONLY REFERENCE
JOSHUA 17:7

EPHES-DAMMIM OT1
Boundary of blood drops

A place where the Philistine army established a camp. From here Goliath challenged the Israelites to battle.

ONLY REFERENCE
I SAMUEL 17:1

EPHESUS NT17

Capital of the Roman province of Asia, in the western part of Asia Minor. On his way to Jerusalem, Paul stopped in Ephesus and spoke to the Jews in its synagogue. Apollos preached in the city, knowing only the baptism of John the Baptist, but when Priscilla and Aquila heard his preaching, they taught him the full way of God.

The idol maker Demetrius stirred up a riot against Paul in Ephesus, because the apostle's preaching hurt his business. He made his case against Paul with his fellow silversmiths, who became so angered they took to the streets. A crowd formed, caught up two of Paul's companions, and headed for the theater. For two hours they cried out, "Great is Diana of the Ephesians." Finally the town clerk calmed them and encouraged them to make use of the law instead of continuing this unlawful gathering.

From prison in Rome, Paul wrote an epistle to the Ephesian church focusing on the need for unity in the body of Christ.

In the book of Revelation, John relays Jesus' message to the church in Ephesus. Christ praises them for their good deeds but warns that they have lost their first love.

FIRST REFERENCE
ACTS 18:19
LAST REFERENCE
REVELATION 2:1
KEY REFERENCES
ACTS 18:24–26; 19:21–41; REVELATION 2:1–7

EPHRAIM OT38/NT1
Double fruit

1) A mountainous area that was part of the inheritance of the tribes of Ephraim and Manasseh. Joshua, son of Nun, received the city of Timnath-serah in Mount Ephraim, where he lived and was buried.

Mount Ephraim was also the home of a man named Micah, who established a "house of gods" and asked a Levite to become his priest. The Danites took Micah's priest and his idols from him and used them to fall into their own idolatry. King Jehoshaphat of Judah brought Mount Ephraim back to the Lord.

Though Jeremiah saw the people of Mount Ephraim being afflicted by God for their sinfulness, in the end he foretold their satisfaction of the soul.

FIRST REFERENCE
JOSHUA 17:15
LAST REFERENCE
JEREMIAH 50:19
KEY REFERENCES
JOSHUA 24:30; JUDGES 7:24

2) A town near Baal-hazor, where Absalom had sheepshearers.

ONLY REFERENCE
2 SAMUEL 13:23

3) A forest where King David's troops fought the troops of his son Absalom. During the battle Absalom's head became caught in the thick boughs of an oak tree. When David's battle commander Joab heard of this, he went to the tree and killed Absalom, against the king's command.

ONLY REFERENCE
2 SAMUEL 18:6

4) A gate in the wall of Jerusalem. The city's walls were broken down between this gate and the corner gate when, after capturing King Amaziah of Judah, Jehoash, king of Israel, attacked the city.

FIRST REFERENCE
2 KINGS 14:13
LAST REFERENCE
NEHEMIAH 12:39

5) A city near Israel's wilderness where Jesus went after He raised Lazarus from the dead and the Jewish leaders sought to kill Him.

ONLY REFERENCE
JOHN 11:54

EPHRAIN OT1
Fawnlike

A city taken from King Jeroboam of Israel by Abijah, king of Judah.

ONLY REFERENCE
2 CHRONICLES 13:19

EPHRATAH OT3
Fruitfulness

Hometown of Boaz and Ruth. The prophet Micah foretold that the Messiah would come from here. Same as Beth-lehem, Bethlehem, Beth-lehem-judah, and probably Ephrath.

FIRST REFERENCE
RUTH 4:11
LAST REFERENCE
MICAH 5:2

EPHRATH OT4
Fruitfulness

Rachel was buried near this town. Probably the same as Beth-lehem, Bethlehem, Beth-lehem-judah, and Ephratah.

FIRST REFERENCE
GENESIS 35:16
LAST REFERENCE
GENESIS 48:7

EPHRON OT1
Fawnlike

A mountain that formed part of the border of the tribe of Judah.

ONLY REFERENCE
JOSHUA 15:9

ERECH OT1
Length

A city in the kingdom of Nimrod, who ruled the land of Shinar.

ONLY REFERENCE
GENESIS 10:10

ESAU OT4
Handling; rough (that is, sensibly felt)

A mountain in Edom (another name for Esau). The book of Obadiah speaks of God's judgment falling on the Mount of Esau as it loses its understanding and its people are killed. In the end, God will rule Edom.

FIRST REFERENCE
OBADIAH 8
LAST REFERENCE
OBADIAH 21

ESEK OT1
Strife

A well dug by Isaac's servants. When the herdsmen of Gerar found out about it, they tried to claim this well.

ONLY REFERENCE
GENESIS 26:20

ESHCOL OT4

A brook in a valley of the same name where the spies whom Moses sent into Canaan cut down a large cluster of grapes and other fruit to show the bounty of the land.

FIRST REFERENCE
NUMBERS 13:23
LAST REFERENCE
DEUTERONOMY 1:24

ESHEAN OT1
Support

A city that became part of the inheritance of the tribe of Judah following the conquest of the Promised Land.

ONLY REFERENCE
JOSHUA 15:52

ESHTAOL OT7
Intreaty

A city that became part of the inheritance of the tribe of Judah following the conquest of the Promised Land. Later it became part of the inheritance of Dan when Joshua cast lots in Shiloh to provide territory for the seven tribes that had yet to receive their land.

FIRST REFERENCE
JOSHUA 15:33
LAST REFERENCE
JUDGES 18:11

ESHTEMOA OT3
To hear intelligently (with the sense of obedience)

A Levitical city of the tribe of Judah.

David sent some of the spoils from his warfare with the Amalekites to Eshtemoa. Same as Eshtemoh.

FIRST REFERENCE
JOSHUA 21:14
LAST REFERENCE
I CHRONICLES 6:57

ESHTEMOH OT1

A city that became part of the inheritance of the tribe of Judah following the conquest of the Promised Land. See Eshtemoa.

ONLY REFERENCE
JOSHUA 15:50

ETAM OT4
Hawk ground

1) A rock where Samson lived after he attacked the Philistines for giving his wife to another man. The men of Judah came there and bound him, planning to hand him over to their Philistine overlords. But when they reached Lehi, the ropes that bound Samson loosened, and he attacked his enemies with the jawbone of a donkey.

FIRST REFERENCE
JUDGES 15:8
LAST REFERENCE
JUDGES 15:11

2) A village that became part of the inheritance of the tribe of Simeon.

ONLY REFERENCE
I CHRONICLES 4:32

3) A city that King Rehoboam fortified to defend Judah.

ONLY REFERENCE
2 CHRONICLES 11:6

ETHAM OT4

A campsite of the Israelites on their way to the Promised Land.

FIRST REFERENCE
EXODUS 13:20
LAST REFERENCE
NUMBERS 33:8

ETHER OT2
Abundance

A city that became part of the inheritance of the tribe of Judah following the conquest of the Promised Land. Later it became part of the inheritance of Simeon when Joshua cast lots in Shiloh to provide territory for the seven tribes that had yet to receive their land.

FIRST REFERENCE
JOSHUA 15:42
LAST REFERENCE
JOSHUA 19:7

ETHIOPIA OT8/NT1

A nation south of Egypt, stretching along the Nile River from Aswan to Khartoum. Esther's husband, the Persian king Ahasuerus (also called Xerxes), ruled over Ethiopia, which formed a border of his domain. The eunuch whom the apostle Philip met and baptized on his journey from Jerusalem to Gaza came from Ethiopia and served Candace, the queen of that nation. The word translated "Cush" in modern Bible versions often appears as "Ethiopia" in the King James Version of the Bible. Same as Cush.

EUPHRATES
OT19/NT2
To break forth; rushing

FIRST REFERENCE
GENESIS 2:13
LAST REFERENCE
ACTS 8:27

A river that Genesis 2:14 describes as flowing out of Eden's river. The Euphrates River flows from Turkey to the Persian Gulf and is one of the rivers enclosing Mesopotamia.

God covenanted with Abram that the land from the river of Egypt, on Judah's southwestern border, to the Euphrates would be given to his descendants. The Lord renewed the promise with Joshua as Israel entered the Promised Land.

King Solomon's kingdom stretched as far as the Euphrates River in the north, and King Josiah of Judah fought near the Euphrates with Pharaoh Necho of Egypt.

In the book of Revelation, John describes the vial of wrath that will be poured out on the Euphrates, drying it up.

FIRST REFERENCE
GENESIS 2:14
LAST REFERENCE
REVELATION 16:12
KEY REFERENCES
GENESIS 15:18; JOSHUA 1:4;
1 CHRONICLES 18:3

EZEL
OT1
Departure

A stone where Jonathan met David to warn him to flee from Saul.

ONLY REFERENCE
1 SAMUEL 20:19

EZEM
OT1
Bone

A city that became part of the inheritance of the tribe of Simeon.

ONLY REFERENCE
1 CHRONICLES 4:29

EZION-GABER
OT4
Backbone of a man

An Edomite seaport that the Israelites used as a campsite on their way to the Promised Land. Jehoshaphat, king of Judah, joined with Ahaziah, king of Israel, to build a fleet in Ezion-gaber, intending the ships to sail for Tarshish. But the ships were broken by the Lord. Same as Ezion-geber.

FIRST REFERENCE
NUMBERS 33:35
LAST REFERENCE
2 CHRONICLES 20:36

EZION-GEBER
OT3
Backbone of a man

An Edomite seaport at which King Solomon developed a navy for Israel. King Jehoshaphat of Judah made ships he intended to send to Ophir for gold, but they were broken at Ezion-geber. Same as Ezion-gaber.

FIRST REFERENCE
1 KINGS 9:26
LAST REFERENCE
2 CHRONICLES 8:17

-F-

FAIR HAVENS NT1

An anchorage on Crete, near La-sea, where Paul and his companions stopped on their way to Rome. Though Paul warned against putting to sea again, Fair Havens was not a good place to stay for the winter. The vessel set off again and was shipwrecked.

ONLY REFERENCE
ACTS 27:8

-G-

GAASH OT4
A quaking

Joshua was buried on the north side of this hill in Mount Ephraim. One of David's valiant warriors was Hurai of the brooks of Gaash.

FIRST REFERENCE
JOSHUA 24:30
LAST REFERENCE
I CHRONICLES 11:32

GABA OT3
A hillock

A city that became part of the inheritance of Benjamin when Joshua cast lots in Shiloh to provide territory for the seven tribes that had yet to receive their land. Exiles returned here from Babylon. Same as Geba.

FIRST REFERENCE
JOSHUA 18:24
LAST REFERENCE
NEHEMIAH 7:30

GABBATHA NT1
The knoll

Also called the Pavement, Gabbatha was the place where Pilate judged cases. Here he heard the Jews' complaints against Jesus and gave Him over to be crucified.

ONLY REFERENCE
JOHN 19:13

GADARA NT3

The land of the Gadarenes. The name Gadara never actually appears in scripture, only the name of its people. Here Jesus healed the man with a legion of unclean spirits who lived among the tombs. Despite this amazing miracle, the Gadarenes requested that Jesus and His disciples leave their land.

FIRST REFERENCE
MARK 5:1
LAST REFERENCE
LUKE 8:37

GALATIA NT6

A Roman province in the center of Asia Minor. For a time, the Holy Spirit forbade Paul and Silas to preach here. But later, on his third missionary journey, Paul strengthened the disciples in the provinces of Galatia and Phrygia. The apostle reminded the church of Galatia that he first preached to them because of an illness he suffered (Galatians 4:13).

Paul wrote an epistle to the Galatians to establish the authority for his apostleship, to counter the influence of the law-bound Judaizers who had swayed some Galatians away from the gospel, and to encourage these Christians to believe in salvation by grace.

FIRST REFERENCE
ACTS 16:6
LAST REFERENCE
I PETER 1:1

GALEED   OT2
Heap of testimony

Jacob's name for the memorial mound that commemorated his covenant with his father-in-law, Laban. Laban called it Jegar-sahadutha. Same as Jegar-sahadutha and Mizpah 1.

FIRST REFERENCE
GENESIS 31:47
LAST REFERENCE
GENESIS 31:48

GALILEE   OT6/NT66
A circle

An area in the north of Israel that may originally have been part of the inheritance of the tribe of Naphtali. Israel did not overpower the people who inhabited the area, so it became a racially mixed area, earning it the name "Galilee of the Gentiles."

When King Solomon gave twenty Galilean towns to Hiram, king of Tyre, the area also included the tribe of Asher's land. Same as Cabul 2.

Following the Jews' return from exile, this name referred to a much larger territory that included the northernmost of the three provinces of Palestine.

King Tiglath-pileser of Assyria overthrew Pekah, king of Israel; the victor captured Galilee and transported captives to his own land.

In Nazareth, a city of Galilee, Mary received the news that she would bear the Messiah. Following Jesus' birth and the family's flight into Egypt, Joseph received an angelic message that he was to return to Israel. He brought his family to Galilee to avoid the rule of Archelaeus, a son of Herod the Great. Jesus grew up in Nazareth but moved to another Galilean town, Capernaum, at the beginning of His ministry, to fulfill Isaiah's prophecy that the lands of Zebulun (the tribe of Nazareth) and Naphtali (the tribe of Capernaum) would see a great light.

At the Sea of Galilee, Jesus called the disciples Simon, Andrew, James, John, and Philip. He preached to the people of Galilee, drawing crowds to Himself. In Cana of Galilee, He performed the first miracle, followed by healings. When the Jews sought His life, at the time of the Feast of Tabernacles, Jesus remained for a while in Galilee. When He finally went to Jerusalem, many questioned whether a prophet would come from Galilee. At the Last Supper, Jesus promised that after His resurrection He would go before His disciples to Galilee.

When the Jews wanted to kill Jesus, Pilate, discovering that Jesus was from Galilee, sent Him to its tetrarch, Herod Antipas, to be judged. But Herod, unwilling to take on this hot issue, sent Jesus back to Pilate for judgment.

When the women who had followed Jesus from Galilee discovered that His body was missing from the tomb, both an angel and the Lord gave them a message that the disciples should return to Galilee, where they would see Him again. When they obeyed, they were reunited with the Master.

FIRST REFERENCE
JOSHUA 20:7
LAST REFERENCE
ACTS 13:31
KEY REFERENCES
1 KINGS 9:10–13; 2 KINGS 15:29;
MATTHEW 4:12–16

GALLIM   OT2
Springs

Hometown of Mical's second husband, Phalti. Isaiah foretold that this Benjaminite city would rejoice at the Assyrians' destruction.

FIRST REFERENCE
1 SAMUEL 25:44
LAST REFERENCE
ISAIAH 10:30

GAREB   OT1
Scabby

A hill that Jeremiah foretold will be used as a measurement for the final rebuilding of Jerusalem when the city is restored.

ONLY REFERENCE
JEREMIAH 31:39

GATH   OT33
Treading out grapes; a winepress

One of the few Anakite cities in which Joshua did not entirely eradicate that people. But Gath did not remain under Israel's control, instead becoming one of Philistia's five most important cities. During the time of the judge Samuel, the Philistines captured the ark of the covenant and it was moved to Gath. After the people of that city were afflicted with tumors for their possession of the ark, they sent it to Ekron. During Samuel's rule, Gath was returned to Israel (1 Samuel 7:14).

Goliath came from this city. After David killed the giant, Israel's troops chased the Philistines as far as Gath. But when Saul sought to kill David, Israel's popular warrior fled to Gath and pretended he was mad. King Achish objected to having him there, so David escaped to the cave of Adullam. Eventually David and his troops returned to Gath and served the Philistine king.

Shimei, who had cursed King David and been forgiven, was required by King Solomon to stay in Jerusalem, because David had warned his son against the man. When Shimei traveled to Gath to recover an escaped slave, Solomon had Shimei executed.

Ownership of Gath went back and forth between Judah and its enemies. King Rehoboam of Judah built up the defenses of the city to defend his country, but Hazael, king of Aram, captured it. King Uzziah of Judah conquered Gath again and broke down the city walls.

FIRST REFERENCE
JOSHUA 11:22
LAST REFERENCE
MICAH 1:10
KEY REFERENCES
I SAMUEL 21:10; 27:2; I CHRONICLES 18:1

GATH-HEPHER
OT1

Winepress of the well

Hometown of the prophet Jonah.

ONLY REFERENCE
2 KINGS 14:25

GATH-RIMMON
OT4

Winepress of the pomegranate

1) A city that became part of the inheritance of Dan when Joshua cast lots in Shiloh to provide territory for the seven tribes that had yet to receive their land. It was later one of the forty-eight cities given to the Levites as God had commanded.

FIRST REFERENCE
JOSHUA 19:45
LAST REFERENCE
JOSHUA 21:24

2) One of the forty-eight cities given to the Levites as God had commanded. Gath-rimmon was given to them by the tribe of Manasseh.

FIRST REFERENCE
JOSHUA 21:25
LAST REFERENCE
I CHRONICLES 6:69

GAZA
OT18/NT1

Strong

1) An ancient Canaanite city that was conquered by the Philistines and became one of their most important cities. Joshua subdued Gaza, and it became part of the inheritance of Judah, but some Canaanites remained in the city.

Samson tore loose Gaza's city gates, where his enemies lay in wait to attack him. After the Philistines finally captured him and made him their slave, they took him to Gaza. As his hair grew, Samson regained his strength and pulled down the pillars of the temple of Dagon, killing himself and the worshippers.

King Hezekiah of Judah defeated the Philistines as far as Gaza. The prophets foresaw God's judgment of the Philistines and Gaza's destruction.

On the road to Gaza, Philip met the Ethiopian eunuch and led him to the Lord.

FIRST REFERENCE
GENESIS 10:19
LAST REFERENCE
ACTS 8:26
KEY REFERENCES
JUDGES 16:1, 21

2) A city of the tribe of Ephraim. At the time of Gideon, the Midianites destroyed the land of Israel up to Gaza.

FIRST REFERENCE
JUDGES 6:4
LAST REFERENCE
I CHRONICLES 7:28

GAZER OT2
Something cut off; a portion

God commanded David to fight the Philistines from Gibeon to this city. Same as Gezer.

FIRST REFERENCE
2 SAMUEL 5:25
LAST REFERENCE
I CHRONICLES 14:16

GEBA OT12
A hillock

One of the forty-eight cities given to the Levites as God had commanded. Geba was given to them by the tribe of Benjamin. When the city was in Philistine hands, Jonathan attacked this garrison, and David fought the Philistines up to Geba. King Josiah of Judah defiled Geba, which had become a place of pagan worship. After the return from exile, the people of this city lived at Michmash, Aija, and Bethel. Same as Gaba.

FIRST REFERENCE
JOSHUA 21:17
LAST REFERENCE
ZECHARIAH 14:10

GEBAL OT2
Chain of hills; mountain

1) A nation near the Dead Sea that joined other persistent enemies of Israel in opposing God's people.

ONLY REFERENCE
PSALM 83:7

2) Another name for the Phoenician city of Byblos, which traded extensively in papyrus scrolls.

ONLY REFERENCE
EZEKIEL 27:9

GEBIM OT1
Cisterns

A village above Jerusalem. Isaiah foresaw Gebim attempting to hide from God's wrath.

ONLY REFERENCE
ISAIAH 10:31

GEDER OT1
A circumvallation or siege wall

A Canaanite city on the western side of the Jordan River that Joshua and his men overthrew.

ONLY REFERENCE
JOSHUA 12:13

GEDERAH OT1
Enclosure (especially for flocks)

A city that became part of the inheritance of the tribe of Judah following the conquest of the Promised Land.

ONLY REFERENCE
JOSHUA 15:36

GEDEROTH OT2
Enclosures (especially for flocks)

A city that became part of the inheritance of the tribe of Judah following the conquest of the Promised Land. During the reign of King Ahaz of Judah, it was one of the cities of the southern low country of Judah that was invaded and occupied by the Philistines.

FIRST REFERENCE
JOSHUA 15:41
LAST REFERENCE
2 CHRONICLES 28:18

GEDEROTHAIM OT1
Double wall

A city that became part of the inheritance of the tribe of Judah following the conquest of the Promised Land.

ONLY REFERENCE
JOSHUA 15:36

GEDOR OT3
Enclosure

1) A city that became part of the inheritance of the tribe of Judah following the conquest of the Promised Land.

ONLY REFERENCE
JOSHUA 15:58

2) Hometown of Jehoram, whose sons Joelah and Zebadiah joined David's mighty men at Ziklag.

ONLY REFERENCE
1 CHRONICLES 12:7

3) A valley that the descendants of Simeon conquered, displacing the Hamites and Meunites, so they would have pastures for their flocks.

ONLY REFERENCE
1 CHRONICLES 4:39

GELILOTH OT1
Circles

A place on the border of the tribe of Benjamin's territory.

ONLY REFERENCE
JOSHUA 18:17

GENNESARET NT3

A plain along the northwest border of the Sea of Galilee. The Lake of Gennesaret is another name for the Sea of Galilee.

FIRST REFERENCE
MATTHEW 14:34
LAST REFERENCE
LUKE 5:1

GERAR OT10
A rolling country

A Canaanite city where Abraham and Sarah lived. Because the couple had said they were brother and sister, Abimelech, king of Gerar, took Sarah as one of his women. When God revealed their marriage to Abimelech, he gave Abraham and Sarah many gifts and told them to live wherever they wanted in his land.

Isaac lived in Gerar at God's command. When Abimelech's people became jealous over Abraham's wells, the king of Gerar told Isaac to leave. The patriarch settled in the valley of Gerar, but the herdsmen there demanded the wells Isaac's servants had dug, so Isaac moved again.

King Asa of Judah conquered the cities around Gerar.

FIRST REFERENCE
GENESIS 10:19
LAST REFERENCE
2 CHRONICLES 14:14

GERIZIM OT4
Cut up

A mountain in Samaria, near Shechem, where the Israelite leaders were to bless the people after they entered the Promised Land. From this mountain Jotham also spoke to the men of Shechem about making Abimelech their king.

FIRST REFERENCE
DEUTERONOMY 11:29
LAST REFERENCE
JUDGES 9:7

GESHUR OT8
Bridge

Maacah, daughter of the Syrian king of Geshur, married David and bore him a son, Absalom. After killing his half brother Amnon, Absalom fled to Geshur for three years. When King David commanded that his son return to Jerusalem, Joab traveled to Geshur and brought Absalom back.

FIRST REFERENCE
2 SAMUEL 3:3
LAST REFERENCE
1 CHRONICLES 3:2

GETHSEMANE NT2
Oil press

A garden across the Kidron Valley from Jerusalem, on the Mount of Olives. Jesus brought His disciples to Gethsemane, where He prayed, asking the Father to take the cup of crucifixion from Him. Despite His deep sorrow, Jesus accepted His Father's will, while His nearby disciples, Peter, James, and John, fell asleep. An armed crowd came to Gethsemane, and Jesus was arrested after Judas betrayed Him with a kiss. The disciples fled as their Master was led away to face the Sanhedrin.

FIRST REFERENCE
MATTHEW 26:36
LAST REFERENCE
MARK 14:32

GEZER OT13
Something cut off; a portion

A Canaanite city on the west side of the Jordan River whose king, Horam, fought against Joshua and his people at Lachish. Israel killed all of Horam's troops and conquered the city. Gezer fell to the lot of Ephraim, but that tribe did not drive out the Canaanites, only made them do forced labor for Israel. Ephraim gave Gezer to the Levites as a city of refuge as God had commanded. During King David's reign, war erupted with the Philistines at Gezer, and these enemies of Israel were conquered.

The pharaoh of Egypt, King

Solomon's father-in-law, conquered Gezer, taking it from the Canaanites and burning the city. Then he gave it as a present or dowry to his daughter. Solomon rebuilt and fortified the city. Same as Gazer.

FIRST REFERENCE
JOSHUA 10:33
LAST REFERENCE
I CHRONICLES 20:4
KEY REFERENCE
I KINGS 9:15–17

GIAH   OT1
A fountain

A place near the wilderness of Gibeon where Abner attempted to make peace between his tribe (the tribe of Benjamin) and Joab, commander of King David's troops.

ONLY REFERENCE
2 SAMUEL 2:24

GIBBETHON   OT6
A hilly spot

A city that became part of the inheritance of Dan when Joshua cast lots in Shiloh to provide territory for the seven tribes that had yet to receive their land. One of the forty-eight cities given to the Levites as God had commanded, Gibbethon was given to them by the tribe of Dan.

The Philistines controlled Gibbethon when Baasha killed King Nadab of Israel, who was besieging the city, then took his throne. Later, Zimri murdered Baasha's son, King Elah, in an attempt to make himself king. Omri, Israel's battle commander, withdrew from Gibbethon and laid siege to Zimri's capital of Tirzah.

FIRST REFERENCE
JOSHUA 19:44
LAST REFERENCE
I KINGS 16:17

GIBEAH   OT48
A hillock

A city that became part of the inheritance of the tribe of Judah following the conquest of the Promised Land. Scripture implies that it became part of the inheritance of Benjamin when Joshua cast lots in Shiloh to provide territory for the seven tribes that had yet to receive their land.

The wickedness of the men of Gibeah was indicated by their attempt to abuse a Levite, a visitor to their city. When his host would not allow it, the Levite sent his concubine out to them. They sexually abused and killed her. That Levite roused Israel against Gibeah. After a three-day battle, the Israelites withdrew to Baal-tamar, drawing the Benjaminites out of Gibeah. Then the Israelites entered the city and conquered it. The Israelites outside the city surrounded their enemies as they fled, and Israel won the battle.

Gibeah was Saul's home, and the book of 1 Samuel often places him there. Hosea several times refers to the sinfulness of the incident in Judges. Same as Gibeath.

FIRST REFERENCE
JOSHUA 15:57
LAST REFERENCE
HOSEA 10:9
KEY REFERENCE
JUDGES 19:1–20:48

GIBEATH   OT1
Hilliness

A city that became part of the inheritance of Benjamin when Joshua cast lots in Shiloh to provide territory for the seven tribes that had yet to receive their land. Same as Gibeah.

ONLY REFERENCE
JOSHUA 18:28

GIBEON   OT35
Hilly

This Hivite city's wily leaders saw that the invading Israelites were a danger and sent representatives to Joshua, who tricked him into believing they came from a distant country that wanted to make peace with Israel. After Joshua made an agreement with them, he discovered they were near neighbors.

The Gibeonites called on Joshua to defend them against five Amorite kings who besieged their city because they had made peace with Israel. Joshua kept his agreement and supported Gibeon in battle. When Joshua asked God to make the sun stand still so the battle could continue, it remained in the sky until they had avenged their allies. Gibeon was the only city that made peace with Israel as the Israelites conquered the Promised Land.

Gibeon became part of the inheritance of Benjamin when Joshua cast lots in Shiloh to provide territory for the seven tribes that had yet to receive their land. It later became one of the forty-eight cities given to the Levites as God had commanded.

At Gibeon, Joab, David's battle commander, fought and overcame Abner, commander of Saul's host. But Abner killed Joab's brother Asahel, beginning a feud that brought about Abner's death. Later, on a stone at Gibeon, Joab killed Amasa, commander of David's army.

Before the Jerusalem temple was built, sacrifices were made to the Lord at Gibeon. Solomon sacrificed here after he became king.

FIRST REFERENCE
JOSHUA 9:3
LAST REFERENCE
JEREMIAH 41:16
KEY REFERENCE
I KINGS 3:4–5

GIDOM   OT1
A cutting (that is, desolation)

After the men of Gibeah abused and killed a visiting Levite's concubine, the Israelites rose up against the tribe of Benjamin, chased them, and fought them as far as Gidom, killing two thousand men.

ONLY REFERENCE
JUDGES 20:45

GIHON OT6
Stream

1) An Ethiopian river that was one of the four fed by Eden's river.

ONLY REFERENCE
GENESIS 2:13

2) A spring near Jerusalem where Solomon was anointed king by Zadok the priest at King David's command. King Hezekiah, threatened by war with Babylon, cut a shaft that redirected the water of this spring directly into Jerusalem.

FIRST REFERENCE
I KINGS 1:33
LAST REFERENCE
2 CHRONICLES 33:14

GILBOA OT8
Fountain of ebullition

A mountain southeast of the city of Jezreel 2. On Mount Gilboa, the Philistines fought and killed the Israelites in their last battle with King Saul. King Saul's sons died in battle. When the king realized he would lose the battle, he killed himself there.

FIRST REFERENCE
I SAMUEL 28:4
LAST REFERENCE
I CHRONICLES 10:8

GILEAD OT87
Probably derived from "heap of testimony"

1) From this mountainous area east of the Jordan River, sometimes called Mount Gilead, came the Ishmaelite spice merchants who took Joseph to Egypt as a slave. Gilead was well known for its trade in spices and medicinal herbs. In perhaps the best-known reference to this, Jeremiah ironically asked, "Is there no balm in Gilead?" (Jeremiah 8:22).

Here Jacob fled when he left his father-in-law, Laban.

Before the Israelites entered the Promised Land, Gilead was ruled by Og, king of Bashan, and Sihon, king of the Amorites. Before they entered the Promised Land, Reuben and Gad requested that Moses allot them the rich pasturelands of Gilead as their inheritance, since these tribes owned many cattle. Manasseh inherited the northernmost area of Gilead and dispossessed the Amorites who lived there.

In the time of the judges, the Ammonites camped in Gilead while the Israelites gathered at Mizpeh. The Israelites called on the outcast Jephthah to command them, and he led their troops to victory in battle. Later he led the men of Gilead in battle against Ephraim.

Abner, commander of Saul's army, made Saul's son Ish-bosheth king of Gilead after his father's death. But Ish-bosheth ruled only two years before David was made king. The Syrian king Hazael conquered Gilead, taking it from Jehu, king of Israel.

The prophet Hosea denounced Gilead for its wickedness.

But Zechariah promised that God would bring so many of His scattered people back to the land that they would not all fit there.

FIRST REFERENCE
GENESIS 31:21
LAST REFERENCE
ZECHARIAH 10:10
KEY REFERENCES
NUMBERS 32:1; JUDGES 10:17–11:33;
2 SAMUEL 2:8–9; JEREMIAH 8:22

2) A mountain range from which Gideon sent the fearful portion of his troops home.

ONLY REFERENCE
JUDGES 7:3

3) A city of Gilead, possibly Ramoth-gilead. Or it may be the Gilead referred to in Judges 10:17. See Gilead 1.

ONLY REFERENCE
HOSEA 6:8

GILGAL OT41
A wheel

1) The first Israelite encampment in the Promised Land, "in the east border of Jericho." Here Joshua made a memorial of the twelve stones the Israelites took out of the Jordan River after they crossed it. Joshua circumcised the Israelites at Gilgal, and God removed the reproach of Egypt from them there.

Samuel judged Israel at Gilgal in a kind of circuit court. And here he made Saul king, with public sacrifices. Later, when Saul and his people faced war with the Philistines, and Samuel did not come to Gilgal, Saul wrongly took the prophet's place and sacrificed a burnt offering. At Gilgal Samuel confronted Saul for another disobedience, his failure to obey God's command to kill all the Amalekites' cattle following Israel's victorious battle over that nation.

The men of Judah met King David at Gilgal after he had fled from Jerusalem and his traitorous son, Absalom, and put down the rebellion. From Gilgal, the men escorted the rightful king back over the Jordan River.

The prophets repeatedly condemned Israel's sin at Gilgal, which had become a site of pagan worship.

FIRST REFERENCE
DEUTERONOMY 11:30
LAST REFERENCE
MICAH 6:5
KEY REFERENCES
JOSHUA 4:19; 5:9–10; 2 SAMUEL 19:12–15

2) A city between Dor and Tirzah. Gilgal was conquered by Joshua and the Israelites.

ONLY REFERENCE
JOSHUA 12:23

3) A place Elijah and Elisha passed through before God took Elijah up in a whirlwind. Elisha returned there during a famine and performed a miracle when Gilgal's prophets had eaten a poisonous stew. Elisha put meal or flour in the pot, and it was no longer harmful.

FIRST REFERENCE
2 KINGS 2:1
LAST REFERENCE
2 KINGS 4:38

GILOH OT2
Open

A city that became part of the inheritance of the tribe of Judah following the conquest of the Promised Land. It was the home of Ahithophel, King David's counselor who traitorously supported the claim of David's son Absalom to the throne.

FIRST REFERENCE
JOSHUA 15:51
LAST REFERENCE
2 SAMUEL 15:12

GIMZO OT1

A city of the southern low country of Judah that the Philistines invaded and occupied during the reign of King Ahaz.

ONLY REFERENCE
2 CHRONICLES 28:18

GITTAH-HEPHER OT1
Winepress of the well

A city that became part of the inheritance of Zebulun when Joshua cast lots in Shiloh to provide territory for the seven tribes that had yet to receive their land.

ONLY REFERENCE
JOSHUA 19:13

GITTAIM OT2
Double winepress

1) A city, possibly of Benjamin, that the non-Jewish Beerothites fled to and made their home.

ONLY REFERENCE
2 SAMUEL 4:3

2) A town of Benjamin resettled by the Jews after the Babylonian exile.

ONLY REFERENCE
NEHEMIAH 11:33

GOATH OT1
Lowing

A place near Jerusalem that Jeremiah foretold would be encompassed by the restored Jerusalem as it was finally "built to the LORD" (Jeremiah 31:38).

ONLY REFERENCE
JEREMIAH 31:39

GOB OT2
Pit

During King David's reign, Israel twice fought the Philistines here, and his mighty men killed some Philistine giants.

FIRST REFERENCE
2 SAMUEL 21:18
LAST REFERENCE
2 SAMUEL 21:19

GOLAN OT4

Captive

A city of refuge established by Moses on the east bank of the Jordan River, before Israel entered the Promised Land. It became part of the inheritance of the tribe of Manasseh.

FIRST REFERENCE
DEUTERONOMY 4:43
LAST REFERENCE
1 CHRONICLES 6:71

GOLGOTHA NT3

The skull

The place near Jerusalem where Jesus was crucified. Golgotha is mentioned by all the Gospel writers except Luke, who calls it by the Latin name, Calvary. Scripture tells us Golgotha was beyond the walls of the city: "Jesus also suffered outside the city gate" (Hebrews 13:12 NIV). John adds that there was a garden there, as well as an unused tomb in which He was buried (John 19:41–42). Same as Calvary.

FIRST REFERENCE
MATTHEW 27:33
LAST REFERENCE
JOHN 19:17

GOMORRAH OT19/NT1

A ruined heap

One of five Canaanite "cities of the plain" at the southern end of the Dead Sea. In scripture Gomorrah is most often connected with its sister city of the plain, Sodom. Both lay in the well-watered plain of the Jordan River, where Lot decided to settle. When the cities of the plain were attacked by the king of Shinar and his allies, Lot was taken captive.

Because of their sinfulness, God destroyed these cities by raining down fire and brimstone upon them until the smoke went up as if they were furnaces. In the Prophets, Sodom and Gomorrah's names became bywords for God's judgment of sin. Same as Gomorrha.

FIRST REFERENCE
GENESIS 10:19
LAST REFERENCE
2 PETER 2:6
KEY REFERENCES
GENESIS 13:10; 19:24, 28

GOMORRHA NT4

This Greek form of the name Gomorrah refers to the Canaanite city destroyed by God. Same as Gomorrah.

FIRST REFERENCE
MATTHEW 10:15
LAST REFERENCE
JUDE 7

GOSHEN OT15

1) A section east of the Nile River delta that the Israelites settled in after Joseph brought them to Egypt. Here Joseph first met his father after many years of separation. In Goshen the Jews lived separately from the Egyptians because foreign shepherds were not held

in high esteem. Yet Pharaoh approved of their resettlement in his land. When God sent the plagues against Egypt, they did not affect His people in Goshen.

FIRST REFERENCE
GENESIS 45:10
LAST REFERENCE
EXODUS 9:26
KEY REFERENCES
GENESIS 46:29, 34; EXODUS 8:22

2) An area in the southern part of what would later become Judah. Joshua and the Israelites conquered Goshen, along with the rest of the south country.

FIRST REFERENCE
JOSHUA 10:41
LAST REFERENCE
JOSHUA 11:16

3) A city that became part of the inheritance of the tribe of Judah following the conquest of the Promised Land.

ONLY REFERENCE
JOSHUA 15:51

GOZAN OT5
A quarry

An Assyrian river and probably the area around it to which the Samaritans were transported after Shalmaneser, king of Assyria, conquered Israel.

FIRST REFERENCE
2 KINGS 17:6
LAST REFERENCE
ISAIAH 37:12

GRECIA OT3
Latin form of Greece

This variation of the name Greece is used only in the book of Daniel, describing the prophet's vision about the empires of Media, Persia, and Greece.

FIRST REFERENCE
DANIEL 8:21
LAST REFERENCE
DANIEL 11:2

GREECE OT1/NT1

Though Greece was a mighty ancient European empire, it is infrequently mentioned in scripture. Zechariah spoke of Greece as an enemy of God's people. The book of Acts only once uses the nation's name to describe Paul's mission there. More often, scripture speaks of the individual Greek cities or provinces that were stops on the apostle's second and third missionary journeys.

FIRST REFERENCE
ZECHARIAH 9:13
LAST REFERENCE
ACTS 20:2

GUDGODAH OT1
Cleft

An encampment of the Israelites after God gave Moses the second tablets of the law and after Aaron's death.

ONLY REFERENCE
DEUTERONOMY 10:7

GUR OT1

A place near Ibleam where Ahaziah, king of Judah, was attacked by the soldiers of Israel's king Jehu.

ONLY REFERENCE
2 KINGS 9:27

GUR-BAAL OT1

An area in Arabia conquered by King Uzziah of Judah.

ONLY REFERENCE
2 CHRONICLES 26:7

-H-

HABOR OT3
United

A district of Assyria to which King Shalmaneser of Assyria transported the Israelites after he conquered Samaria.

FIRST REFERENCE
2 KINGS 17:6
LAST REFERENCE
1 CHRONICLES 5:26

HACHILAH OT3
Dark

While King Saul was pursuing David, twice the Ziphites reported to him that David was hiding in this wooded hill south of Jeshimon. When Saul went to capture David, the first time he received a report that the Philistines were attacking Israel, and he had to leave. The second time, David's spies warned their leader. David entered Saul's camp at night and took a spear and water jar to prove he had been there. The next day, he confronted Saul and proved he did not want to harm the king.

FIRST REFERENCE
1 SAMUEL 23:19
LAST REFERENCE
1 SAMUEL 26:3

HADADRIMMON
OT1

A place in the valley of Megiddo that the prophet Zechariah spoke of as suffering deep mourning.

ONLY REFERENCE
ZECHARIAH 12:11

HADASHAH OT1
New

A city that became part of the inheritance of the tribe of Judah following the conquest of the Promised Land.

ONLY REFERENCE
JOSHUA 15:37

HADATTAH OT1

A city that became part of the inheritance of the tribe of Judah following the conquest of the Promised Land.

ONLY REFERENCE
JOSHUA 15:25

HADID OT3

A place in Benjamin resettled by the Jews after the Babylonian exile.

FIRST REFERENCE
EZRA 2:33
LAST REFERENCE
NEHEMIAH 11:34

HADRACH OT1

A part of Syria that is mentioned nowhere else in scripture. The prophet Zechariah proclaimed that the word of the Lord was against this land by the Orontes River.

ONLY REFERENCE
ZECHARIAH 9:1

HAI OT2

Abram camped at this city, building an altar near Hai, when he first entered the Promised Land. Same as Ai.

FIRST REFERENCE
GENESIS 12:8
LAST REFERENCE
GENESIS 13:3

HALAH OT3

A district in Assyria to which King Shalmaneser transported the Israelites after he conquered Samaria.

FIRST REFERENCE
2 KINGS 17:6
LAST REFERENCE
1 CHRONICLES 5:26

HALAK OT2
Bare

A mountain in southern Canaan that Joshua and his warriors conquered.

FIRST REFERENCE
JOSHUA 11:17
LAST REFERENCE
JOSHUA 12:7

HALHUL OT1
Contorted

A city that became part of the inheritance of the tribe of Judah following the conquest of the Promised Land.

ONLY REFERENCE
JOSHUA 15:58

HALI OT1
A trinket (as polished)

A city that became part of the inheritance of Asher when Joshua cast lots in Shiloh to provide territory for the seven tribes that had yet to receive their land.

ONLY REFERENCE
JOSHUA 19:25

HAMATH OT34
Walled

Capital of a kingdom, called by the same name, in northern Syria, held by the Hivites. When God used the Philistines, Canaanites, Sidonians, and Hivites to teach the children of Israel war as they conquered the Promised Land, it was in the area from Baal-hermon "unto the entering in of Hamath" (Judges 3:3; translated "Lebo Hamath" in some Bible versions). Later, when King David conquered Hadadezer, king of Zobah, King Toi (or Tou) of Hamath sent his son to David "to salute him, and to bless him" and bring him gifts (2 Samuel 8:9–10; 1 Chronicles 18:9–10).

At least part of the area of Hamath eventually belonged to Israel. When King Solomon dedicated the temple, all Israel from Hamath to the river of Egypt joined in the celebration. Solomon also made Hamath a store city that housed provisions for his nation. Though it once belonged to Judah, Hamath came into Israel's grasp when King Jeroboam recovered both it and Damascus.

After the king of Assyria conquered Samaria, he repeopled it with pagan men from Hamath. When Rabshakeh tried to win Jerusalem without a fight, he warned the people in that holy city of his master's power, pointing out that the gods of Hamath had not protected its people during the Assyrian conquest.

After being conquered by Pharaoh Necho, King Jehoahaz of Judah was imprisoned in the land of Hamath. Here also Nebuchadnezzar killed Israel's chief priests, King Zedekiah's sons, and all the princes of Judah after the fall of Jerusalem.

Isaiah prophesied that when the Messiah established His kingdom, God's people from Hamath would be recovered. But Isaiah also asked where the gods of that land were, to point out their total lack of power and complete destruction. The prophet Ezekiel foretold a day when Hamath would be a border of the restored Israel.

FIRST REFERENCE
NUMBERS 13:21
LAST REFERENCE
ZECHARIAH 9:2
KEY REFERENCES
1 KINGS 8:65; 2 KINGS 14:28;
2 CHRONICLES 8:4

HAMATH-ZOBAH
OT 1

Walled station

A city conquered by King Solomon. Scholars disagree on whether this is the same city as Hamath.

ONLY REFERENCE
2 CHRONICLES 8:3

HAMMATH
OT 1

Hot springs

A fortified or walled city that became part of the inheritance of Naphtali when Joshua cast lots in Shiloh to provide territory for the seven tribes that had yet to receive their land.

ONLY REFERENCE
JOSHUA 19:35

HAMMON
OT 2

Warm spring

1) A city that became part of the inheritance of Asher when Joshua cast lots in Shiloh to provide territory for the seven tribes that had yet to receive their land.

ONLY REFERENCE
JOSHUA 19:28

2) One of the forty-eight cities given to the Levites as God had commanded. Hammon was given to them by the tribe of Naphtali. Same as Hammoth-dor.

ONLY REFERENCE
1 CHRONICLES 6:76

HAMMOTH-DOR
OT 1

Hot springs of Dor

One of the forty-eight cities given to the Levites as God had commanded. Hammoth-dor was given to them by the tribe of Naphtali. Same as Hammon 2.

ONLY REFERENCE
JOSHUA 21:32

HAMONAH
OT 1

Multitude

A town in the valley of Hamongog that the prophet Ezekiel foretold would become a graveyard.

ONLY REFERENCE
EZEKIEL 39:16

HAMON-GOG
OT 2

The multitude of Gog

Following God's destruction of Israel's enemy Gog, Ezekiel foresaw that Gog's dead troops would be buried in this valley. It would take seven months to bury all the dead there.

FIRST REFERENCE
EZEKIEL 39:11
LAST REFERENCE
EZEKIEL 39:15

HANANEEL
OT 4

God has favored

One of Jerusalem's towers, Hananeel was sanctified by the high priest Eliashib after Nehemiah rebuilt the walls. Jeremiah foretold that this tower will be part of the eternal Jerusalem of God's kingdom.

FIRST REFERENCE
NEHEMIAH 3:1
LAST REFERENCE
ZECHARIAH 14:10

HANES OT1

Isaiah warned God's people against trusting in Egypt and its power. Egypt's ambassadors, he said, would come to this place, which was probably in Egypt.

ONLY REFERENCE
ISAIAH 30:4

HANNATHON OT1
Favored

A city on the border of the tribe of Zebulun's territory.

ONLY REFERENCE
JOSHUA 19:14

HAPHRAIM OT1
Double pit

A city that became part of the inheritance of Issachar when Joshua cast lots in Shiloh to provide territory for the seven tribes that had yet to receive their land.

ONLY REFERENCE
JOSHUA 19:19

HARA OT1
Mountainousness

Because of the idolatry of the tribes of Reuben, Gad, and Manasseh, God stirred up the Assyrians, who conquered these tribes and carried them to this Assyrian province.

ONLY REFERENCE
I CHRONICLES 5:26

HARADAH OT2
Fear; anxiety

A campsite of the Israelites on their way to the Promised Land.

FIRST REFERENCE
NUMBERS 33:24
LAST REFERENCE
NUMBERS 33:25

HARAN OT10
Parched

A Mesopotamian city where Terah and his family settled after they left Ur of the Chaldees. Terah died in Haran, but God sent Terah's son Abram and his family on to the Promised Land.

When Jacob was threatened by his brother, Esau, Rebekah sent her favorite son to her brother, Laban, who lived in Haran.

Rabshakeh's message to King Hezekiah of Judah uses Haran as an example of a city destroyed by Assyria's troops, and Isaiah spoke of its destruction by that nation. Same as Charran.

FIRST REFERENCE
GENESIS 11:31
LAST REFERENCE
EZEKIEL 27:23

HARETH OT1
Forest

A forest in Judah where David hid from King Saul.

ONLY REFERENCE
1 SAMUEL 22:5

HAROD OT1
To shudder with terror; to fear; to hasten with anxiety

A spring that Gideon and his men camped by before God had Gideon send home the fearful warriors. God used the way the warriors drank water to whittle down the number that would battle against Midian.

ONLY REFERENCE
JUDGES 7:1

HAROSHETH OT3
Mechanical work

Home of Sisera, commander of the army of Jabin, king of Canaan. After God gave His people the victory, Israel's battle commander Barak pursued the Canaanites to this city, where all Sisera's troops were killed.

FIRST REFERENCE
JUDGES 4:2
LAST REFERENCE
JUDGES 4:16

HASHMONAH OT2
Fertile

A campsite of the Israelites on their way to the Promised Land.

FIRST REFERENCE
NUMBERS 33:29
LAST REFERENCE
NUMBERS 33:30

HAURAN OT2
Cavernous

A province southeast of Damascus and east of the Sea of Galilee and the Jordan River. The prophet Ezekiel describes it as part of the border of the land of the twelve tribes when Jerusalem is finally restored.

FIRST REFERENCE
EZEKIEL 47:16
LAST REFERENCE
EZEKIEL 47:18

HAVILAH OT3
Circular

1) An area fed by the Pison River, which flowed from the river of the Garden of Eden. Havilah was a land that had gold.

ONLY REFERENCE
GENESIS 2:11

2) An area whose name the Bible always connects with the Shur Desert. It was described as being "before Egypt, as thou goest toward Assyria," and it belonged to the Ishmaelites.

FIRST REFERENCE
GENESIS 25:18
LAST REFERENCE
1 SAMUEL 15:7

HAVOTH-JAIR OT2
Hamlets of Jair

Some small towns of Gilead that were part of the land of Manasseh. They belonged to the thirty sons of Jair, a judge of Israel.

FIRST REFERENCE
NUMBERS 32:41
LAST REFERENCE
JUDGES 10:4

HAZAR-ADDAR OT1
Village of Addar

A place that God used to identify the southern border of Israel when He first gave it to His people.

ONLY REFERENCE
NUMBERS 34:4

HAZAR-ENAN OT4
Village of springs

A place that God used to identify the northern border of Israel when he first gave it to His people. Ezekiel foretold it will be part of the border of the land of the twelve tribes when Jerusalem is finally restored.

FIRST REFERENCE
NUMBERS 34:9
LAST REFERENCE
EZEKIEL 48:1

HAZAR-GADDAH OT1
Village of fortune

A city that became part of the inheritance of the tribe of Judah when Joshua cast lots in Shiloh to provide territory for the seven tribes that had yet to receive their land.

ONLY REFERENCE
JOSHUA 15:27

HAZAR-HATTICON OT1
Village of the middle

Part of the border of the land of the twelve tribes when Jerusalem is finally restored. Hazar-hatticon lay by the coast of Hauran.

ONLY REFERENCE
EZEKIEL 47:16

HAZAR-SHUAL OT4
Village of the fox

A city that became part of the inheritance of the tribe of Judah following the conquest of the Promised Land. It became part of the inheritance of Simeon when Joshua cast lots in Shiloh to provide territory for the seven tribes that had yet to receive their land. After the Babylonian exile, Hazar-shual was resettled by the Jews.

FIRST REFERENCE
JOSHUA 15:28
LAST REFERENCE
NEHEMIAH 11:27

HAZAR-SUSAH OT1

Village of cavalry

A city that became part of the inheritance of Simeon when Joshua cast lots in Shiloh to provide territory for the seven tribes that had yet to receive their land. Same as Hazar-susim.

ONLY REFERENCE
JOSHUA 19:5

HAZAR-SUSIM OT1

Village of horses

A city that became part of the inheritance of the tribe of Simeon. Same as Hazar-susah.

ONLY REFERENCE
1 CHRONICLES 4:31

HAZAZON-TAMAR OT1

Division of the palm tree

Those who warned Jehoshaphat, king of Judah, used this name to describe the location of the encampment of the Moabites, Ammonites, and other enemies of Judah who were poised to attack Judah. Same as En-gedi and Hazezon-tamar.

ONLY REFERENCE
2 CHRONICLES 20:2

HAZERIM OT1

Yards

The territory belonging to a people who were displaced by the Philistines (Caphtorim) who came from Caphtor and settled in Palestine.

ONLY REFERENCE
DEUTERONOMY 2:23

HAZEROTH OT6

Yards

A campsite of the Israelites on their way to the Promised Land.

FIRST REFERENCE
NUMBERS 11:35
LAST REFERENCE
DEUTERONOMY 1:1

HAZEZON-TAMAR OT1

Another name for En-gedi. It was called by this name when Chedorlaomer, king of Elam, and his allies attacked the kings of Sodom, Gommorah, Admah, Zeboiim, and Zoar. Same as En-gedi and Hazazon-tamar.

ONLY REFERENCE
GENESIS 14:7

HAZOR OT19

Village

1) Joshua fought and killed King Jabin of Hazor, destroyed all the people in his city, and burned it. Later Hazor became part of the

inheritance of the tribe of Naphtali. When Israel disobeyed the Lord, He "sold them into the hand of [another] Jabin king of Canaan, that reigned in Hazor" (Judges 4:2). King Solomon raised a levy to fortify Hazor. When King Tiglath-pileser captured Israel, Hazor's people were taken captive to Assyria.

FIRST REFERENCE
JOSHUA 11:1
LAST REFERENCE
1 KINGS 9:15
KEY REFERENCES
JOSHUA 19:32–36; JUDGES 4:2; 2 KINGS 15:29

2) A city that became part of the inheritance of the tribe of Judah following the conquest of the Promised Land.

ONLY REFERENCE
JOSHUA 15:23

3) Another city that became part of the inheritance of the tribe of Judah following the conquest of the Promised Land.

ONLY REFERENCE
JOSHUA 15:25

4) A place resettled by the tribe of Benjamin after the Babylonian exile.

ONLY REFERENCE
NEHEMIAH 11:33

5) A district in Arabia captured by King Nebuchadnezzar of Babylon.

FIRST REFERENCE
JEREMIAH 49:28
LAST REFERENCE
JEREMIAH 49:33

1) A city that became part of the inheritance of Asher when Joshua cast lots in Shiloh to provide territory for the seven tribes that had yet to receive their land.

ONLY REFERENCE
JOSHUA 19:28

2) A place in Palestine where Abram lived and built an altar to the Lord. Sarah died and was buried here. Abraham (Abram) and Isaac lived in the city of Hebron.

During Israel's conquest of the Promised Land, Hoham, king of Hebron, joined an alliance to attack Gibeon, because that city had made peace with Joshua. Joshua came to Gibeon's aid and won the battle, killing Hebron's king and his allies. Then Israel attacked the city, destroying all the people within.

Hebron was one of the forty-eight cities given to the Levites by the tribe of Judah as God had commanded. But the fields and villages became the inheritance of Caleb, as Moses and Joshua had promised. Caleb expelled the three sons of Anak from Hebron.

David sent some of the spoils from his warfare with the Amalekites to Hebron. Here David lived and was anointed king of Judah, and he ruled in Hebron for seven and a half years. After the Israelites came to Hebron to make David their king, too, he moved to Jerusalem.

David's son Absalom had himself declared king in Hebron after telling his father he wanted to go there to fulfill a vow.

Under King Rehoboam of Judah, Hebron became a fortified or walled city. Same as Arbah and Kirjath-arba.

FIRST REFERENCE
GENESIS 13:18
LAST REFERENCE
2 CHRONICLES 11:10
KEY REFERENCES
JOSHUA 10:23–39; 14:13–14; 21:11–13

HELAM OT2
Fortress

A place where King David conquered King Hadarezer of Zobah, who led the Syrians against Israel. After this loss, the Syrians were afraid to continue helping the Ammonites.

FIRST REFERENCE
2 SAMUEL 10:16
LAST REFERENCE
2 SAMUEL 10:17

HELBAH OT1
Fertility

A town that became part of the inheritance of the tribe of Asher. The tribe did not drive the original inhabitants from this place.

ONLY REFERENCE
JUDGES 1:31

HELBON OT1
Fruitful

A city near Damascus that produced wine and traded with Tyre.

ONLY REFERENCE
EZEKIEL 27:18

HELEPH OT1
Change

A city that became part of the inheritance of Naphtali when Joshua cast lots in Shiloh to provide territory for the seven tribes that had yet to receive their land.

ONLY REFERENCE
JOSHUA 19:33

HELKATH OT2
Smoothness

A city that became part of the inheritance of Asher when Joshua cast lots in Shiloh to provide territory for the seven tribes that had yet to receive their land. Helkath became one of the forty-eight cities given to the Levites as God had commanded.

FIRST REFERENCE
JOSHUA 19:25
LAST REFERENCE
JOSHUA 21:31

HELKATH-HAZZURIM OT1
Smoothness of the rocks

A place near the pool of Gibeon where selected warriors of David and Ish-boseth competed with and killed each other. In the ensuing battle, David's troops won.

ONLY REFERENCE
2 SAMUEL 2:16

HENA   OT2

A city conquered by Assyria. Rab-shakeh used its destruction as an example of why Jerusalem should side with his nation.

FIRST REFERENCE
2 KINGS 18:34
LAST REFERENCE
ISAIAH 37:13

HEPHER   OT2
A pit or shame

A kingdom east of the Jordan River conquered by Joshua and his army. Under King Solomon's governmental organization, this region was responsible for supplying provisions for the king.

FIRST REFERENCE
JOSHUA 12:17
LAST REFERENCE
I KINGS 4:10

HEPHZI-BAH   OT1
My delight is in her

A symbolic name that Isaiah used for Jerusalem. It showed God's love for her.

ONLY REFERENCE
ISAIAH 62:4

HERES   OT1
Shining

An Amorite mountain in Aijalon that was subject to the tribe of Ephraim.

ONLY REFERENCE
JUDGES 1:35

HERMON   OT13
Abrupt

A mountain north and slightly east of the Sea of Galilee. Og, king of Bashan, ruled this land before he was defeated by Joshua and his army. Joshua conquered "unto Baal-gad in the valley of Lebanon under mount Hermon" (Joshua 11:17). The psalms speak of Hermon in terms of blessing. Same as Senir, Shenir, Sion 1, and Sirion.

FIRST REFERENCE
DEUTERONOMY 3:8
LAST REFERENCE
SONG OF SOLOMON 4:8
KEY REFERENCES
JOSHUA 12:4–5; 13:5, 11

HESHBON   OT38
Contrivance (implying intelligence)

Capital city of King Sihon of the Amorites. It was conquered by the Israelites after Sihon refused to let Moses and his people pass through on the King's Highway on their way to the Promised Land. Before entering the Promised Land, the tribes of Gad and Reuben requested that Moses make this rich cattle land their inheritance. The prophets Isaiah and Jeremiah speak repeatedly of Heshbon's destruction.

FIRST REFERENCE
NUMBERS 21:25
LAST REFERENCE
JEREMIAH 49:3
KEY REFERENCE
NUMBERS 21:21–26

HESHMON OT1
Opulent

A city that became part of the inheritance of the tribe of Judah following the conquest of the Promised Land.

ONLY REFERENCE
JOSHUA 15:27

HETHLON OT2
Enswathed

A landmark on the border of the land of the twelve tribes when Jerusalem is finally restored.

FIRST REFERENCE
EZEKIEL 47:15
LAST REFERENCE
EZEKIEL 48:1

HEZRON OT2
Courtyard

A town that formed part of the border of the tribe of Judah's territory following the conquest of the Promised Land.

FIRST REFERENCE
JOSHUA 15:3
LAST REFERENCE
JOSHUA 15:25

HIDDEKEL OT2

One of the rivers that flowed out of Eden's river. The Hiddekel River flowed into Assyria. It was identified in the Septuagint as the Tigris River.

FIRST REFERENCE
GENESIS 2:14
LAST REFERENCE
DANIEL 10:4

HIERAPOLIS NT1
Holy city

A Phrygian city with a church that was served and possibly founded by Epaphras.

ONLY REFERENCE
COLOSSIANS 4:13

HILEN OT1
Fortress

One of the forty-eight cities given to the Levites as God had commanded. Hilen was given to them by the tribe of Judah.

ONLY REFERENCE
1 CHRONICLES 6:58

HINNOM OT13

A valley southwest of Jerusalem that identifies the borders of the inheritance of the tribes of Judah and Benjamin. Here Kings Ahaz and Manasseh led Judah into idolatry, worshipping Baal in its high places. When good King

Josiah of Judah put down idolatry in his land, he defiled Topheth, a site in the valley where the previous kings had sacrificed their children to the pagan god Moloch.

The prophet Jeremiah foresaw that Hinnom would become known as "the valley of slaughter" and would become a graveyard (Jeremiah 7:32). Also called "the valley of the son of Hinnom."

FIRST REFERENCE
JOSHUA 15:8
LAST REFERENCE
JEREMIAH 32:35
KEY REFERENCES
2 KINGS 23:10; 2 CHRONICLES 28:3; 33:6

HOBAH   OT1
Hiding place

Chedorlaomer, king of Elam, and his Mesopotamian allies captured Abram's nephew Lot in Sodom. When Abram discovered this, he attacked the allies and pursued them to Hobah, near Damascus, to rescue Lot.

ONLY REFERENCE
GENESIS 14:15

HOLON   OT3
Sandy

1) A city that became part of the inheritance of the tribe of Judah following the conquest of the Promised Land. It became one of the forty-eight cities given to the Levites as God had commanded.

FIRST REFERENCE
JOSHUA 15:51
LAST REFERENCE
JOSHUA 21:15

2) A Moabite city that the prophet Jeremiah foresaw would be judged by God.

ONLY REFERENCE
JEREMIAH 48:21

HOR   OT12
Mountain

1) A mountain in Edom to which the Israelites came after traveling to Kadesh and being refused passage through Edom by its king. At the age of 123, Aaron died at Mount Hor. His son Eleazar was made high priest in his place.

FIRST REFERENCE
NUMBERS 20:22
LAST REFERENCE
DEUTERONOMY 32:50
KEY REFERENCE
NUMBERS 20:22–28

2) A mountain that God used to mark the northern border of Canaan when He gave it to His people.

FIRST REFERENCE
NUMBERS 34:7
LAST REFERENCE
NUMBERS 34:8

HOREB   OT17
Desolate

On this mountain range Moses grazed the sheep belonging to his father-in-law, Jethro, before he brought God's message to Israel. Scholars have debated whether Horeb is another name for Mount Sinai or is simply in the range of mountains in which Mount Sinai lay.

Here Moses struck the rock, at

God's command, to provide water for the Israelites during the Exodus. After the Israelites rebelled by worshipping the golden calf, God met Moses at Horeb. But He could not show the prophet His face. Instead He put Moses in a cleft of the rock and let him see His back.

The last chapters of the book of Exodus and Numbers 1–11 take place at Horeb. Here God made a covenant with His people and provided them with a second set of the tablets of the Ten Commandments, since Moses had destroyed the originals in his anger at their idolatry. Then God sent the Israelites to the land of the Amorites and on into the land of Canaan.

At Horeb, the prophet Elijah met God after fleeing from Queen Jezebel. God encouraged and strengthened the prophet, telling him that he was not alone in faithful service to the Lord.

FIRST REFERENCE
EXODUS 3:1
LAST REFERENCE
MALACHI 4:4
KEY REFERENCES
EXODUS 34:6–23; DEUTERONOMY 1:6–8

HOREM   OT1
Devoted

A fortified or walled city that became part of the inheritance of Naphtali when Joshua cast lots in Shiloh to provide territory for the seven tribes that had yet to receive their land.

ONLY REFERENCE
JOSHUA 19:38

HOR-HAGIDGAD   OT2
Hole in the cleft

A campsite of the Israelites on their way to the Promised Land.

FIRST REFERENCE
NUMBERS 33:32
LAST REFERENCE
NUMBERS 33:33

HORMAH   OT9
Devoted

A city the Canaanites called Zephath, which the Israelites promised God they would destroy if God gave it into their hand. Joshua and his men won the battle and destroyed the city. Hormah became part of the inheritance of the tribe of Judah and then became part of the inheritance of Simeon. This occurred when Joshua cast lots in Shiloh to provide territory for the seven tribes that had yet to receive their land.

Following their conquest of Canaan, the Israelites renamed the city and rebuilt it. David sent some of the spoils from his warfare with the Amalekites to Hormah. Same as Zephath.

FIRST REFERENCE
NUMBERS 14:45
LAST REFERENCE
1 CHRONICLES 4:30

HORONAIM OT4
Double cave town

A city of Moab. Isaiah and Ezekiel described its judgment by God.

FIRST REFERENCE
ISAIAH 15:5
LAST REFERENCE
JEREMIAH 48:34

HOSAH OT1
Hopeful

A city that became part of the inheritance of Asher when Joshua cast lots in Shiloh to provide territory for the seven tribes that had yet to receive their land.

ONLY REFERENCE
JOSHUA 19:29

HUKKOK OT1
Appointed

A city that became part of the inheritance of Naphtali when Joshua cast lots in Shiloh to provide territory for the seven tribes that had yet to receive their land.

ONLY REFERENCE
JOSHUA 19:34

HUKOK OT1
Appointed

One of the forty-eight cities given to the Levites as God had commanded. Hukok was given to them by the tribe of Asher.

ONLY REFERENCE
1 CHRONICLES 6:75

HUMTAH OT1
Low

A city that became part of the inheritance of the tribe of Judah following the conquest of the Promised Land.

ONLY REFERENCE
JOSHUA 15:54

HUZZAB OT1

Scholars disagree on the meaning of this name, used poetically only in Nahum 2:7. Some think it describes a queen of Assyria, while others think it is a personification of the nation of Assyria or a region within it.

ONLY REFERENCE
NAHUM 2:7

IBLEAM OT3
Devouring people

A city that became part of the inheritance of the tribe of Manasseh, though it seems to have been in Issachar or Asher's territory. The original inhabitants were not driven out of Ibleam after Israel's conquest of the land. Near here Ahaziah, king of Judah, was killed at Jehu's orders.

FIRST REFERENCE
JOSHUA 17:11
LAST REFERENCE
2 KINGS 9:27

ICONIUM NT6
Imagelike

Paul and Barnabas first came to this city of Asia Minor after the Jews in Antioch of Pisidia incited the leading people of their city against the apostles. The two men spoke to the Iconian Jews first, but many Greeks of the city were also converted. The city became split, some supporting Paul and Barnabas, others supporting the unbelieving Jews who stirred up trouble for them.

When the Jews sought to stone them, Paul and Barnabas fled to Lystra. But their enemies from Antioch and Iconium followed, and Paul was stoned in Lystra. After moving on to Derbe and preaching there, Paul and Barnabas returned to Iconium and the other cities where they had encountered trouble. They strengthened the churches there, appointing elders to lead them.

When Paul considered adding Timothy to his ministry, the Christians at Iconium recommended the young disciple.

FIRST REFERENCE
ACTS 13:51
LAST REFERENCE
2 TIMOTHY 3:11

IDALAH OT1

A city that became part of the inheritance of the tribe of Zebulun when Joshua cast lots in Shiloh to provide territory for the seven tribes that had yet to receive their land.

ONLY REFERENCE
JOSHUA 19:15

IDUMAEA NT1

A Greek name for Edom. Some people from this area, southeast of Judah, were part of the crowd that followed Jesus to the Sea of Galilee. So many people surrounded Him that He had to preach from a boat. Same as Edom and Idumea.

ONLY REFERENCE
MARK 3:8

IDUMEA OT4
Edom; red

Another name for Edom, used by the prophets Isaiah and Ezekiel. Isaiah foretold the judgment of this land and a great slaughter there. Ezekiel foresaw that the land would be desolate. Same as Edom and Idumaea.

FIRST REFERENCE
ISAIAH 34:5
LAST REFERENCE
EZEKIEL 36:5

IIM OT2
Ruins

1) A campsite of the Israelites on their way to the Promised Land. Same as Ije-abarim.

ONLY REFERENCE
NUMBERS 33:45

2) A city that became part of the inheritance of the tribe of Judah following the conquest of the Promised Land.

ONLY REFERENCE
JOSHUA 15:29

IJE-ABARIM OT2
Ruins of the passers

A campsite of the Israelites on their way to the Promised Land. It lay in the wilderness before Moab. Same as Iim 1.

FIRST REFERENCE
NUMBERS 21:11
LAST REFERENCE
NUMBERS 33:44

IJON OT3
Ruin

A town of Naphtali that the Syrian prince Ben-hadad conquered at the instigation of King Ada of Judah. During the reign of Pekah, king of Israel, the Assyrian king Tiglath-pileser conquered Ijon and carried away all the people to his own land.

FIRST REFERENCE
I KINGS 15:20
LAST REFERENCE
2 CHRONICLES 16:4

ILLYRICUM NT1

A Roman province that lay on the northwest border of Macedonia. When he wrote the book of Romans, Paul said he had preached the Gospel from Jerusalem to this area.

ONLY REFERENCE
ROMANS 15:19

INDIA OT2

An eastern border of the empire ruled by King Ahasuerus. His Jewish bride, Esther, was queen over this huge territory.

FIRST REFERENCE
ESTHER 1:1
LAST REFERENCE
ESTHER 8:9

IRON OT1

A city that became part of the inheritance of Naphtali when Joshua cast lots in Shiloh to provide territory for the seven tribes that had yet to receive their land.

ONLY REFERENCE
JOSHUA 19:38

IRPEEL OT1
God will heal

A city that became part of the inheritance of Benjamin when Joshua cast lots in Shiloh to provide territory for the seven tribes that had yet to receive their land.

ONLY REFERENCE
JOSHUA 18:27

IR-SHEMESH OT1
City of the sun

A city that became part of the inheritance of Dan when Joshua cast lots in Shiloh to provide territory for the seven tribes that had yet to receive their land.

ONLY REFERENCE
JOSHUA 19:41

ISH-TOB OT2
Man of Tob

A small Palestinian kingdom, possibly in Syria, that provided the Ammonites with twelve thousand troops to fight against King David.

FIRST REFERENCE
2 SAMUEL 10:6
LAST REFERENCE
2 SAMUEL 10:8

ISRAEL OT2511
He will rule as God

The nation of God's chosen people, named with the covenant name He gave to Jacob. The Lord originally covenanted with Abraham, calling him to Canaan from Ur of the Chaldees and promising him that he would become a great nation and God would bless him (Genesis 12:1–3). Though Abraham was old, God gave Abraham his son Isaac as the child of promise through whom the blessing would come true. God renewed His covenant with Isaac's son Jacob, promising He would make a nation from his descendants and give them the Promised Land. The nation of Israel was established from Jacob's line and consisted of the twelve tribes named for his sons.

When famine struck, Jacob's sons traveled to Egypt to buy food and discovered that their brother Joseph, whom they had sold into slavery, was second in command of that land and in charge of the food supplies. Joseph invited his family to move to Egypt's land of Goshen, where they could thrive during the famine. The people of Israel stayed in Egypt for four hundred years (Genesis 15:13) and were enslaved by a new pharaoh, who feared their numbers.

Finally, under the leadership

of Moses and Aaron, all Israel left Egypt in a huge exodus. But at the doorstep of the Promised Land, the fearful people refused to enter. So this faithless generation lived in the wilderness until they all died. Under the leadership of Joshua, the next generation of Israelites conquered many nations around the Promised Land, as God again led them toward their new country. After conquering the nations of Canaan, they took possession of the land to which God had brought them forty years before.

Unlike the nations around them, Israel was ruled by judges until the people asked the prophet-judge Samuel for a king. Saul became Israel's first king, followed by David, one of Israel's greatest kings. David's line ruled the nation, and God promised to continue his kingly line if his descendants would follow Him. But his son Solomon fell into idolatry, and under David's grandson Rehoboam, the nation split. Only the tribes of Judah and Benjamin followed Rehoboam, who was then crowned king of Judah. The rest of the tribes made Jeroboam king of the nation then called Israel or later Samaria (after the newly established capital).

Many of the kings of both nations turned away from the Lord. During the rule of Israel's king Hoshea, Assyria conquered Israel, or the northern kingdom. Finding Hoshea unfaithful, Assyria imprisoned him, invaded his land, and eventually captured Samaria. The Israelites were sent to Assyria as captives.

Judah was captured by the Chaldean (Babylonian) Empire, which succeeded Assyria as the major Mesopotamian power. In turn, the Persian king Cyrus conquered Assyria and sent many Jews back to their homeland. Following the Jews' return from exile, the name Israel was again used to refer to the whole nation.

In the intertestamental period, Israel was ruled by various foreign empires, existed a short time as an independent nation, then was conquered by Rome. During the New Testament era, this pagan empire continued to rule the often rebellious nation.

FIRST REFERENCE
GENESIS 32:32
LAST REFERENCE
MALACHI 2:11
KEY REFERENCES
I KINGS 9:4–5; 12:16–24; 2 KINGS 17:1–6

ITALY NT4

A peninsula south of the Alps whose major city was Rome, capital of the Roman Empire.

Aquila, a Jew who aided Paul in his ministry, had to leave Italy with his wife, Priscilla, because Emperor Claudius expelled the Jews from Rome. Paul sailed for Italy when Herod Agrippa II decided to send him to Rome to be judged by the emperor.

FIRST REFERENCE
ACTS 18:2
LAST REFERENCE
HEBREWS 13:24

ITHNAN   OT1
Extensive

A city that became part of the inheritance of the tribe of Judah following the conquest of the Promised Land.

ONLY REFERENCE
JOSHUA 15:23

ITTAH-KAZIN   OT1
Time of a judge

A city that became part of the inheritance of Zebulun when Joshua cast lots in Shiloh to provide territory for the seven tribes that had yet to receive their land.

ONLY REFERENCE
JOSHUA 19:13

ITURAEA   NT1

A tetrarchy in the northwest part of Palestine, near Mount Hermon. Herod Antipas's brother Philip ruled over Ituraea.

ONLY REFERENCE
LUKE 3:1

IVAH   OT3

A city conquered by Assyria. Rabshakeh used its destruction as an example to Judah of why Jerusalem should side with his nation.

FIRST REFERENCE
2 KINGS 18:34
LAST REFERENCE
ISAIAH 37:13

-J-

JAAZER   OT2
Helpful

Moses sent spies to this Amorite city. Israel attacked and took the villages around it, driving out the Amorites who lived there. It became part of the inheritance of the tribe of Gad, which turned it into a fortified city.

FIRST REFERENCE
NUMBERS 21:32
LAST REFERENCE
NUMBERS 32:35

JABBOK   OT7
Pouring forth

This river flows from the mountains of Gilead into the Jordan River. Jacob met the Lord near here, at Peniel, after he sent his family across the ford of Jabbok. When the Amorite king Sihon refused to let the Israelites pass through his land on their way to the Promised Land, Israel conquered his land, north to the Jabbok. The Amorite territory east of the Jordan became the inheritance of the tribes of Reuben and Gad. Later the Ammonites demanded that Israel return the land south of the Jabbok to them, but Israel refused their claim.

FIRST REFERENCE
GENESIS 32:22
LAST REFERENCE
JUDGES 11:22

JABESH OT9
Dry

A city of Gad that tried to make peace with Nahash the Ammonite. Nahash declared he would only make peace if the city would let him put out their right eyes. When Saul heard of Jabesh's situation, he rallied all Israel to come to the aid of the city. The tribes gathered and defeated Nahash and his troops. The people were so impressed with Saul's leadership that they confirmed Saul as king of Israel.

After Saul and his sons were killed in battle with the Philistines, the inhabitants of Jabesh, perhaps remembering Saul's defense of their city, recovered the royal family's bodies and burned them. Their bones were buried at Jabesh. Same as Jabesh-gilead.

FIRST REFERENCE
I SAMUEL 11:1
LAST REFERENCE
I CHRONICLES 10:12

JABESH-GILEAD OT12
Dry Gilead

When Israel attacked the Benjaminites for disregarding the rules of hospitality toward a Levite and his concubine and abusing the concubine until she died, the town of Jabesh-gilead did not come to battle. So the Israelites attacked Jabesh-gilead and killed everyone in the city except four hundred young virgins, whom they gave to the remaining Benjaminites as wives.

After Saul and his sons were killed in battle with the Philistines, the inhabitants of Jabesh-gilead recovered their bodies and burned them. Their bones were buried at Jabesh-gilead. Same as Jabesh.

FIRST REFERENCE
JUDGES 21:8
LAST REFERENCE
I CHRONICLES 10:11
KEY REFERENCE
JUDGES 21:8–14

JABEZ OT1
Sorrowful

A city of Judah where Kenite scribes lived.

ONLY REFERENCE
I CHRONICLES 2:55

JABNEEL OT2
Built of God

1) A city that formed part of the border of the tribe of Judah's territory.

ONLY REFERENCE
JOSHUA 15:11

2) A city that became part of the inheritance of Naphtali when Joshua cast lots in Shiloh to provide territory for the seven tribes that had yet to receive their land.

ONLY REFERENCE
JOSHUA 19:33

JABNEH OT1
A building

A city of the Philistines that was conquered by Judah's king Uzziah.

ONLY REFERENCE
2 CHRONICLES 26:6

JACHIN OT2
He will establish

The right pillar on the porch of Solomon's temple.

FIRST REFERENCE
1 KINGS 7:21
LAST REFERENCE
2 CHRONICLES 3:17

JAGUR OT1
A lodging

A city that became part of the inheritance of the tribe of Judah following the conquest of the Promised Land.

ONLY REFERENCE
JOSHUA 15:21

JAHAZ OT5
Threshing floor

A city where the Amorite king Sihon fought and lost to Israel after he would not let the Israelites travel through his land on their way to the Promised Land. Same as Jahaza, Jahazah, and Jahzah.

FIRST REFERENCE
NUMBERS 21:23
LAST REFERENCE
JEREMIAH 48:34

JAHAZA OT1
Threshing floor

A city east of the Dead Sea that became part of the inheritance of Reuben. Same as Jahaz, Jahazah, and Jahzah.

ONLY REFERENCE
JOSHUA 13:18

JAHAZAH OT2
Threshing floor

One of the forty-eight cities given to the Levites as God had commanded. Jahazah was given to them by the tribe of Reuben. Jeremiah foresaw its judgment by God. Same as Jahaz, Jahaza, and Jahzah.

FIRST REFERENCE
JOSHUA 21:36
LAST REFERENCE
JEREMIAH 48:21

JAHZAH OT1
Threshing floor

One of the forty-eight cities given to the Levites as God had commanded. Jahzah was given to them by the tribe of Reuben. Same as Jahaza and Jahazah.

ONLY REFERENCE
1 CHRONICLES 6:78

JAIR OT2
Enlightener

An area of Bashan that became part of the inheritance of the tribe of Manasseh.

FIRST REFERENCE
JOSHUA 13:30
LAST REFERENCE
1 CHRONICLES 2:23

JANOAH OT1
Quiet

During the reign of Pekah, king of Israel, the Assyrian king Tiglath-pileser conquered this city of the tribe of Naphtali, captured its people, and carried them to his own land.

ONLY REFERENCE
2 KINGS 15:29

JANOHAH OT2
Quiet

A border city of Ephraim that lay between Taanath-shiloh and Naarath.

FIRST REFERENCE
JOSHUA 16:6
LAST REFERENCE
JOSHUA 16:7

JANUM OT1
Asleep

A city that became part of the inheritance of the tribe of Judah following the conquest of the Promised Land.

ONLY REFERENCE
JOSHUA 15:53

JAPHIA OT1
Bright

A town that became part of the inheritance of Zebulun when Joshua cast lots in Shiloh to provide territory for the seven tribes that had yet to receive their land.

ONLY REFERENCE
JOSHUA 19:12

JAPHLETI OT1
He will deliver

"The coast of Japhleti" marked the border of the inheritance of the children of Joseph (Ephraim and Manasseh).

ONLY REFERENCE
JOSHUA 16:3

JAPHO OT1
Beautiful

A city that became part of the inheritance of Dan when Joshua cast lots in Shiloh to provide territory for the seven tribes that had yet to receive their land.

ONLY REFERENCE
JOSHUA 19:46

JARMUTH OT7
Elevation

1) An Amorite city that fought Gibeon because Gibeon made a covenant with the Israelites. After Israel joined its ally and won the battle, Joshua killed Jarmuth's king. Jarmuth became part of the inheritance of the tribe of Judah following the conquest of the Promised Land. It was resettled after the return from the Babylonian exile.

FIRST REFERENCE
JOSHUA 10:3
LAST REFERENCE
NEHEMIAH 11:29

2) One of the forty-eight cities given to the Levites as God had commanded. Jarmuth was given to them by the tribe of Issachar.

ONLY REFERENCE
JOSHUA 21:29

JATTIR   OT4
Redundant

A city that became part of the inheritance of the tribe of Judah following the conquest of the Promised Land. It later became one of the forty-eight cities given to the Levites as God had commanded. David sent Jattir some of the spoils from his warfare with the Amalekites.

FIRST REFERENCE
JOSHUA 15:48
LAST REFERENCE
1 CHRONICLES 6:57

JAVAN   OT2
Dregs; mud

A city of southern Arabia that traded with Tyre, selling goods in its fairs and marketplaces.

FIRST REFERENCE
EZEKIEL 27:13
LAST REFERENCE
EZEKIEL 27:19

JAZER   OT11
Helpful

An Amorite city east of the Jordan River that the tribe of Gad requested as part of its inheritance. It later became one of the forty-eight cities given to the Levites as God had commanded. The prophets Isaiah and Jeremiah speak of the city's mourning over a destroyed harvest.

FIRST REFERENCE
NUMBERS 32:1
LAST REFERENCE
JEREMIAH 48:32

JEARIM   OT1
Forests

A mountain that formed part of the border of the tribe of Judah's territory. Same as Chesalon.

ONLY REFERENCE
JOSHUA 15:10

JEBUS   OT4
Trodden (that is, threshing place)

The name of Jerusalem when it belonged to the Jebusites. A Levite refused to stay overnight in Jebus and went on to Gibeah, where his concubine was abused and died. After David was anointed king of Israel, the Jebusites refused to have him come to the city, so David captured it. In this battle, Joab earned the position as commander of David's troops. Same as Jebusi, Jerusalem, Salem, and Zion.

FIRST REFERENCE
JUDGES 19:10
LAST REFERENCE
1 CHRONICLES 11:5

JEBUSI   OT2
A Jebusite

An early name for Jerusalem. When Joshua cast lots in Shiloh to provide territory for the seven tribes that had yet to receive their land, Jebusi was the name used to describe this city on the border of the tribe of Benjamin's territory. Same as Jebus, Jerusalem, Salem, and Zion.

FIRST REFERENCE
JOSHUA 18:16
LAST REFERENCE
JOSHUA 18:28

JEGAR-SAHADUTHA OT1
Heap of the testimony

A stone that Jacob set up as a pillar of testimony to the covenant he made with his father-in-law, Laban. Jegar-sahadutha was the name Laban gave to the stone, which Jacob called Galeed. Same as Galeed and Mizpah 1.

ONLY REFERENCE
GENESIS 31:47

JEHOSHAPHAT OT2
Jehovah judged

A valley where God will plead with the nations for His people, Israel, and where He will judge the ungodly.

FIRST REFERENCE
JOEL 3:2
LAST REFERENCE
JOEL 3:12

JEHOVAH-JIREH OT1
Jehovah will see to it

Another name for Mount Moriah, where God stopped Abraham from sacrificing his son Isaac and instead provided a ram for the offering. Same as Moriah.

ONLY REFERENCE
GENESIS 22:14

JEHOVAH-NISSI OT1
Jehovah is my banner

An altar that Moses built to commemorate God's promise to save His people by fighting the Amalekites Himself, from generation to generation.

ONLY REFERENCE
EXODUS 17:15

JEHOVAH-SHALOM OT1
Jehovah is peace

Gideon was amazed at the visit of an angel of the Lord, who called him a mighty man of valor. This angel also told him that God would be with him as he fought the Midianites, who controlled Israel. Gideon built an altar to God in Ophrah of the Abi-ezrites and called it by this name.

ONLY REFERENCE
JUDGES 6:24

JEHUD OT1
Judah

A city that became part of the inheritance of Dan when Joshua cast lots in Shiloh to provide territory for the seven tribes that had yet to receive their land.

ONLY REFERENCE
JOSHUA 19:45

JEKABZEEL   OT1
God will gather

A city of Judah resettled by the Jews after the Babylonian exile.

ONLY REFERENCE
NEHEMIAH 11:25

JERICHO   OT57/NT7
Fragrant

A Moabite city next to Mount Nebo, west of the Jordan River, Jericho was also called the "city of palm trees." The Israelites entered Canaan, crossing the Jordan River near Jericho, and camped in the Jericho plain as they conquered the Midianites and for some time afterward.

From Shittim, before they crossed the Jordan River, Joshua sent two spies to Jericho. When the men were caught inside the city, Rahab hid them and then helped them escape by lowering them out a window, using a rope. In return the spies promised that she and her family would be safe when Israel conquered her city.

God gave Joshua an unusual battle plan to take Jericho: For six days Israel's soldiers were to walk once around the city; on the seventh day they were to go around the city seven times, with the priests walking before the troops, blowing their trumpets and carrying the ark of the covenant. When the priests made a long blast, the people were to shout, and Jericho would be theirs. Joshua and his troops followed these instructions, captured Jericho, and destroyed it.

Jericho became part of the inheritance of the tribe of Benjamin. But Eglon, king of Moab, captured the city and held it for eighteen years. Then Ehud killed him and led Israel into battle against the Moabites, regaining the city.

Elijah and Elisha went to Jericho on the day Elijah was carried into heaven by a chariot of fire. That city's prophets were aware of the event that was to come.

As He left Jericho, Jesus healed two blind men, one of whom was Bartimaeus. As He passed through another time, Jesus saw Zacchaeus in a tree and brought him salvation.

FIRST REFERENCE
NUMBERS 22:1
LAST REFERENCE
HEBREWS 11:30
KEY REFERENCES
JOSHUA 2, 6; LUKE 19:1–10

JERUEL   OT1
Founded of God

A wilderness near the place where King Jehoshaphat of Judah and his army fought the Moabites and Ammonites.

ONLY REFERENCE
2 CHRONICLES 20:16

When Abraham lived in Canaan, Jerusalem (known as "Salem") was ruled by Mechizedec, "priest of the most high God" (Genesis 14:18–20). But before Israel entered the Promised Land, the Jebusite king Adoni-zedec and some neighboring kings went to war against Gibeon, which had made a covenant with the Israelites. Joshua supported Gibeon, conquered and burned Jerusalem, and killed the kings of Adoni-zedec's alliance. Though the Israelites conquered the land and the Benjaminites held Jerusalem as part of their inheritance, they could not expel the Jebusites.

When David became king of Israel, the Jebusites refused to let him into their city, which they called Jebus, so he conquered the city and made it his capital. Israel called it "the city of David" or Jerusalem. David brought the ark of the covenant into the city.

Jerusalem became part of a power struggle between David and his son Absalom, when Absalom sought to overthrow his father. Rather than having the city destroyed, David left it for a time, until his son had been killed and the rebellion ended. After David sinned by numbering the people of Israel, God afflicted Israel with a pestilence. But instead of destroying Jerusalem, God turned back his hand. David built an altar on the threshing floor of Araunah the Jebusite, and the plague ended.

David passed his throne to his son Solomon, who in seven years built the temple in Jerusalem, with the aid of King Hiram of Tyre's skilled workmen. Solomon had the ark of the covenant brought in, and God's glory filled the temple. Because it was the center of worship, Psalm 46:4 refers to Jerusalem as "the city of God, the holy place of the tabernacles of the most High." Solomon's building projects did not end there. He also built his own palace, which took thirteen years to complete.

King Rehoboam took the throne following Solomon's death, but he alienated ten tribes of Israel, leaving Rehoboam with Judah, Simeon, and part of Benjamin. Jerusalem was the capital of the kingdom of Judah. In the fifth year of Rehoboam's reign, Shishak, king of Egypt, attacked and conquered Jerusalem and took all the treasures of the king's house and the temple. Later, Pharaoh Necho conquered Judah, killing King Josiah and taking King Jehoahaz prisoner. He made Jehoiakim king in his place and exacted tribute from Judah.

The last king of Judah, Zedekiah, reinstituted the celebration of Passover in Jerusalem and rebuilt the watercourse of Gihon so that it fed directly into the city. But when Zedekiah rebelled in 586 B.C., Nebuchadnezzar, king of Babylon, besieged and defeated Jerusalem, destroying much of the city and all of the temple, and took Zedekiah captive. After killing the rest of Israel's leaders, Nebuchadnezzar took the people of Judah captive and carried them to Babylon. Yet the prophet Joel prophesied that Judah would "dwell for ever" and Jerusalem would last "from generation to generation" (Joel 3:20).

When Cyrus, king of Persia, came to power in Babylon, he commanded that the Jews rebuild their temple. He returned the temple vessels to them and sent some Jews back to Jerusalem. The temple they rebuilt was not as glorious as Solomon's. Later, after more Jews returned to their homeland, Nehemiah rebuilt the walls of the city at the command of the Persian king Artaxerxes.

During the New Testament era, Rome held sway over Israel. Herod the Great, king of Judea, began a massive building project to restore the temple, nearly doubling its size. He also rebuilt Jerusalem's walls. When Herod heard that the wise men were seeking the king of the Jews, both he and all Jerusalem were troubled. Though Herod did his best to kill the king whom the magi sought, God saved Jesus and His earthly parents.

Shortly after His birth, Jesus was brought to the temple so His parents could offer a sacrifice. Here Simeon and the prophetess Anna recognized God's salvation in Jesus. After their return to Nazareth, Joseph and Mary went to Jerusalem each year at Passover. When Jesus was twelve, they found him in the temple, talking with the teachers of the law.

In Jerusalem, Satan tempted Jesus to throw Himself down from the temple. Early in His ministry, Jesus went to the temple and cleared it of the cattle, sheep, and doves that were sold for sacrifice, declaring, "How dare you turn my Father's house into a market!" (John 2:16 NIV). Many people, including the Pharisees, came from Jerusalem to hear His preaching. But because the religious and civil leaders did not accept His message and even sought to kill Him, Jesus did not spend large amounts of time in the city. Only the feasts or major Jewish holidays seemed to draw Him to the city.

As He headed toward Jerusalem, just before His death, Jesus recognized that His death had to take place in the city. He grieved over Jerusalem's history of killing the prophets and expressed a wish to gather its people together, like a hen protecting her chicks. Jesus was arrested outside Jerusalem, tried within it, and crucified and buried just outside the city, near Golgotha.

At Pentecost in Jerusalem, the Holy Spirit filled believers and they spoke with other tongues. Here Stephen preached the Gospel with power, doing miracles. Unable to counter this powerful testimony, the leaders of a synagogue stirred up people against him. Setting false witnesses against him, they brought Stephen before the Sanhedrin. Angered by his testimony, these Jews attacked and stoned Stephen. In the persecution that followed the faithful disciple's death, many Christians left Jerusalem, preaching as they traveled.

Saul and Barnabas delivered a relief offering, collected from the other churches, to the persecuted Christians of Jerusalem.

Jerusalem remained important even as the church spread beyond Israel. When Paul and Barnabas disagreed with the Judaizers, they met with the church's council in Jerusalem, where it was decided that Gentiles need not be circumcised in order to become Christians.

When Paul again returned to Jerusalem, he reported to James, who led the church in that city, and all the elders. After Paul completed a ritual of purification at the temple, he was seized by some Jews of Asia, who accused him of bringing Greeks into the temple. As they attempted to kill Paul, the Roman guard rescued him. But it was two years before Porcius Festus came to Jerusalem, heard his case, and sent him to Rome for judgment.

In the book of Revelation, the apostle John foresaw the New Jerusalem coming down out of heaven. Here God will live with His people in a beautiful city without sin. Same as Jebus, Jebusi, Salem, and Zion.

FIRST REFERENCE
JOSHUA 10:1
LAST REFERENCE
REVELATION 21:10
KEY REFERENCES
2 SAMUEL 5:6–7; 6:12; I KINGS 8:1–11; LUKE 13:33–34; REVELATION 21:2–27

JESHANAH OT1
Old

King Abijah of Judah took this city, along with its towns, from King Jeroboam of Israel.

ONLY REFERENCE
2 CHRONICLES 13:19

JESHIMON OT6
A desolation

1) An area visible from the Pisgah mountain range and Mount Peor.

FIRST REFERENCE
NUMBERS 21:20
LAST REFERENCE
NUMBERS 23:28

2) A wilderness area near the hill of Hachilah where David hid from King Saul.

FIRST REFERENCE
I SAMUEL 23:19
LAST REFERENCE
I SAMUEL 26:3

JESHUA OT1
He will save

A city of Judah resettled by the Jews after the Babylonian exile.

ONLY REFERENCE
NEHEMIAH 11:26

JETHLAH OT1
It will hang (that is, be high)

A city that became part of the inheritance of Dan when Joshua cast lots in Shiloh to provide territory for the seven tribes that had yet to receive their land.

ONLY REFERENCE
JOSHUA 19:42

JEZREEL   OT32
God will sow

1) A city that became part of the inheritance of the tribe of Judah following the conquest of the Promised Land. David's wife Ahinoam came from Jezreel. David and his men camped by a fountain in this city when he served King Achish and the Philistines were gathering in Aphek. As the Israelites moved to the rear of the troops, the Philistine army refused to fight with them, since David had once been associated with Saul's army.

FIRST REFERENCE
JOSHUA 15:56
LAST REFERENCE
I SAMUEL 29:11

2) A city that became part of the inheritance of Issachar when Joshua cast lots in Shiloh to provide territory for the seven tribes that had yet to receive their land. King Ahab of Israel had a palace here. When he coveted a nearby vineyard belonging to Naboth, his wife, Jezebel, had Naboth killed so her husband could get it. By the walls of this city, Elijah prophesied, dogs would eat the body of the queen who had done this wicked deed. Near Jezreel, Jehu killed King Joram, Ahab's son, as God had commanded him to do. Then he ordered Jezebel killed in the manner the prophet had foretold. Finally, he ordered the rulers of Samaria to kill all Ahab's sons and send their heads to him in Jezreel.

FIRST REFERENCE
JOSHUA 19:18
LAST REFERENCE
2 CHRONICLES 22:6
KEY REFERENCES
I KINGS 21:1–16, 23; 2 KINGS 9:30–37

3) The tribes of Ephraim and Manasseh told Joshua they feared the Canaanites in this valley because they had iron chariots. The Midianites and Amalekites camped at Jezreel before they fought Gideon and the three hundred men God chose for him according to the way they drank water. Hosea foretold that God would "break the bow of Israel, in the valley of Jezreel" (Hosea 1:5), but the valley would also become a blessing for Israel (Hosea 2:22–23).

FIRST REFERENCE
JOSHUA 17:16
LAST REFERENCE
HOSEA 2:22

JIPHTAH   OT1
He will open

A city that became part of the inheritance of the tribe of Judah following the conquest of the Promised Land.

ONLY REFERENCE
JOSHUA 15:43

JIPHTHAH-EL OT2
God will open

A valley that marked the border of the inheritances of Zebulun and Asher when Joshua cast lots in Shiloh to provide territory for the seven tribes that had yet to receive their land.

FIRST REFERENCE
JOSHUA 19:14
LAST REFERENCE
JOSHUA 19:27

JOGBEHAH OT2
Hillock

A fortified or walled city built by the tribe of Gad.

FIRST REFERENCE
NUMBERS 32:35
LAST REFERENCE
JUDGES 8:11

JOKDEAM OT1
Burning of the people

A city that became part of the inheritance of the tribe of Judah following the conquest of the Promised Land.

ONLY REFERENCE
JOSHUA 15:56

JOKMEAM OT1
The people will be raised

One of the six cities of refuge established in Israel for those who had committed accidental murder. Jokmeam was given to the Levites by the tribe of Ephraim.

ONLY REFERENCE
1 CHRONICLES 6:68

JOKNEAM OT4
People will be lamented

1) Jokneam of Carmel was a city on the west side of the Jordan River. After the Israelites conquered it, it became part of the inheritance of the tribe of Zebulun. Jokneam and its suburbs became one of the forty-eight cities given to the Levites as God had commanded.

FIRST REFERENCE
JOSHUA 12:22
LAST REFERENCE
JOSHUA 21:34

2) Under King Solomon's governmental organization, a city responsible for supplying provisions for the king.

ONLY REFERENCE
1 KINGS 4:12

JOKTHEEL OT2
Veneration of God

1) A city that became part of the inheritance of the tribe of Judah following the conquest of the Promised Land.

ONLY REFERENCE
JOSHUA 15:38

2) A name that King Amaziah of Judah gave to the city of Selah after he conquered it. Same as Sela and Selah.

ONLY REFERENCE
2 KINGS 14:7

JOPPA OT3/NT10
Beautiful

A Mediterranean seaport city in the territory of the tribe of Dan. Huram (or Hiram) of Tyre shipped cedar logs to King Solomon through Joppa for his building projects in Jerusalem. When the Israelites rebuilt the temple following the Babylonian exile, they used the same route. To escape God's command to go to Nineveh, the prophet Jonah went to Joppa, seeking a ship bound for Tarshish.

The disciple Tabitha (Dorcas) lived in Joppa. When she died, her friends called Peter to come and heal her. At Simon the tanner's house in Joppa, Peter saw a vision in which God told him, "What God hath cleansed, that call not thou common" (Acts 10:15). From this the apostle understood that he should accept Gentiles who believed in Jesus. Therefore he received the messengers of the centurion Cornelius, visited his household, and preached there. When the Holy Spirit fell upon his hearers, Peter baptized them.

FIRST REFERENCE
2 CHRONICLES 2:16
LAST REFERENCE
ACTS 11:13
KEY REFERENCES
JONAH 1:3; ACTS 9:36–38; ACTS 10

JORDAN OT183/NT15
A descender

A river flowing from Palestine's Lake Huleh south to the Sea of Galilee and on to the Dead Sea; the Jordan River defined the eastern edge of Canaan. Abram's nephew Lot settled in the well-watered plain of the Jordan, north of the Dead Sea, when his uncle commanded him to choose his own land.

On their way toward Canaan, the Israelites conquered lands east of the Jordan River, including the eastern part of the Amorite holdings. Before they crossed into Canaan, the tribes of Reuben and Gad asked Moses for lands east of the Jordan River as their inheritance.

After these tribes agreed to help in the conquest of Canaan, Moses allowed them this inheritance (Numbers 32). Following the conquest of the Promised Land, most of Israel's land lay west of the Jordan. Only Reuben, Gad, and some of Manasseh's land lay to the east, encompassing Gilead and Bashan.

Under Joshua, Israel crossed the Jordan River into Canaan. God commanded that the ark of the covenant be carried into the Jordan and remain in the channel while Israel crossed over. The waters stood up in a heap so the people could pass safely. From the riverbed, God told Joshua to take twelve stones that were made into a memorial of the crossing.

Before the prophet Elijah was taken up into heaven in a fiery chariot, he and his disciple, Elisha, crossed the Jordan River. On their way across, Elijah struck the river with his mantle, and the water divided. On his way back, alone, Elisha performed the same miracle.

The prophet Elijah told the Syrian captain Naaman to wash himself seven times in the Jordan River to be healed of leprosy. Though Naaman would have preferred to wash in one of the rivers of his own land, his servants persuaded him to follow the prophet's directions, and the captain was healed.

John the Baptist performed many baptisms in the Jordan River, including the baptism of Jesus.

FIRST REFERENCE
GENESIS 13:10
LAST REFERENCE
JOHN 10:40
KEY REFERENCES
JOSHUA 1:2; 3:11–17; 2 KINGS 2:6–14; 5:1–14;
MATTHEW 3:6, 13

JOTBAH   OT1

Pleasantness

Hometown of Meshullemeth, the mother of King Amon of Judah.

ONLY REFERENCE
2 KINGS 21:19

JOTBATH   OT1

Pleasantness

A campsite of the Israelites during the Exodus, Jotbath was "a land of rivers of waters." Same as Jotbathah.

ONLY REFERENCE
DEUTERONOMY 10:7

JOTBATHAH   OT2

Pleasantness

A campsite of the Israelites on their way to the Promised Land. Same as Jotbath.

FIRST REFERENCE
NUMBERS 33:33
LAST REFERENCE
NUMBERS 33:34

JUDAEA   NT43

A Roman district, part of the province of Syria, that included Jerusalem and Bethlehem, which was ruled by King Herod the Great. Following Herod's death, his son Archelaus ruled in his place. Fearing the ruler's revenge, Joseph took Mary and Jesus to Galilee when they discovered that Archelaus was ruling Judaea. Later, Pontius Pilate became governor there.

John the Baptist preached and baptized in Judaea's wilderness, and many from this area followed Jesus. There He baptized them and preached the Sermon on the Mount. Jesus warned the Judaeans that when they saw the abomination of desolation prophesied by Daniel, they should flee to the mountains. Though Judaea had become a dangerous place for Jesus, He chose to return there to raise Lazarus, despite the warnings of His disiciples.

Following the death of Stephen, the Christians of Jerusalem were scattered through Judaea and elsewhere because of persecution.

The Judaizers, who wanted Gentiles to receive circumcision, came from Judaea. They attempted to "correct" Paul's missionary efforts with non-Jewish people. Sometimes translated "Judah." Same as Judea.

FIRST REFERENCE
MATTHEW 2:1
LAST REFERENCE
1 THESSALONIANS 2:14
KEY REFERENCES
MATTHEW 3:1; MARK 3:7;
LUKE 6:17; JOHN 11:7

JUDAH   OT581
Celebrated

When Solomon's son Rehoboam inherited the kingdom of Israel and began to rule it unwisely, all the tribes except Judah, Simeon, and part of Benjamin broke off. The northern tribes followed Jeroboam, who was crowned king of Israel. Rehoboam subsequently ruled over the nation of Judah.

Rehoboam wisely built fortified cities to defend his nation. During his reign, Shishak, king of Egypt, attacked Jerusalem and took away the treasures of the temple and the king's house. In addition, Rehoboam and Jeroboam were constantly at war.

The priests and Levites of Israel were thrown out after Jeroboam's institution of idolatry as the national religion. They reacted by moving to Judah and Jerusalem.

Judah had a succession of good and bad kings and one bad queen. Idolatry was a constant threat to the kingdom, and some rulers gave in to it easily. Judah faced numerous enemies: Israel, Syria, Assyria, and Babylon. Though the Assyrian king Sennacherib tried to take Jerusalem, he was unsuccessful. But the Chaldean king Nebuchadnezzar put down the rebellious King Zedekiah of Judah. Judah's king was captured, his sons were killed as he watched, his eyes were put out, and he was taken prisoner to Babylon. Jerusalem's temple was destroyed, along with the king's house and the great homes of the city. Many of Judah's people were taken captive to Babylon, along with their king. The top spiritual leaders of Jerusalem were killed.

After Israel's return from the Babylonian exile, Judah was a district in the Persian Empire.

FIRST REFERENCE
I KINGS 12:17
LAST REFERENCE
MALACHI 3:4
KEY REFERENCES
I KINGS 12; 2 KINGS 25; 2 CHRONICLES 11:1–15

JUDEA   OT1
Celebrated

Following the Babylonian exile, the land of Judah became a Persian province called Judea. In some Bible versions it is translated "Judah." Same as Judaea.

ONLY REFERENCE
EZRA 5:8

JUTTAH   OT2
Extended

A city that became part of the inheritance of the tribe of Judah following the conquest of the Promised Land. It later became one of the forty-eight cities given to the Levites as God had commanded.

FIRST REFERENCE
JOSHUA 15:55
LAST REFERENCE
JOSHUA 21:16

-K-

KABZEEL   OT3
God has gathered

A city that became part of the inheritance of the tribe of Judah following the conquest of the Promised Land. It was the home of Benaiah, one of David's three most valiant warriors.

FIRST REFERENCE
JOSHUA 15:21
LAST REFERENCE
1 CHRONICLES 11:22

KADESH   OT17
Sanctuary

A place in the Desert of Zin from which Chedorlaomer, king of Elam, and his allies attacked the Amalekites and Amorites. From Kadesh, Moses sent the twelve spies into the Promised Land. After Israel refused to enter the Promised Land, the Israelites lived in a camp in Kadesh "many days" (Deuteronomy 1:46). Miriam died in Kadesh, and the rock of Meribah, which Moses disobediently struck two times, was near here.

When Israel wanted to pass through Edom on the way to the Promised Land, Moses sent the king of Edom a message from Kadesh, asking permission. He described Kadesh as "a city in the uttermost of thy border."

When Ezekiel described the extent of the restored Jerusalem, he used Kadesh as a border marker. Same as En-mishpat, Kadesh-barnea, and Kedesh 4.

FIRST REFERENCE
GENESIS 14:7
LAST REFERENCE
EZEKIEL 48:28
KEY REFERENCE
NUMBERS 20:14–17

KADESH-BARNEA   OT10
Desert of a fugitive

The site of the Israelite camp from which Moses sent the twelve spies into the Promised Land. In Kadesh-barnea, Moses promised Caleb the mountain of Hebron as an inheritance. Because they had refused to enter the land when God originally commanded them to, it took the Israelites thirty-eight years to travel from Kadesh-barnea to the brook Zered. Same as En-mishpat, Kadesh, and Kedesh 4.

FIRST REFERENCE
NUMBERS 32:8
LAST REFERENCE
JOSHUA 15:3

KANAH   OT3
Reediness

1) A river that formed a portion of the border of the inheritance of the tribes of Ephraim and Manasseh.

FIRST REFERENCE
JOSHUA 16:8
LAST REFERENCE
JOSHUA 17:9

2) A city that became part of the inheritance of the tribe of Asher

following the conquest of the Promised Land.

ONLY REFERENCE
JOSHUA 19:28

KARKAA OT1
Ground floor

A city that formed part of the border of the tribe of Judah's territory.

ONLY REFERENCE
JOSHUA 15:3

KARKOR OT1
Foundation

A place where the Midianite kings Zebah and Zalmunna gathered their troops against Gideon, after the Midianite–Amalekite army had lost 120,000 men. The Israelites attacked them and both kings fled, then were captured.

ONLY REFERENCE
JUDGES 8:10

KARNAIM OT1

A city where Chedorlaomer, king of Elam, and his Mesopotamian allies conquered the Rephaims.

ONLY REFERENCE
GENESIS 14:5

KARTAH OT1
City

One of the forty-eight cities given to the Levites as God had commanded. Kartah was given to them by the tribe of Zebulun.

ONLY REFERENCE
JOSHUA 21:34

KARTAN OT1
City plot

One of the forty-eight cities given to the Levites as God had commanded. Kartan was given to them by the tribe of Naphtali.

ONLY REFERENCE
JOSHUA 21:32

KATTATH OT1
Littleness

A city that became part of the inheritance of Zebulun when Joshua cast lots in Shiloh to provide territory for the seven tribes that had yet to receive their land.

ONLY REFERENCE
JOSHUA 19:15

KEDEMOTH OT4
Beginnings

1) A wilderness area from which Moses sent messengers to the Amorite king Sihon, asking him to allow Israel to pass through his territory.

ONLY REFERENCE
DEUTERONOMY 2:26

2) A border city of the tribe of Reuben that became one of the forty-eight cities given to the Levites as God had commanded.

FIRST REFERENCE
JOSHUA 13:18
LAST REFERENCE
1 CHRONICLES 6:79

KEDESH OT11
A sanctum

1) A kingdom on the west side of the Jordan River that was conquered by Joshua and his troops. It became a fortified ("fenced" in the KJV) city in the inheritance of the tribe of Naphtali.

FIRST REFERENCE
JOSHUA 12:22
LAST REFERENCE
JOSHUA 19:37

2) One of the six cities of refuge established in Israel for those who had committed accidental murder. Kedesh was in the land of the tribe of Naphtali. Before the battle with Sisera and his troops, Barak called the men of Zebulun and Naphtali to come to this Galilean city. Heber the Kenite had pitched his tent nearby.

Tiglath-pileser, king of Assyria, conquered Kedesh, and its people were taken captive to Assyria. Same as Kedesh-Naphtali.

FIRST REFERENCE
JOSHUA 20:7
LAST REFERENCE
I CHRONICLES 6:76

3) One of the forty-eight cities given to the Levites as God had commanded. Kedesh was given to them by the tribe of Issachar.

ONLY REFERENCE
I CHRONICLES 6:72

4) A city that became part of the inheritance of the tribe of Judah following the conquest of the Promised Land. Same as En-mishpat, Kadesh, and Kadesh-barnea.

ONLY REFERENCE
JOSHUA 15:23

KEDESH-NAPHTALI OT1
A sanctum my wrestling

A city from which the prophet Deborah called Barak when he and the tribes of Naphtali and Zebulun were to fight Sisera and his troops. Same as Kedesh 2.

ONLY REFERENCE
JUDGES 4:6

KEHELATHAH OT2
Convocation

A campsite of the Israelites on their way to the Promised Land.

FIRST REFERENCE
NUMBERS 33:22
LAST REFERENCE
NUMBERS 33:23

KEILAH OT17
Enclosing or citadel

A city that became part of the inheritance of the tribe of Judah following the conquest of the Promised Land.

After David fled from King Saul, the Philistines attacked Keilah. David inquired twice of the Lord, who told him to attack the Philistines and He would deliver the enemy into David's hands. Israel slaughtered the Philistines and saved the city. Saul planned to capture David in Keilah. But David again inquired of God and learned the people of the city would turn him over to Saul, so he and his men left.

FIRST REFERENCE
JOSHUA 15:44
LAST REFERENCE
NEHEMIAH 3:18
KEY REFERENCE
I SAMUEL 23:1–13

KENATH   OT2
Possession

A city that Nobah took, along with its surrounding villages. He renamed the city for himself. Same as Nobah.

FIRST REFERENCE
NUMBERS 32:42
LAST REFERENCE
I CHRONICLES 2:23

KERIOTH   OT3
Buildings

1) A city that became part of the inheritance of the tribe of Judah following the conquest of the Promised Land.

ONLY REFERENCE
JOSHUA 15:25

2) A Moabite city that Jeremiah foretold would be judged. The city would be taken, and its men would be as weak as a woman in labor.

FIRST REFERENCE
JEREMIAH 48:24
LAST REFERENCE
JEREMIAH 48:41

KEZIZ   OT1
Abrupt

A valley that became part of the inheritance of Benjamin when Joshua cast lots in Shiloh to provide territory for the seven tribes that had yet to receive their land.

ONLY REFERENCE
JOSHUA 18:21

KIBROTH-HATTAAVAH   OT5
Graves of the longing

A campsite of the Israelites on their way to the Promised Land. Here God sent a plague on His people for their greediness in collecting the quail He had sent for them to eat.

FIRST REFERENCE
NUMBERS 11:34
LAST REFERENCE
DEUTERONOMY 9:22

KIBZAIM   OT1
A double heap

One of the forty-eight cities given to the Levites as God had commanded. Kibzaim was given to them by the tribe of Ephraim.

ONLY REFERENCE
JOSHUA 21:22

KIDRON   OT11
Dusky place

A brook and valley just east of Jerusalem, between Jerusalem and the Mount of Olives, that David passed over when he left Jerusalem to keep his rebellious son Absalom from destroying the city. Kings Asa and Josiah burned idols near the Kidron Brook. Josiah also burned former kings' pagan altars there. When the temple was purified under King Hezekiah's rule, the priests used this area for ridding the nation of all the unclean things that had been in the temple. Jeremiah predicted that when Jerusalem was rebuilt, this area would be holy to the Lord. Same as Cedron.

FIRST REFERENCE
2 SAMUEL 15:23
LAST REFERENCE
JEREMIAH 31:40

KINAH   OT1
Short

A city that became part of the inheritance of the tribe of Judah following the conquest of the Promised Land.

ONLY REFERENCE
JOSHUA 15:22

KIR   OT4
Fortress

1) Tiglath-pileser, king of Assyria, took the people of Damascus captive and brought them to this district of his own land. According to the prophet Amos, God brought them out of Kir.

FIRST REFERENCE
2 KINGS 16:9
LAST REFERENCE
AMOS 9:7

2) A city of Moab that the prophet Isaiah foretold would be destroyed and "brought to silence."

ONLY REFERENCE
ISAIAH 15:1

KIR-HARASETH   OT1
Fortress of earthenware

A Moabite city that was conquered by King Jehoram of Israel and his allies, King Jehoshaphat of Judah and the king of Edom. After Mesha, king of Moab, sacrificed his son on the city wall and the fighting became very intense, the Israelites withdrew. Same as Kir-hareseth, Kir-haresh, and Kir-heres.

ONLY REFERENCE
2 KINGS 3:25

KIR-HARESETH   OT1
Fortress of earthenware

A Moabite city that the prophet Isaiah foretold would be stricken because of that nation's pride. Same as Kir-haraseth, Kir-haresh, and Kir-heres.

ONLY REFERENCE
ISAIAH 16:7

KIR-HARESH   OT1
Fortress of earthenware

A Moabite city over which the prophet Isaiah lamented. Same as Kir-haraseth, Kir-hareseth, and Kir-heres.

ONLY REFERENCE
ISAIAH 16:11

KIR-HERES   OT2
Fortress of earthenware

The prophet Jeremiah mourned for this Moabite city, whose riches had perished. Same as Kir-haraseth, Kir-hareseth, and Kir-haresh.

FIRST REFERENCE
JEREMIAH 48:31
LAST REFERENCE
JEREMIAH 48:36

KIRIATHAIM   OT4
Double city

1) King Chedorlaomer of Elam and his Mesopotamian allies attacked the Emims, a race of giants who inhabited this plain.

ONLY REFERENCE
GENESIS 14:5

2) A city of Moab that the prophet Jeremiah foretold would be conquered. God's judgment would come upon it in part because Moab declared that Judah was like all the heathen nations.

FIRST REFERENCE
JEREMIAH 48:1
LAST REFERENCE
EZEKIEL 25:9

KIRIOTH   OT1
Buildings

A Moabite city with palaces that Amos foretold would be burned with tumult, shouting, and "the sound of the trumpet."

ONLY REFERENCE
AMOS 2:2

KIRJATH   OT1
City

A city that became part of the inheritance of Benjamin when Joshua cast lots in Shiloh to provide territory for the seven tribes that had yet to receive their land.

ONLY REFERENCE
JOSHUA 18:28

KIRJATHAIM   OT3
Double city

1) A city built by the tribe of Reuben, Kirjathaim was on the tribe's border, between Mephaath and Sibmah.

FIRST REFERENCE
NUMBERS 32:37
LAST REFERENCE
JOSHUA 13:19

2) One of the forty-eight cities given to the Levites as God had commanded. Kirjathaim was given to them by the tribe of Naphtali.

ONLY REFERENCE
I CHRONICLES 6:76

KIRJATH-ARBA
OT6

City of Arba or city of the four giants

A city of the Anakims, among whom Arba was a great man. Here Sarah died. Kirjath-arba became part of the inheritance of the tribe of Judah following the conquest of the Promised Land. It became one of the six cities of refuge established in Israel for those who had committed accidental murder. After the death of

Joshua, Judah fought the Canaanites of this city. It was resettled following the Babylonian exile. Same as Arbah and Hebron.

FIRST REFERENCE
GENESIS 23:2
LAST REFERENCE
NEHEMIAH 11:25

KIRJATH-ARIM
OT1
City of forests or city of towns

A city in Judah to which captives returned after the Babylonian exile.

ONLY REFERENCE
EZRA 2:25

KIRJATH-BAAL
OT2
City of Baal

A city that became part of the inheritance of the tribe of Judah following the conquest of the Promised Land. Kirjath-baal became part of the inheritance of Benjamin when Joshua cast lots in Shiloh to provide territory for the seven tribes that had yet to receive their land. Same as Baalah 1, Baale of Judah, and Kirjath-jearim.

FIRST REFERENCE
JOSHUA 15:60
LAST REFERENCE
JOSHUA 18:14

KIRJATH-HUZOTH
OT1
City of streets

A Moabite city where King Balak brought the prophet Balaam after he asked Balaam to curse Israel.

Balak made offerings of oxen and sheep and took Balaam to the high places of Baal. But Balaam would not curse Israel.

ONLY REFERENCE
NUMBERS 22:39

KIRJATH-JEARIM
OT15
City of forests or city of towns

A city of the Gibeonites that the Israelites did not conquer because they had made a covenant with these people. The Gibeonites persuaded Joshua they had come from far away when really they were close neighbors. Later the city became part of the inheritance of the tribe of Judah. Here the tribe of Dan camped when they went to the house of Micah and stole his priest and idols.

When the Philistines returned the ark of the covenant to Israel, the ox cart came to Beth-shemesh. God killed some of the men of that town because they had looked into the ark. So the people of Beth-shemesh sent a message to Kirjath-jearim to bring the ark of the covenant into their city. The ark stayed there twenty years until David took it to Jerusalem. Same as Baalah 1, Baale of Judah, and Kirjath-baal.

FIRST REFERENCE
JOSHUA 9:17
LAST REFERENCE
JEREMIAH 26:20
KEY REFERENCES
JUDGES 18:12; 1 SAMUEL 6:21–7:2;
1 CHRONICLES 13:5–6

KIRJATH-SANNAH
OT1
City of branches or city of a book

A city that became part of the inheritance of the tribe of Judah following the conquest of the Promised Land. Same as Debir and Kirjath-sepher.

ONLY REFERENCE
JOSHUA 15:49

KIRJATH-SEPHER
OT4
City of branches or city of a book

A city of Judah that was not fully conquered at the time Joshua died. When he went up against Kirjath-sepher, Caleb promised that whatever man conquered this city would gain his daughter Achsah as his wife. Caleb's brother Othniel captured the city and gained his bride. Same as Debir and Kirjath-sannah.

FIRST REFERENCE
JOSHUA 15:15
LAST REFERENCE
JUDGES 1:12

KISHION
OT1
Hard place

A city that became part of the inheritance of Issachar when Joshua cast lots in Shiloh to provide territory for the seven tribes that had yet to receive their land. Same as Kishon 1.

ONLY REFERENCE
JOSHUA 19:20

KISHON
OT6
Hard place (1) or winding (2)

1) One of the forty-eight cities given to the Levites as God had commanded. Kishon was given to them by the tribe of Issachar. Same as Kishion.

ONLY REFERENCE
JOSHUA 21:28

2) A river in the middle of Palestine, running from Mount Gilboa north to the Mediterranean Sea. Sisera gathered his army from Harosheth to this river, where he engaged in battle with Barak and his troops. Barak and Deborah's song tells us that the river swept some of the warriors away.

At this river, after his confrontation with the prophets of Baal on Mount Carmel, the prophet Elijah killed the pagan prophets. Same as Kison.

FIRST REFERENCE
JUDGES 4:7
LAST REFERENCE
I KINGS 18:40

KISON
OT1
Winding

A river near which Barak, the leader of Israel's army, defeated King Jabin of Hazor and his commander Sisera. Same as Kishon 2.

ONLY REFERENCE
PSALM 83:9

KITHLISH   OT 1
Wall of a man

A city that became part of the inheritance of the tribe of Judah following the conquest of the Promised Land.

ONLY REFERENCE
JOSHUA 15:40

KITRON   OT 1
Fumagative

A city from which the tribe of Zebulun never drove out the native Canaanites.

ONLY REFERENCE
JUDGES 1:30

-L-

LABAN   OT 1
White

A place in the wilderness "over against the Red Sea." Near here Moses reviewed the Law with the Israelites before they entered the Promised Land.

ONLY REFERENCE
DEUTERONOMY 1:1

LACHISH   OT 24

An Amorite city ruled by Japhia when Joshua and his troops conquered the Promised Land. Japhia joined with Adoni-zedek and his other allies in attacking Gibeon. Joshua and his forces came to Gibeon's aid because they had an agreement with that city. Japhia was one of the five kings who fled to the cave at Makkedah and became trapped there. After the battle, all five kings were killed by Joshua. The Israelites besieged Lachish, took it in two days, and killed all its inhabitants. The city became part of the inheritance of the tribe of Judah following the conquest of the Promised Land.

King Rehoboam fortified Lachish to defend his nation. King Amaziah of Judah fled from a conspiracy in Jerusalem, escaped to Lachish, and was killed there by his enemies.

Sennacherib, king of Assyria, laid siege to Lachish as his messengers visited Jerusalem, to threaten that city with attack.

FIRST REFERENCE
JOSHUA 10:3
LAST REFERENCE
MICAH 1:13
KEY REFERENCE
JOSHUA 10:3–35

LAHAI-ROI   OT2
Of the Living One, my seer

Isaac lived near this well in the south country, near Beersheba. Same as Beer-lahai-roi.

FIRST REFERENCE
GENESIS 24:62
LAST REFERENCE
GENESIS 25:11

LAHMAM   OT1
Foodlike

A city that became part of the inheritance of the tribe of Judah following the conquest of the Promised Land.

ONLY REFERENCE
JOSHUA 15:40

LAISH   OT5
Crushing

A Sidonian (or Zidonian) city captured and burned by the tribe of Dan. The tribe renamed it the city of Dan, rebuilt it, and lived there. Same as Leshem.

FIRST REFERENCE
JUDGES 18:7
LAST REFERENCE
ISAIAH 10:30

LAKUM   OT1
Stop up by a barricade (perhaps a fortification)

A city that became part of the inheritance of Naphtali when Joshua cast lots in Shiloh to provide territory for the seven tribes that had yet to receive their land.

ONLY REFERENCE
JOSHUA 19:33

LAODICEA   NT6
Just people

A city of the Roman province of Phrygia. Paul had not yet visited the church in Laodicea when he wrote the Colossians. Paul told the nearby church at Colossae that Epaphras, "a servant of Christ" (Colossians 4:12), had a great zeal for their congregation and the church at Laodicea. The epistle to the Colossians was written to be read in both churches. In the book of Revelation, John relays Jesus' message to the church in Laodicea.

FIRST REFERENCE
COLOSSIANS 2:1
LAST REFERENCE
REVELATION 1:11

LASEA   NT1

A Cretan city near the port called the Fair Havens, where Paul and his companions took shelter before a storm.

ONLY REFERENCE
ACTS 27:8

LASHA OT1
To break through; a boiling spring

An early border place in the land settled by the descendants of Noah's grandson Canaan.

ONLY REFERENCE
GENESIS 10:19

LASHARON OT1
Plain

A Canaanite city on the west side of the Jordan River that was conquered by Joshua and his army.

ONLY REFERENCE
JOSHUA 12:18

LEBANON OT71
The white mountain

A Syrian mountain range of northern Palestine that runs along the Mediterranean Sea; it consists of two lines of mountains, the Lebanon Mountains in the west and the Anti-Lebanon Mountains in the east, with a valley between them. This was a richly wooded land in the Old Testament era and is used in scripture as a sign of a land filled with plenty.

God promised Israel that it would own the land to Lebanon. When Israel began to claim the Promised Land, the kings of this area fought Joshua and his troops. When Joshua was old, God promised to drive out the inhabitants of Lebanon, from Baal-gad to the entering into Hamath. But God left the nations of this area "to prove Israel" (Judges 3:1, 3).

Lebanon was famed for its cedar trees. When King Solomon began to build the temple in Jerusalem, he arranged with King Hiram of Tyre to have Lebanon cedar, fir, and algum trees cut and floated down by sea to Israel. When the temple was rebuilt after the Babylonian exile, Israel again secured timber from Lebanon.

The prophets foretold Lebanon's destruction by the Lord.

FIRST REFERENCE
DEUTERONOMY 1:7
LAST REFERENCE
ZECHARIAH 11:1
KEY REFERENCES
JOSHUA 1:4; 1 KINGS 5:1–10; 2 CHRONICLES 2:8, 16

LEBONAH OT1
Frankincense

A place near Shiloh and Bethel. The Israelites fought the tribe of Benjamin and refused to allow their daughters to marry into that tribe because it condoned the abuse and killing of a Levite's concubine at Gibeah. Afterward they debated how the few men left in Benjamin should find wives. South of Lebonah there was an annual feast, and the Israelites decided that here the men of Benjamin should capture wives from the daughters of Shiloh.

ONLY REFERENCE
JUDGES 21:19

LEHI OT3
To be soft; the cheek; jawbone

A place in Judah where Samson battled the Philistines and killed a thousand men with the jawbone of a donkey.

FIRST REFERENCE
JUDGES 15:9
LAST REFERENCE
JUDGES 15:19

LESHEM OT1
A gem, perhaps a jacinth

A city captured by the tribe of Dan. They renamed the city Dan, after their forefather. Same as Laish.

ONLY REFERENCE
JOSHUA 19:47

LIBNAH OT18
A whitish tree, perhaps the storax

1) A campsite of the Israelites on their way to the Promised Land.

FIRST REFERENCE
NUMBERS 33:20
LAST REFERENCE
NUMBERS 33:21

2) A Canaanite city conquered by Joshua and his troops. Libnah became part of the inheritance of the tribe of Judah following the conquest of the Promised Land. It became one of the forty-eight cities given to the Levites as God had commanded.

Libnah revolted against the rule of wicked King Jehoram (Joram) of Judah, who did not follow the Lord. Later, King Sennacherib of Assyria besieged the city after he fought Lachish and before he attacked Jerusalem.

FIRST REFERENCE
JOSHUA 10:29
LAST REFERENCE
JEREMIAH 52:1
KEY REFERENCE
JOSHUA 10:29–31

LIBYA OT2/NT1
Put, a son of Ham

A country west of Egypt that Ezekiel foretold would fall by the sword, along with Egypt, Persia, and Ethiopia. People from Libya were part of the crowd that observed the coming of the Holy Spirit at Pentecost.

FIRST REFERENCE
EZEKIEL 30:5
LAST REFERENCE
ACTS 2:10

LOD OT4

A city built by the sons of Elpaal, who were of the tribe of Benjamin. Lod was resettled by the tribe of Benjamin following the Babylonian exile.

FIRST REFERENCE
I CHRONICLES 8:12
LAST REFERENCE
NEHEMIAH 11:35

LO-DEBAR OT3
Pastureless

A city where Mephibosheth, Jonathan's son, lived in the home of Machir, son of Ammiel, until King David brought Mephibosheth to Jerusalem.

FIRST REFERENCE
2 SAMUEL 9:4
LAST REFERENCE
2 SAMUEL 17:27

LUHITH OT2
Floored

A Moabite hill or city that probably was near Zoar and Horonaim.

FIRST REFERENCE
ISAIAH 15:5
LAST REFERENCE
JEREMIAH 48:5

LUZ OT8
Probably derived from a nut tree, perhaps the almond

1) Luz is the Canaanite name for the city that Jacob called Bethel. After his sons revenged the rape of Dinah, God told Jacob to take his household to this city and build an altar there. Later Jacob testified to Joseph that God appeared to him there and blessed him (Genesis 48:3). Luz became part of the inheritance of the tribe of Benjamin following the conquest of the Promised Land. Same as Bethel.

FIRST REFERENCE
GENESIS 28:19
LAST REFERENCE
JUDGES 1:23

2) A city built in the land of the Hittites by the man who showed the spies of the house of Joseph how to enter the city of Bethel (which was also called Luz).

ONLY REFERENCE
JUDGES 1:26

LYCAONIA NT2
Perhaps derived remotely from wolf

An area of Asia Minor that included the cities of Lystra and Derbe. The people there must have spoken a distinctive dialect, since Luke specifically mentions their unusual speech.

FIRST REFERENCE
ACTS 14:6
LAST REFERENCE
ACTS 14:11

LYCIA NT1
Perhaps derived remotely from wolf

A Roman province in Asia Minor that included the city of Myra. The centurion in charge of getting Paul to Rome found a ship in Myra to take them to their destination.

ONLY REFERENCE
ACTS 27:5

LYDDA NT3

A Judean city where Peter healed a man named Aeneas. Many people came to the Lord through this miracle. Then believers asked Peter to come to Joppa to heal Tabitha.

FIRST REFERENCE
ACTS 9:32
LAST REFERENCE
ACTS 9:38

LYSTRA NT6

A Lycaonian city to which Paul and Barnabas fled after the Jews of Iconium tried to stone them. In Lystra Paul healed a lame man. The people of the city responded by declaring Paul and Barnabas gods. But the Jews of Antioch and Iconium followed the apostles to Lystra and stoned Paul. Though they left Lystra, Paul and Barnabas later returned to encourage the believers there.

The Christians of Lystra and Iconium gave a good report about Timothy, so Paul took him on his missionary travels.

FIRST REFERENCE
ACTS 14:6
LAST REFERENCE
2 TIMOTHY 3:11

-M-

MAACAH OT1
Depression

A small Syrian kingdom north of Lake Huleh that supported the Ammonites after their king insulted King David's messengers. The Syrians fled before Israel's battle commander Joab and his troops. Same as Maachah.

ONLY REFERENCE
2 SAMUEL 10:8

MAACHAH OT1
Depression

A small Syrian kingdom north of Lake Huleh that supported the Ammonites after their king insulted King David's messengers. The Syrians fled before Israel's battle commander Joab and his troops. Same as Maachah.

ONLY REFERENCE
1 CHRONICLES 19:7

MAALEH-ACRABBIM OT1
Steep of scorpions

A pass that formed part of the southern border of the tribe of Judah's territory.

ONLY REFERENCE
JOSHUA 15:3

MAARATH OT1
Waste

A city that became part of the inheritance of the tribe of Judah following the conquest of the Promised Land.

ONLY REFERENCE
JOSHUA 15:59

MACEDONIA NT28

Famed homeland of Alexander the Great, in the New Testament era Macedonia was a Roman province north of Greece; it included the cities of Philippi, Berea, and Thessalonica. The apostle Paul began his ministry there after he had a vision of a Macedonian who requested him to come to his land. In response, Paul and his ministry companions traveled to Philippi, the chief city of the eastern part of the province. There Lydia became the first European convert (Acts 16:14–15).

But ministry in Macedonia was not always easy. The apostle declared that in Macedonia "our flesh had no rest, but we were troubled on every side" (2 Corinthians 7:5). During his first visit to Philippi, Paul and Silas were beaten and imprisoned. But their suffering bore fruit, as their jailor came to faith. Paul and Silas moved on to Thessalonica, where a multitude of devout Greeks believed, not a few of whom were the chief women of the city. Trouble again arose, and Paul and Silas moved on to Berea, where the Jews to whom he preached studied the scriptures to see if he spoke the truth.

But again, after some people believed, Paul's opponents from Thessalonica stirred up trouble, so Paul traveled on, leaving Timothy and Silas to continue the ministry. Paul took Macedonians Gaius and Aristarchus as companions in his ministry. They visited Ephesus with Paul and became part of the riot inspired by the silversmith Demetrius (Acts 19:29). After the uproar died down, Paul returned to the Macedonian ministry.

The Thessalonians became examples to the fledgling church of Macedonia as they turned away from idolatry. And the apostle commends them as successful Gospel preachers (1 Thessalonians 1:8). The churches of this province also gave to the collection of funds for the beleaguered church of Jerusalem.

Paul closely connected his visits to Macedonia with those to Corinth, and he spoke to the churches about each other. The apostle confronted Corinthian pride, telling the church at Corinth that where it did not provide for him, Macedonia supplied his needs. But Philippi had also provided for him when Macedonia failed.

FIRST REFERENCE
ACTS 16:9
LAST REFERENCE
1 TIMOTHY 1:3
KEY REFERENCES
ACTS 16:9–12; 2 CORINTHIANS 7:5

MACHPELAH OT6
A fold

A cave of Shechem that, along with the surrounding field, Abraham bought from Ephron the Hittite as a burial place for Sarah. Also buried there were Abraham, Isaac, Rebekah, and Leah. Joseph brought the body of his father, Jacob, out of Egypt to be buried at Machpelah as well.

FIRST REFERENCE
GENESIS 23:9
LAST REFERENCE
GENESIS 50:13

MADIAN NT1

A variation of the name Midian. Moses fled here after he killed an Egyptian. Same as Midian.

ONLY REFERENCE
ACTS 7:29

MADMANNAH OT1
Dunghill

A city that became part of the inheritance of the tribe of Judah following the conquest of the Promised Land.

ONLY REFERENCE
JOSHUA 15:31

MADMEN OT1
Dunghill

A Moabite town whose people the prophet Jeremiah foresaw being cut down and pursued with a sword.

ONLY REFERENCE
JEREMIAH 48:2

MADMENAH OT1
Dunghill

The people of this place would flee before the Assyrians, according to the prophet Isaiah's prophecy.

ONLY REFERENCE
ISAIAH 10:31

MADON OT2
Extensiveness (that is, height)

A Canaanite city whose king supported Jabin, king of Hazor, when Israel arrived in the Promised Land. Joshua and his troops conquered Madon.

FIRST REFERENCE
JOSHUA 11:1
LAST REFERENCE
JOSHUA 12:19

MAGDALA NT1
The tower

A city on the Sea of Galilee that was the home of Mary Magdalene.

ONLY REFERENCE
MATTHEW 15:39

MAHANAIM OT13
Double camp

A place east of the Jordan River where Jacob met angels of God after making a covenant with his father-in-law, Laban. Mahanaim became a border indicator for the tribes of Gad and Manasseh and later became one of the six cities of refuge established in Israel for those who had committed accidental murder. Mahanaim was given to the Levites by the tribe of Gad.

Here Abner made Ish-bosheth king of Gilead. When King David fled from his son Absalom, supporters brought David's men supplies in Mahanaim.

FIRST REFERENCE
GENESIS 32:2
LAST REFERENCE
1 CHRONICLES 6:80
KEY REFERENCES
2 SAMUEL 2:8–11; 17:26–27

MAHANEH-DAN OT1
Camp of Dan

A place behind Kirjath-jearim where the Danites camped before they stole the idols from Micah in Mount Ephraim.

ONLY REFERENCE
JUDGES 18:12

MAKAZ OT1
End

Under King Solomon's governmental organization, a town responsible for supplying provisions for the king.

ONLY REFERENCE
1 KINGS 4:9

MAKHELOTH OT2
Assemblies

A campsite of the Israelites on their way to the Promised Land.

FIRST REFERENCE
NUMBERS 33:25
LAST REFERENCE
NUMBERS 33:26

MAKKEDAH OT9
Herding fold

Site of a cave where Joshua trapped five Amorite kings who fled during battle. Later, Joshua killed them here.

FIRST REFERENCE
JOSHUA 10:10
LAST REFERENCE
JOSHUA 15:41

MAKTESH OT1
Dell

A district in or near Jerusalem that the prophet Zephaniah foresaw would howl at the destruction of its merchants.

ONLY REFERENCE
ZEPHANIAH 1:11

MAMRE OT8
Lusty (in the sense of vigor)

A plain in Hebron where Abram (later called Abraham) lived and built an altar. Here he received the news that Sarah would have a child. Near Mamre, Sarah, Abraham, Isaac, Rebekah, Leah, and Jacob would be buried.

FIRST REFERENCE
GENESIS 13:18
LAST REFERENCE
GENESIS 50:13

MANAHATH OT1
To rest

A Benjaminite city to which the people of Geba were taken as captives.

ONLY REFERENCE
I CHRONICLES 8:6

MANASSEH OT91
Causing to forget

The land of the tribe of Manasseh, which included the conquered kingdom of Og of Bashan. This tribe's split inheritance lay on both the east and west sides of the Jordan River. Before the conquest of the land west of the Jordan River, Manasseh evidently joined with Reuben and Gad in desiring land east of the Jordan River. The sons of Machir, the firstborn son of Manasseh, conquered Gilead, displacing the Amorites. So Moses gave this northeastern corner of Israel's conquest to Machir and his descendants. Jair and Nobah added

to their land, winning a further city and villages (Numbers 32:39–42). Moses confirmed Manasseh's inheritance (Numbers 34:13–15).

This was the largest portion of the tribe's holdings, but the rest of the tribe received land west of the Jordan, in a territory north of Ephraim and Dan, stretching from the Jordan River to the Mediterranean Sea. Manasseh thrived in the Promised Land.

But the tribe of Manasseh never drove out some of the original inhabitants of their cities and therefore fell into idolatry. So God sent the Assyrian king Pul (Tiglath-pileser III), who took captive the people of Manasseh east of the Jordan River and exported them to his own land (1 Chronicles 5:25–26). When Josiah became king of Judah, he destroyed idolatrous images in the towns of Manasseh and burned the pagan priests on their altars.

FIRST REFERENCE
NUMBERS 1:10
LAST REFERENCE
EZEKIEL 48:5
KEY REFERENCES
JOSHUA 17:1–17; 2 CHRONICLES 34:4–6

MAON OT6
A residence

1) A village that became part of the inheritance of the tribe of Judah following the conquest of the Promised Land. Maon was the home of Nabal, the wealthy man who refused to help David and his men, though they had protected

Nabal's lands during David's warfare with Saul.

FIRST REFERENCE
JOSHUA 15:55
LAST REFERENCE
I SAMUEL 25:2

2) A wilderness in the plain south of Jeshimon. Here King Saul pursued David, who fled until the king was distracted by a Philistine attack.

FIRST REFERENCE
I SAMUEL 23:24
LAST REFERENCE
I SAMUEL 23:25

MARAH   OT5
Bitter

A campsite of the Israelites on their way to the Promised Land. The waters here were bitter.

FIRST REFERENCE
EXODUS 15:23
LAST REFERENCE
NUMBERS 33:9

MARALAH   OT1
Earthquake

A city that became part of the inheritance of Zebulun when Joshua cast lots in Shiloh to provide territory for the seven tribes that had yet to receive their land.

ONLY REFERENCE
JOSHUA 19:11

MARESHAH   OT6
Summit

A city that became part of the inheritance of the tribe of Judah following the conquest of the Promised Land. King Rehoboam of Judah fortified Mareshah to defend his nation. Here King Asa of Judah met in battle with Zerah the Ethiopian. The prophet Micah foretold this city's conquest by Assyria.

FIRST REFERENCE
JOSHUA 15:44
LAST REFERENCE
MICAH 1:15

MAROTH   OT1
Bitter springs

A Judean city that awaited good but saw evil come upon it when the Assyrians attacked.

ONLY REFERENCE
MICAH 1:12

MARS' HILL   NT1

Also called "the Areopagus," this hill near Athens's Acropolis was where the ancient Athenian court and council met. In Paul's day, the council was in charge of religious matters in the city. Paul had taught Christ in the synagogues; the philosophers of Athens heard his message and began to debate with him about the "foreign gods" he was preaching (Acts 17:18 NIV). They brought him to a meeting of the council of the Areopagus at Mars' Hill and asked him about his teaching. The apostle took the opportunity to speak to them about Christ, and a few people came to the Lord as a result of his message. Same as Areopagus.

ONLY REFERENCE
ACTS 17:22

MASHAL OT1
Request

One of the forty-eight cities given to the Levites as God had commanded. Mashal was given to them by the tribe of Asher.

ONLY REFERENCE
1 CHRONICLES 6:74

MASREKAH OT2
Vineyard

Home of an Edomite king, Samlah, who inherited his throne from Hadad, son of Bedad.

FIRST REFERENCE
GENESIS 36:36
LAST REFERENCE
1 CHRONICLES 1:47

MASSAH OT4
A testing

Another name for Meribah, where God's people murmured against Him. Their grumbling provoked Him to wrath, though He provided water for them there.

FIRST REFERENCE
EXODUS 17:7
LAST REFERENCE
DEUTERONOMY 33:8

MATTANAH OT2
A present; an offering; a bribe

A camp of the Israelites during their forty years in the wilderness.

FIRST REFERENCE
NUMBERS 21:18
LAST REFERENCE
NUMBERS 21:19

MEAH OT2
A hundred or a hundredth

A tower in Jerusalem that was sanctified by the high priest Eliashib and dedicated by Nehemiah.

FIRST REFERENCE
NEHEMIAH 3:1
LAST REFERENCE
NEHEMIAH 12:39

MEARAH OT1
Cave

A place near Sidon that Israel had not yet possessed when Joshua was old.

ONLY REFERENCE
JOSHUA 13:4

MEDEBA OT5
Water of quiet

An Amorite city that became part of the inheritance of the tribe of Reuben. After the new king of Ammon offended David's messengers, he hired the king of Maacha and his troops as mercenaries. Maacha's men assembled against Israel at Medeba.

victorious. During King Solomon's rule, Baana was the provisions officer in charge of Megiddo.

Fleeing from Jehu, King Azahiah of Judah was set upon by Jehu's men and died in Megiddo. King Josiah of Judah also died here in a battle with Pharaoh Necho, having been shot by the pharaoh's archers.

FIRST REFERENCE
JOSHUA 12:21
LAST REFERENCE
2 CHRONICLES 35:22

MEGIDDON   OT1
Rendezvous

The prophet Zechariah compares the day when Israel will recognize the crucified Messiah to the great mourning in this valley. Same as Megiddo.

ONLY REFERENCE
ZECHARIAH 12:11

ME-JARKON   OT1
Water of the yellowness

A town that became part of the inheritance of Dan when Joshua cast lots in Shiloh to provide territory for the seven tribes that had yet to receive their land.

ONLY REFERENCE
JOSHUA 19:46

FIRST REFERENCE
NUMBERS 21:30
LAST REFERENCE
ISAIAH 15:2

MEDIA   OT6
Madai (in Hebrew)

A Mesopotamian nation that lay northeast of Babylon and north of Elam. Media was conquered by the Assyrians, whose king, Shalmaneser, transported the conquered Israelites to Media. For a time the Media established themselves as an independent nation but were again conquered by Persia. The army and leaders of Media were part of the Persian king Ahasuerus's feast.

FIRST REFERENCE
ESTHER 1:3
LAST REFERENCE
DANIEL 8:20

MEGIDDO   OT11
Rendezvous

A fortress city northwest of Taanach that guarded a strategic mountain pass west of the Jordan River, Megiddo was conquered by Joshua and his troops. Though it was within the tribe of Issachar's territory, Megiddo became part of the inheritance of the tribe of Manasseh. The tribe did not drive out its original inhabitants.

Deborah and Barak's victory song says, "The kings of Canaan fought at Taanach by the waters of Megiddo" (Judges 5:19 NIV), but the kings did not leave the field with plunder. Instead Israel was

MEKONAH — OT1
A base

A town of Judah resettled by the Jews after the Babylonian exile.

ONLY REFERENCE
NEHEMIAH 11:28

MELITA — NT1

The island on which Paul and his fellow travelers to Rome landed after they were shipwrecked. The people of Melita were kind to them.

ONLY REFERENCE
ACTS 28:1

MEMPHIS — OT1

An ancient Egyptian city, capital of the northern part of that country, that was famed for its burial places. The prophet Hosea foretold that Memphis would bury the people of Israel who had turned away from God.

ONLY REFERENCE
HOSEA 9:6

MEONENIM — OT1
To cover; to cloud over; to act covertly (that is, to practice magic)

A plain near Shechem.

ONLY REFERENCE
JUDGES 9:37

MEPHAATH — OT4
Illuminative

One of the forty-eight cities given to the Levites as God had commanded. Mephaath was given to them by the tribe of Reuben. In his oracle against Moab, the prophet Jeremiah foresaw judgment falling on Mephaath.

FIRST REFERENCE
JOSHUA 13:18
LAST REFERENCE
JEREMIAH 48:21

MERATHAIM — OT1
Double bitterness

A name for Babylon that the prophet Jeremiah used when he foretold Israel's return to its land and the righteousness of Israel and Judah. God commanded the two nations to destroy Merathaim.

ONLY REFERENCE
JEREMIAH 50:21

MERIBAH — OT6
Quarrel

1) The rock of Horeb that God commanded Moses to strike to provide water for His people in the wilderness. Because the Israelites quarreled and tested God there, Moses called the place Massah (meaning "a testing") and Meribah (meaning "quarrel").

ONLY REFERENCE
EXODUS 17:7

2) During the Israelites' forty years in the desert, in a second incident

in the desert of Zin, God commanded Moses to speak to a rock that would produce water. Instead Moses struck the rock twice. Here God provided the water but told Moses and Aaron they would not enter the Promised Land. Same as Meribah-kadesh.

FIRST REFERENCE
NUMBERS 20:13
LAST REFERENCE
PSALM 81:7

MERIBAH-KADESH
OT 1

A place in the wilderness (or desert) of Zin where the Israelites disobeyed God. Same as Meribah 2.

ONLY REFERENCE
DEUTERONOMY 32:51

MEROM   OT 2
Altitude, elevated place, or elation

The "waters of Merom" were the site of a battle between Jabin, king of Hazor, and his allies and Joshua and his troops. The Israelites defeated their enemies and chased them to Zidon and beyond. Some have identified Merom with Lake Huleh, but the Jewish historian Josephus places the Israelites' camp elsewhere.

FIRST REFERENCE
JOSHUA 11:5
LAST REFERENCE
JOSHUA 11:7

MEROZ   OT 1

A city on which Deborah and Barak called down a curse because its inhabitants did not assist in Israel's battle with Sisera.

ONLY REFERENCE
JUDGES 5:23

MESHA   OT 1
A sowing or a possession

A place where Shem's descendants lived.

ONLY REFERENCE
GENESIS 10:30

MESOPOTAMIA
OT5/NT2
In the middle of two rivers

The territory between the Tigris and Euphrates rivers. From this area came a number of great ancient empires, including the Old Babylonian, Assyrian, and Neo-Babylonian empires. Abraham, who was originally from Ur, a city of Mesopotamia, sent a servant to the city of Nahor, also in Mesopotamia, to find a bride from his own family for his son Isaac.

In the time of the judges, when Israel sinned, God put the nation under the hand of Mesopotamia's king for eight years. Othniel delivered Israel from his rule. The Mesopotamians joined the Ammonites in war against King David.

People from Mesopotamia

saw the Christians filled with the Holy Spirit at Pentecost. See Assyria and Babylon.

FIRST REFERENCE
GENESIS 24:10
LAST REFERENCE
ACTS 7:2

METHEG-AMMAH OT1
Bit of the metropolis

A figurative name for a major city that King David won in a battle with the Philistines.

ONLY REFERENCE
2 SAMUEL 8:1

MICHMAS OT2
Hidden

A city whose people returned to Israel after the Babylonian exile. Same as Michmash.

FIRST REFERENCE
EZRA 2:27
LAST REFERENCE
NEHEMIAH 7:31

MICHMASH OT9
Hidden

A village of Israel where Saul's troops gathered to fight the Philistines. Afterward the Philisitnes set up a garrison at the pass of Michmash. Jonathan and his armor bearer attacked the Philistines here, and in the ensuing battle their enemies fled. Michmash was resettled by the tribe of Benjamin following the Babylonian exile. Same as Michmas.

FIRST REFERENCE
I SAMUEL 13:2
LAST REFERENCE
ISAIAH 10:28

MICHMETHAH OT2
Concealment

A city on the border of the territory of the tribes of Ephraim and Manasseh.

FIRST REFERENCE
JOSHUA 16:6
LAST REFERENCE
JOSHUA 17:7

MIDDIN OT1
A contest or a quarrel

A city that became part of the inheritance of the tribe of Judah following the conquest of the Promised Land.

ONLY REFERENCE
JOSHUA 15:61

MIDIAN OT35
A contest or a quarrel

A land east of the Sinai Peninsula, in the northwest portion of Arabia. Midian lay east of the Gulf of Aqaba and south of Edom. Moses fled here after he killed an Egyptian. He married Zipporah, daughter of the Midian priest Jethro. When Israel conquered the Promised Land, Midianites sought to lure Israel into idolatry and intermarriage. Cozbi, daughter of a Midianite prince, was killed when an Israelite brought her to his tent as Moses called Israel to turn away from foreign women.

God called Moses to fight Midian, bringing His vengeance down on it. Israel killed Midian's five kings and their prophet Balaam, who had plotted with Midian and Moab to draw Israel into pagan practices. Israel killed the Midianite men but brought the women and children as captives to their camp. Moses reminded them that these women had caused Israel's downfall. He commanded them to kill all but the women who were virgins.

After the prophetess Deborah and the battle commander Barak freed Israel from the rule of Canaan, God gave the nation over to Midian for seven years. Then God called Gideon to fight the Midianites and liberate Israel from their rule. With three hundred men he attacked the Midian campsite at night, and the enemy ran. Following the attack, Israel captured and killed two of Midian's kings and made peace with two more. During Solomon's reign, Midian supported Hadad the Edomite against Israel. Same as Madian.

FIRST REFERENCE
GENESIS 36:35
LAST REFERENCE
HABAKKUK 3:7
KEY REFERENCES
NUMBERS 25; 31:1–18; JUDGES 7:8–8:28

MIGDAL-EL OT1
Tower of God

A fortified or walled city that became part of the inheritance of Naphtali when Joshua cast lots in Shiloh to provide territory for the seven tribes that had yet to receive their land.

ONLY REFERENCE
JOSHUA 19:38

MIGDAL-GAD OT1
Tower of fortune

A city that became part of the inheritance of the tribe of Judah following the conquest of the Promised Land.

ONLY REFERENCE
JOSHUA 15:37

MIGDOL OT4

1) A campsite of the Israelites on their way to the Promised Land. Migdol lay on the northeastern border of Egypt.

FIRST REFERENCE
EXODUS 14:2
LAST REFERENCE
NUMBERS 33:7

2) A city in Egypt where the people of Judah settled after their nation was devastated by the Babylonians. Jeremiah prophesied that because they did not follow the Lord, they would die in Egypt.

FIRST REFERENCE
JEREMIAH 44:1
LAST REFERENCE
JEREMIAH 46:14

MIGRON OT2
Precipice

A town on the outskirts of Gibeah. Here, under a pomegranate tree, Saul tarried while Jonathan attacked a Philistine outpost.

FIRST REFERENCE
I SAMUEL 14:2
LAST REFERENCE
ISAIAH 10:28

MILETUM NT1

A city south of Ephesus where Paul told Timothy he had left his companion Trophimus, who was sick. Same as Miletus.

ONLY REFERENCE
2 TIMOTHY 4:20

MILETUS NT2

A city south of Ephesus where Paul met with the Ephesian elders before he left for Jerusalem. Same as Melitum.

FIRST REFERENCE
ACTS 20:15
LAST REFERENCE
ACTS 20:17

MILLO OT10
A rampart (that is, a citadel)

1) A fortification somewhere in the area of Shechem, where the men of Millo supported Abimelech as king after Gideon died. It is called Beth Millo in some translations.

FIRST REFERENCE
JUDGES 9:6
LAST REFERENCE
JUDGES 9:20

2) A fortification of ancient Jerusalem. David lived here after the Israelites first made him their king. He rebuilt Jerusalem around Millo. King Solomon repaired the breaches in the fort's wall and refortified it.

Joash, king of Judah, was killed at Millo. King Hezekiah of Judah repaired Millo as the Assyrians threatened his nation.

FIRST REFERENCE
2 SAMUEL 5:9
LAST REFERENCE
2 CHRONICLES 32:5

MINNI OT1

An Armenian province that the prophet Jeremiah called to attack Babylon as part of God's judgment of that nation.

ONLY REFERENCE
JEREMIAH 51:27

MINNITH OT2
Enumeration

An Ammonite town where Jephthah the Gileadite ended his battle that subdued the Ammonites. Minnith grew wheat that was exported to Tyre.

FIRST REFERENCE
JUDGES 11:33
LAST REFERENCE
EZEKIEL 27:17

MIPHKAD — OT1
Assignment

A gate in Jerusalem during Nehemiah's rebuilding of the city that designated the area to be repaired by Malchiah.

ONLY REFERENCE
NEHEMIAH 3:31

MISGAB — OT1
A cliff; altitude; refuge

A place in Moab that the prophet Jeremiah described as "confounded and dismayed" in his prophecy against that nation.

ONLY REFERENCE
JEREMIAH 48:1

MISHAL — OT1

One of the forty-eight cities given to the Levites as God had commanded. Mishal was given to them by the tribe of Asher.

ONLY REFERENCE
JOSHUA 21:30

MISREPHOTH-MAIM — OT2
Burnings of water

Joshua and his troops chased their Canaanite enemies to this place after the battle at the waters of Merom. When Joshua was old, Misrephoth-maim had not yet been possessed by Israel.

FIRST REFERENCE
JOSHUA 11:8
LAST REFERENCE
JOSHUA 13:6

MITHCAH — OT2
Sweetness

A campsite of the Israelites on their way to the Promised Land.

FIRST REFERENCE
NUMBERS 33:28
LAST REFERENCE
NUMBERS 33:29

MITYLENE — NT1

A city on the Greek island of Lesbos. Paul stopped here on his way to Jerusalem at the end of his third missionary journey.

ONLY REFERENCE
ACTS 20:14

MIZAR — OT1
Petty; short (time)

A hill or mountain that the psalmist remembered as he longed for God.

ONLY REFERENCE
PSALM 42:6

MIZPAH — OT23

1) A heap of stones set up by Laban and Jacob as a sign of the covenant between them. Same as Galeed and Jegar-sahadutha.

2) A city of Benjamin built by King Asa of Judah with stones and timber that King Baasha of Israel had been using to build Ramah.

FIRST REFERENCE
I KINGS 15:22
LAST REFERENCE
NEHEMIAH 3:7

3) At his home base in Mizpah, Gedaliah, the ruler placed over Judah by Babylon's king Nebuchadnezzar, was visited by the captains of Judah's armies. He encouraged them not to fear serving Nebuchadnezzar. But because the Israelites dreaded their Chaldean overlords, Ishmael, son of Nethaniah, and his men in Mizpah killed Gedaliah and his followers.

Ishmael also met eighty men who were headed to Jerusalem with offerings for the Lord. Ishmael left Mizpah, met the men, and invited them into the city, where he killed all but ten of the group. Then he made the rest of the inhabitants of the city captives. Army officer Johanan discovered Ishmael's crimes and fought him and his men. The people of Mizpah supported Johanan, but Ishmael and a few of his men escaped.

FIRST REFERENCE
2 KINGS 25:23
LAST REFERENCE
HOSEA 5:1
KEY REFERENCES
JEREMIAH 40:8–10; 41:1–15

4) The territory co-ruled by Shallum, who made repairs to the gate of the fountain in Jerusalem under Nehemiah's rule.

ONLY REFERENCE
NEHEMIAH 3:15

5) An area ruled by Ezer, who made repairs in Jerusalem under Nehemiah's rule.

ONLY REFERENCE
NEHEMIAH 3:19

MIZPEH — OT23

1) A Hivite valley near Mount Hermon where Joshua and the Israelites fought Jabin, king of Hazor, and his allies.

FIRST REFERENCE
JOSHUA 11:3
LAST REFERENCE
JOSHUA 11:8

2) A city that became part of the inheritance of the tribe of Judah following the conquest of the Promised Land. Here the Israelites gathered before they went to war against the Benjaminites, who had abused and killed a Levite's concubine. In Mizpeh the Israelites swore that they would never give their daughters as wives to the Benjaminites.

The prophet Samuel called the Israelites to Mizpeh after he told them to give up idolatry. As they were confessing their sin, the Philistines took advantage of the opportunity to attack. The Lord thundered over the Philistines, terrifying them. Israel's army engaged and subdued its enemies. Mizpeh became part of Samuel's regular circuit court as he judged Israel. When Israel demanded a king, Samuel called the people to Mizpeh, where Saul was chosen to rule the nation.

FIRST REFERENCE
JOSHUA 15:38
LAST REFERENCE
I SAMUEL 10:17
KEY REFERENCE
JUDGES 20:1–3

3) A city that became part of the inheritance of Benjamin when Joshua cast lots in Shiloh to provide territory for the seven tribes that had yet to receive their land.

4) A city where Israel camped before Jephthah the Gileadite led them into battle against the Ammonites. Mizpeh was Jephthah's hometown.

5) A city in Moab where David went to ask the king of Moab to protect his parents while he battled King Saul.

MOAB — OT169

From her [the mother's] father

At the time of the Israelites' return to the Promised Land, this nation, which was composed of the descendants of Lot and his older daughter (Genesis 19:37), lay east of the Dead Sea and below the Arnon River. Though it had once covered land north of the river, the Amorite king Sihon had taken Heshbon and the land to the north from Moab's grasp.

At God's command, when they headed for the Promised Land, the Israelites skirted Moab and went through the Amorites' territory. But Moab's king Balak feared the Israelites and asked the pagan prophet Balaam to curse them. When Balaam could not, he counseled Balak to lead Israel into idolatry (Numbers 31:16). His tactic was successful and its effects were long lasting.

Following the death of the judge Othniel, Moab's king Eglon put together an alliance of nations that attacked Israel. As the loser, Israel served Moab for eighteen years until Gera delivered the nation. Ehud killed Eglon, raised up the men of Mount Ephraim, and subdued their former overlords.

Moab periodically took up arms against God's people. It joined Sisera in his attack on Israel. Saul defended his nation from Moab. But when David escaped to the cave Adullam, he asked the king to allow his parents to live in Moab until he could settle his own future. David's parents remained in Moab as long as David was in that land. But as Israel's king, David fought Moab, which became a tributary to Israel.

After Ahab's death Moab rebelled, and Israel and Judah joined forces against King Mesha of Moab. When the battle went against him, Mesha made a sacrifice of his eldest son, and Israel and Judah withdrew. Moab and the Ammonites fought King Jehoshaphat of Judah. After the nation sought God, Jehoshaphat's army destroyed its enemies.

The prophets speak often of Moab. Isaiah prophesied its destruction and the grief of its people. Jeremiah foretold that Moab's cities would be destroyed and its people would flee. Amos foresaw that Moab would "die with tumult" (Amos 2:2).

FIRST REFERENCE
GENESIS 36:35
LAST REFERENCE
ZEPHANIAH 2:9
KEY REFERENCES
NUMBERS 21:26; 22:1–20; ISAIAH 15–16;
JEREMIAH 48:42

MOLADAH OT4
Birth

A city that became part of the inheritance of the tribe of Judah following the conquest of the Promised Land. It was given to the tribe of Simeon when Joshua cast lots in Shiloh to provide territory for the seven tribes that had yet to receive their land. Moladah was resettled by the Jews after the Babylonian exile.

FIRST REFERENCE
JOSHUA 15:26
LAST REFERENCE
NEHEMIAH 11:26

MOREH OT3
An archer; also a teacher or teaching

1) A Canaanite plain where God promised Abraham He would give the land to his descendants.

FIRST REFERENCE
GENESIS 12:6
LAST REFERENCE
DEUTERONOMY 11:30

2) A hill near the Midianite encampment attacked by Gideon and his three hundred men whom God had chosen by the way they drank water.

ONLY REFERENCE
JUDGES 7:1

MORESHETH-GATH OT1
Possession of Gath

The prophet Micah poetically declared that this place would receive presents (that is, a dowry) because it was going into exile.

ONLY REFERENCE
MICAH 1:14

MORIAH OT2
Seen of God

The land where God sent Abraham to sacrifice his son Isaac, then provided a ram for the sacrifice instead. On Mount Moriah, in the place where the threshing floor of Ornan the Jebusite had been, Solomon built Jerusalem's temple. Same as Jehovah-jireh.

FIRST REFERENCE
GENESIS 22:2
LAST REFERENCE
2 CHRONICLES 3:1

MOSERA OT1
Correction or corrections

A place in the wilderness where Aaron died and was buried.

ONLY REFERENCE
DEUTERONOMY 10:6

MOSEROTH OT2
Correction or corrections

A campsite of the Israelites on their way to the Promised Land.

FIRST REFERENCE
NUMBERS 33:30
LAST REFERENCE
NUMBERS 33:31

MOZAH OT1
Drained

A city that became part of the inheritance of Benjamin when Joshua cast lots in Shiloh to provide territory for the seven tribes that had yet to receive their land.

ONLY REFERENCE
JOSHUA 18:26

MYRA NT1

A city of Lycia where Paul and his companions stopped on their voyage to Rome. Here the centurion who was in charge of their journey found an Alexandrian ship headed for Italy.

ONLY REFERENCE
ACTS 27:5

MYSIA NT2

A northwestern region of the Roman province of Asia. Paul and Silas visited Mysia before they were called to Macedonia.

FIRST REFERENCE
ACTS 16:7
LAST REFERENCE
ACTS 16:8

-N-

NAAMAH OT1
Pleasantness

A city that became part of the inheritance of the tribe of Judah following the conquest of the Promised Land.

ONLY REFERENCE
JOSHUA 15:41

NAARAN OT1
Youthful

A city on the border of the tribe of Ephraim's territory. Naaran lay east of Bethel. Same as Naarath.

ONLY REFERENCE
1 CHRONICLES 7:28

NAARATH OT1
A girl (from infancy to adolescence)

A city on the border of the tribe of Ephraim's territory. Same as Naaran.

ONLY REFERENCE
JOSHUA 16:7

NAHALAL OT1
Pasture

One of the forty-eight cities given to the Levites as God had commanded. Nahalal was given to them by the tribe of Zebulun. Same as Nahallal and Nahalol.

ONLY REFERENCE
JOSHUA 21:35

NAHALIEL — OT 1
Valley of God

A campsite of the Israelites during their years in the wilderness.

ONLY REFERENCE
NUMBERS 21:19

NAHALLAL — OT 1
Pasture

A city that became part of the inheritance of Zebulun when Joshua cast lots in Shiloh to provide territory for the seven tribes that had yet to receive their land. Same as Nahalal and Nahalol.

ONLY REFERENCE
JOSHUA 19:15

NAHALOL — OT 1
Pasture

A city that became part of the inheritance of the tribe of Zebulun. The people of Zebulun never drove the Canaanites out of Nahalol. Same as Nahalal and Nahallal.

ONLY REFERENCE
JUDGES 1:30

NAIN — NT 1

A Galilean city. As Jesus and a crowd of followers approached the city gate, a funeral procession for a young man came out. Jesus had compassion on his mother, a widow, and brought her son back to life.

ONLY REFERENCE
LUKE 7:11

NAIOTH — OT 6
Residence

After David's wife Michal saved him from King Saul's attempts to kill him, David escaped to the prophet Samuel in Ramah. Together the two men went to Naioth, a place where prophets lived, in or near Ramah. When Saul heard that David was there, he sent men to capture him. Though he sent three groups of men, before they could capture David they all began to prophesy. When Saul went himself, he also prophesied. Meanwhile, David left Naioth to seek Jonathan's help.

FIRST REFERENCE
I SAMUEL 19:18
LAST REFERENCE
I SAMUEL 20:1

NAPHTALI — OT 41
My wrestling

The land belonging to the tribe of Naphtali was one of the northernmost inheritances, lying between Asher and the northeastern lands of Manasseh, with Zebulun and Issachar on its southern flank. The western shore of the Sea of Galilee and the northernmost section of the west bank of the Jordan River were part of its territory. Kedesh, Hazor, Dan, and Merom lay within Naphtali's borders. The tribe did not drive out the original inhabitants of Beth-shemesh and Beth-anath, but lived among them and made them pay tribute.

Under King Solomon's governmental organization, the territory of

Naphtali was responsible for supplying provisions for the king.

Ben-hadad, king of Syria, allied himself with King Asa of Judah and fought against Naphtali. During the reign of Pekah, king of Israel, the Assyrian king Tiglath-pileser conquered Naphtali and carried its inhabitants to his own land.

Josiah, king of Judah, broke down the idols of Manasseh, Ephraim, and Simeon as far as Naphtali and burned the bones of the pagan priests on their own altars.

FIRST REFERENCE
NUMBERS 1:15
LAST REFERENCE
EZEKIEL 48:4
KEY REFERENCES
I KINGS 15:20; 2 KINGS 15:29;
2 CHRONICLES 34:1–6

NAZARETH NT29

In this village of Galilee, the virgin Mary heard the news that she would bear the Messiah. After the death of Herod the Great, Joseph brought Mary and Jesus out of Egypt and back to live in Nazareth, which was beyond the reach of Archelaus, son of Herod the Great.

Here Jesus announced the beginning of His ministry and the fulfillment of the promise of the Good News and liberty for God's people. Furious, the people of his hometown tried to kill him (Luke 4:28–29). Matthew's account tells us that their unbelief caused Him not to do many miracles there (Matthew 13:58). Though Jesus moved to Capernaum and stayed there during His early ministry, He is frequently referred to in scripture as Jesus of Nazareth.

Nathanael had no good opinion of the village and wondered if anything good could come from it (John 1:46).

FIRST REFERENCE
MATTHEW 2:23
LAST REFERENCE
ACTS 26:9
KEY REFERENCES
MATTHEW 2:19–23; LUKE 1:26–29; 4:16–19

NEAH OT1
Motion

A city that became part of the inheritance of Zebulun when Joshua cast lots in Shiloh to provide territory for the seven tribes that had yet to receive their land.

ONLY REFERENCE
JOSHUA 19:13

NEAPOLIS NT1
A youth (up to about forty years)

The port of Philippi. Paul and his companions stopped in Neapolis on their way to that important city of Macedonia.

ONLY REFERENCE
ACTS 16:11

NEBALLAT   OT1
Foolish secrecy

A town of Benjamin resettled by the Jews after the Babylonian exile.

ONLY REFERENCE
NEHEMIAH 11:34

NEBO   OT11
Name of a Babylonian god

1) A city east of the Jordan River that the Reubenites requested as part of their inheritance because it had good grazing land for cattle. After inheriting Nebo, the Reubenites built it up. Isaiah foretold that Moab would howl over the city, and Ezekiel foresaw that it would be spoiled in war.

FIRST REFERENCE
NUMBERS 32:3
LAST REFERENCE
JEREMIAH 48:22

2) Mount Nebo was a Moabite mountain near Jericho. Before he died in Moab, Moses went from the plains of Moab to Mount Nebo and on to Mount Pisgah, where he got a clear view of the new land his people would inherit.

FIRST REFERENCE
DEUTERONOMY 32:49
LAST REFERENCE
DEUTERONOMY 34:1

3) A city in Judah to which captives returned after the Babylonian exile.

FIRST REFERENCE
EZRA 2:29
LAST REFERENCE
NEHEMIAH 7:33

NEIEL   OT1
Moved of God

A city that became part of the inheritance of Asher when Joshua cast lots in Shiloh to provide territory for the seven tribes that had yet to receive their land.

ONLY REFERENCE
JOSHUA 19:27

NEKEB   OT1
Dell

A city that became part of the inheritance of Naphtali when Joshua cast lots in Shiloh to provide territory for the seven tribes that had yet to receive their land.

ONLY REFERENCE
JOSHUA 19:33

NEPHTHALIM NT2
To fall down

On the borders of Nephthalim, the land of the tribe of Naphtali, Jesus lived at the beginning of His ministry. By doing so He fulfilled a prophecy that the people of this area would see a great light.

FIRST REFERENCE
MATTHEW 4:13
LAST REFERENCE
MATTHEW 4:15

NEPHTOAH   OT2
Opened

A spring of water near Jerusalem that was on the border of the tribe of Judah's territory.

NETOPHAH   OT2
Distillation

A city in Judah to which captives returned after the Babylonian exile.

FIRST REFERENCE
EZRA 2:22
LAST REFERENCE
NEHEMIAH 7:26

NEZIB   OT1
Station

A city that became part of the inheritance of the tribe of Judah following the conquest of the Promised Land.

ONLY REFERENCE
JOSHUA 15:43

NIBSHAN   OT1

A city that became part of the inheritance of the tribe of Judah following the conquest of the Promised Land.

ONLY REFERENCE
JOSHUA 15:62

NICOPOLIS   NT1
Victorious city

A Greek city where Paul planned to spend the winter when he wrote his epistle to Titus. Though the greeting of Paul's letter describes it as a Macedonian city, scholars believe Nicopolis was probably the Roman-built city at Epirus.

ONLY REFERENCE
TITUS 3:12

NIMRAH   OT1
Clear water

A city east of the Jordan River that the Reubenites and Gadites requested as part of their inheritance because it had good grazing land for cattle.

ONLY REFERENCE
NUMBERS 32:3

NIMRIM   OT2
Clear waters

A Moabite stream that the prophets Isaiah and Jeremiah foretold would become desolate because of God's judgment.

FIRST REFERENCE
ISAIAH 15:6
LAST REFERENCE
JEREMIAH 48:34

NINEVE   NT1
Greek form of Nineveh

Jesus warned the Jews that the people of Nineve, who had repented under Jonah's message, would rise up in judgment of them because they did not repent when they heard His preaching. Same as Nineveh.

ONLY REFERENCE
LUKE 11:32

NINEVEH OT17/NT1

An ancient city built by Asshur that became the capital of the Assyrian Empire. Nineveh was located on the Tigris River's eastern bank. When the Assyrian king Sennacherib attacked Jerusalem, God killed his troops, so the frightened king returned to Nineveh.

God sent Jonah to preach repentance to this large city, which took a journey of three days to cross. Amazingly, Nineveh's king declared that everyone in the city should repent, and the people repented, fasting and putting on sackcloth. Therefore God did not destroy the city as He had warned He would do.

But about a century later, the prophet Nahum spoke of God's anger at the city, which had become the Lord's enemy, and foretold its destruction.

Matthew records Jesus' warning to the Jews that the people of Nineveh would judge them for their lack of repentance. Same as Nineve.

FIRST REFERENCE
GENESIS 10:11
LAST REFERENCE
MATTHEW 12:41
KEY REFERENCES
2 KINGS 19:36; JONAH 3; NAHUM 1:1–2:1; 3:7

NO OT5

Another name for Upper (southern) Egypt's capital, Thebes. The prophet Jeremiah warned that Egypt, including No, would be destroyed from the north. The prophet Ezekiel foresaw the city being judged and its inhabitants being "cut off" and "rent asunder." The prophet Nahum asked Nineveh if it was better than No, which was carried into captivity.

FIRST REFERENCE
JEREMIAH 46:25
LAST REFERENCE
NAHUM 3:8

NOB OT6
Fruit

At this "city of the priests" (1 Samuel 22:19), David came to the high priest, Ahimelech, when he was fleeing from King Saul's wrath. At David's request, the priest gave him the showbread from the altar as well as Goliath's sword. After David fled to Gath, Saul heard from Doeg the Edomite that the priest had supported his enemy. The king commanded Doeg to kill the priests of Nob. The Edomite killed eighty-five priests, as well as men, women, and children and the city's animals.

The tribe of Benjamin resettled Nob after the Babylonian exile.

FIRST REFERENCE
I SAMUEL 21:1
LAST REFERENCE
ISAIAH 10:32

NOBAH OT1
A bark

After he conquered Kenath and its villages, the warrior Nobah renamed the town after himself (Numbers 32:42). Same as Kenath.

ONLY REFERENCE
JUDGES 8:11

NOD
OT1

Vagrancy

A land east of Eden where Cain lived after he murdered his brother Abel.

ONLY REFERENCE
GENESIS 4:16

NOPH
OT7

Another name for Memphis, the ancient capital of Lower (northern) Egypt. In an oracle about Egypt, Isaiah declared that Noph's princes had been deceived and they had seduced their nation.

Following the Babylonian conquest of Judah, some of the Jews fled into Egypt and lived at Noph. But Jeremiah prophesied that Nebuchadnezzar would conquer Egypt as well, and Nopf would be desolate. Ezekiel also predicted the city's destruction.

FIRST REFERENCE
ISAIAH 19:13
LAST REFERENCE
EZEKIEL 30:16

NOPHAH
OT1

A gust

A Moabite city that the Amorites had taken from them. The Israelites destroyed Nophah when they conquered the Amorite lands on their way to the Promised Land.

ONLY REFERENCE
NUMBERS 21:30

OBOTH
OT4

Water skins

A campsite of the Israelites on their way to the Promised Land.

FIRST REFERENCE
NUMBERS 21:10
LAST REFERENCE
NUMBERS 33:44

OLIVET
OT1/NT1

An olive (as yielding illuminating oil)

A mountain ridge east of Jerusalem. King David fled from his son Absalom, grieving as he ascended the Olivet ridge. Luke describes it as "a Sabbath day's journey" outside the city. From here Jesus ascended into heaven. Also called the Mount of Olives.

FIRST REFERENCE
2 SAMUEL 15:30
LAST REFERENCE
ACTS 1:12

ON
OT3

An Egyptian city northeast of Memphis. On was the home of Joseph's wife, Asenath. Her father was a priest there. Same as Aven 1.

FIRST REFERENCE
GENESIS 41:45
LAST REFERENCE
GENESIS 46:20

ONO OT5
Strong

1) A village built by the Benjaminites. It was resettled by them after the Babylonian exile.

FIRST REFERENCE
I CHRONICLES 8:12
LAST REFERENCE
NEHEMIAH 11:35

2) A plain that may be the valley of the craftsmen mentioned in Nehemiah 11:35. In one of the villages here, Sanballat and Geshem wanted to meet Nehemiah to do him harm, but he did not fall for their ploy.

ONLY REFERENCE
NEHEMIAH 6:2

OPHEL OT5
A mound

A walled part of Jerusalem near the Temple Mount. It was the home of the Nethinims, who were temple servants.

FIRST REFERENCE
2 CHRONICLES 27:3
LAST REFERENCE
NEHEMIAH 11:21

OPHIR OT11

A place, possibly in Arabia, Africa, or India, that became a byword for its trade in fine gold. Hiram (or Huram), king of Tyre, sent his navy to bring the precious metal and stones and almug trees from Ophir. King David collected stores of Ophir's gold to line the temple that his son Solomon would build. Solomon joined with Huram to acquire 450 additional talents of gold. King Jehoshaphat of Judah attempted to raise a navy to become part of this trade, but it was destroyed at the port of Ezion-geber.

FIRST REFERENCE
I KINGS 9:28
LAST REFERENCE
ISAIAH 13:12

OPHNI OT1
An inhabitant of Ophen

A city that became part of the inheritance of Benjamin when Joshua cast lots in Shiloh to provide territory for the seven tribes that had yet to receive their land.

ONLY REFERENCE
JOSHUA 18:24

OPHRAH OT7
A female fawn

1) A city that became part of the inheritance of Benjamin when Joshua cast lots in Shiloh to provide territory for the seven tribes that had yet to receive their land.

FIRST REFERENCE
JOSHUA 18:23
LAST REFERENCE
I SAMUEL 13:17

2) A city called Ophrah of the Abiezrites where an angel visited Gideon and called him a "mighty man of valour" (Judges 6:12). Gideon built an altar there and named it Jehovah-shalom. After Gideon was buried in Ophrah, his son Abimelech killed sixty-nine

of his seventy brothers in their father's home.

FIRST REFERENCE
JUDGES 6:11
LAST REFERENCE
JUDGES 9:5

OREB OT1
A raven

A rock where the Midianites were slaughtered. Isaiah compares this event to the scourge God will stir up against Assyria.

ONLY REFERENCE
ISAIAH 10:26

PADAN OT1
A plateau

A name for Padan-aram that Jacob uses when he tells of his leaving there for his homeland. Same as Padan-aram.

ONLY REFERENCE
GENESIS 48:7

PADAN-ARAM OT10
The tableland of Aram

An area of northern Mesopotamia around the city of Haran, Padan-aram was Rebekah's homeland before she married Isaac. When Jacob needed a bride, his father sent him to Padan-aram to marry one of Laban's daughters. Jacob remained there fourteen years, serving his father-in-law for his two daughters, Leah and Rachel. During these years, Jacob's twelve sons were born. When Jacob left Padan-aram, God blessed him and gave him the covenant name Israel. Same as Padan.

FIRST REFERENCE
GENESIS 25:20
LAST REFERENCE
GENESIS 46:15

PAI OT1
Screaming

The capital city of Hadad, king of Edom.

ONLY REFERENCE
1 CHRONICLES 1:50

PALESTINA OT3
Rolling (that is, migratory)

A name for the land of the Philistines, the strip of land next to the Mediterranean Sea. The song of Moses and the Israelites, following the crossing of the Red Sea, spoke of the sorrow that would engulf the people of this land as Israel came to the Promised Land. The prophet Isaiah prophesied against Palestina. By the time of the New Testament, the name had come to describe the entire land of the Jews. Same as Palestine.

FIRST REFERENCE
EXODUS 15:14
LAST REFERENCE
ISAIAH 14:31

PALESTINE OT1
Rolling (that is, migratory)

An ancient name for the land of the Philistines, the strip of land next to the Mediterranean Sea. By the time of the New Testament, the name had come to describe the entire land of the Jews. The name Palestine is used only once in scripture, when the prophet Joel speaks of God's judgment of Palestine for its sins. Same as Palestina.

ONLY REFERENCE
JOEL 3:4

PAMPHYLIA NT5
Every tribal (meaning heterogeneous)

A province on the southern coast of Asia Minor, between Lycia and Cilicia. At Pentecost, people from this province heard the Christians speak in their own tongue. Paul and Barnabas first brought the Gospel to Pamphylia when they preached in the city of Perga. Mark had joined them on this mission but left them here, so Paul refused to take him on his next journey. On his way to Rome, Paul sailed past Pamphylia.

FIRST REFERENCE
ACTS 2:10
LAST REFERENCE
ACTS 27:5

PANNAG OT1
Pastry

Some scholars believe this is the name of a pastry, while others connect it with a place between Damascus and Baalbec.

ONLY REFERENCE
EZEKIEL 27:17

PAPHOS NT2

Cyprus's capital city, where Paul and Barnabas confronted the Jewish sorcerer Elymas, who was perverting the Gospel message. When the two apostles declared the Gospel to the proconsul, Sergius Paulus, Elymas tried to turn him away from the truths of the Gospel. Paul saw Elymas as God's enemy, confronted him, and told him he would be blind for a time. The sorcerer lost his sight, and the proconsul believed.

FIRST REFERENCE
ACTS 13:6
LAST REFERENCE
ACTS 13:13

PARAH   OT I
Heifer

A city that became part of the inheritance of Benjamin when Joshua cast lots in Shiloh to provide territory for the seven tribes that had yet to receive their land.

ONLY REFERENCE
JOSHUA 18:23

PARAN   OT II
Ornamental

The wilderness in Sinai where Ishmael and his mother lived after Abraham sent Hagar away with the boy. During the Exodus, Israel camped here while the twelve spies investigated the Promised Land. After Samuel died, David went to Paran, where he asked Nabal for food and was refused. Nabal's wife, Abigail, came to David's rescue and prevented him from fighting her foolish husband. King Solomon's opponent, Hadad the Edomite, was supported by men of Paran when he fled to Egypt as a boy.

FIRST REFERENCE
GENESIS 21:21
LAST REFERENCE
HABAKKUK 3:3

PARBAR   OT I

Translated "at Parbar westward" in the KJV and "as far as the court to the west" in the NIV, this somewhat obscure phrase refers to an area near the temple, perhaps a suburb by the west wall.

ONLY REFERENCE
1 CHRONICLES 26:18

PARVAIM   OT I

A place from which King Solomon brought gold to decorate the temple.

ONLY REFERENCE
2 CHRONICLES 3:6

PAS-DAMMIM   OT I
Palm (that is, dell) of bloodshed

A place where David and his men fought the Philistines in a field of barley. After fleeing from their enemy, David's troops turned and made their stand in the middle of the field, and God gave them the victory. David's mighty man Eleazar was with him at this battle.

ONLY REFERENCE
1 CHRONICLES 11:13

PATARA   NT I

A city on the coast of Asia Minor in the Roman province of Lycia. On his way to Jerusalem, Paul stopped here to board a ship headed for Phoenicia.

ONLY REFERENCE
ACTS 21:1

PATHROS OT5

A name for Upper (southern) Egypt. From here God promised to recover a remnant of His people when Christ's kingdom is established. But the prophet Jeremiah prophesied to the Jews of his day, who had fled from the Babylonians to Egypt, that they would be destroyed. When Ezekiel prophesied against Egypt, he foretold that after its destruction, God would gather a remnant of that nation in Pathros.

FIRST REFERENCE
ISAIAH 11:11
LAST REFERENCE
EZEKIEL 30:14

PATMOS NT1

An island in the Aegean Sea, west of Asia Minor and southwest of the island of Samos. Here John was imprisoned for the sake of the Gospel and received the revelation that became the last book of the New Testament.

ONLY REFERENCE
REVELATION 1:9

PAU OT1
Screaming

An Edomite city ruled by King Hadar.

ONLY REFERENCE
GENESIS 36:39

PEKOD OT2
Punishment

A symbolic name for the Babylonians (or Chaldeans), used by the prophets as they foretold God's judgment of Babylon.

FIRST REFERENCE
JEREMIAH 50:21
LAST REFERENCE
EZEKIEL 23:23

PENIEL OT1
Face of God

The place near the ford of the Jabbok River where Jacob wrestled with a man and was given the name Israel. The man wrenched Jacob's hip near the tendon, ending the match, and he told Jacob he had struggled with God and man and had overcome. Jacob declared he had met God face-to-face, and his life was preserved. Same as Penuel.

ONLY REFERENCE
GENESIS 32:30

PENUEL OT5
Face of God

The place near the ford of the Jabbok River where Jacob wrestled with a man and was given the name Israel. The man wrenched Jacob's hip near the tendon, ending the match, and Jacob left the place limping.

When Gideon asked the men of the city of Penuel to help his army, they refused. Gideon promised that when he finished chasing the kings of Midian, he would break down their tower. He kept this promise, destroying the tower and killing the men of the city. Same as Peniel.

FIRST REFERENCE
GENESIS 32:31
LAST REFERENCE
JUDGES 8:17

PEOR   OT1
A gap

A Moabite mountain to which King Balak brought Balaam. The king wanted the pagan prophet to curse the Israelites before they entered the Promised Land.

ONLY REFERENCE
NUMBERS 23:28

PERAZIM   OT1

The prophet Isaiah reminded the people of Judah that God had risen up in anger on this mountain. The Lord would rise up again to do His work, the prophet told them. Perhaps the same as Baal-perazim.

ONLY REFERENCE
ISAIAH 28:21

PEREZ-UZZA   OT1
Break of Uzza

The threshing floor of Chidon (also called Nachon), where Uzza put out his hand to steady the ark of the covenant as the oxen stumbled. God killed Uzza. Angered at God's wrath against the man, King David gave the place this name. Same as Perez-uzzah.

ONLY REFERENCE
I CHRONICLES 13:11

PEREZ-UZZAH   OT1
Break of Uzza

The threshing floor of Nachon (also called Chidon), where Uzza put out his hand to steady the ark of the covenant as the oxen stumbled. God killed Uzza. Angered at God's wrath against the man, King David gave the place this name. Same as Perez-uzza.

ONLY REFERENCE
2 SAMUEL 6:8

PERGA   NT3
A tower

A city of Pamphylia and a stop on the first missionary journey of Paul and Barnabas. At this city, John Mark left Barnabas and Paul and returned to Jerusalem. The two apostles later returned to the city on a preaching mission.

FIRST REFERENCE
ACTS 13:13
LAST REFERENCE
ACTS 14:25

PERGAMOS   NT2
Fortified

A city in the Roman province of Mysia in Asia Minor. It is only mentioned in Revelation, in the letter to the seven churches of Asia Minor. Though the Christians of Pergamos held fast to God's name, their doctrine was not pure.

FIRST REFERENCE
REVELATION 1:11
LAST REFERENCE
REVELATION 2:12

PERSIA   OT29

An empire whose original nation lay on the Persian Gulf. It began after Cyrus, later called the Great, became ruler of a small Elamite province; the Persians rebelled against the Medes and began to establish a territory that eventually reached Asia Minor. In the first year of his rule, Cyrus declared that God had charged him with building a temple in Judah. He encouraged the leaders of Judah and Benjamin, along with the priests and Levites, to rebuild the temple. He also returned the temple vessels that Nebuchadnezzar had taken from Jerusalem.

The elderly prophet Daniel was still in Babylonia when Cyrus sent Jews back to their homeland to rebuild the temple. In the third year of this king's rule, the prophet received a vision that described a powerful evil being as the prince of Persia. Daniel foresaw the subsequent rulers of the Persian Empire and the conquest of the Macedonian Alexander the Great.

The Persian king Xerxes I was the Ahasuerus who became Esther's husband. He made her queen after his wife Vashti failed to obey him. When Esther's cousin Mordecai proved his faithfulness by revealing plots against the king, he was rewarded by being made a powerful leader in the Persian Empire.

Opponents of the temple's rebuilding complained to Xerxes' son, King Artaxerxes. Construction of the temple stopped until King Darius took over the rule of Persia. But Artaxerxes made Ezra spiritual leader and Nehemiah governor of Judah.

FIRST REFERENCE
2 CHRONICLES 36:20
LAST REFERENCE
DANIEL 11:2
KEY REFERENCES
2 CHRONICLES 36:20–23; EZRA 1:1–11

PETHOR   OT2

The Mesopotamian hometown of the pagan prophet Balaam. King Balak of Moab sent messengers here to bring Balaam to Moab to curse the Israelites before they entered the Promised Land.

FIRST REFERENCE
NUMBERS 22:5
LAST REFERENCE
DEUTERONOMY 23:4

PHARPAR   OT1
Rushing or rapid

A river of Damascus that Naaman of Syria would have preferred to wash in, rather than the Jordan River. His servants convinced him that the prophet Elisha was not being unreasonable. When he washed in the Jordan River, Naaman was cured of his leprosy.

ONLY REFERENCE
2 KINGS 5:12

PHENICE NT3
Palm country

1) Another name for Phenicia. Some Christians went to Phenice following the death of Stephen. Paul and Barnabas passed through here on their way to Jerusalem. Same as Phenicia.

FIRST REFERENCE
ACTS 11:19
LAST REFERENCE
ACTS 15:3

2) When Paul was traveling to Rome, the master of the ship left Fair Havens and tried to make this port on Crete, where he was planning to spend the winter.

ONLY REFERENCE
ACTS 27:12

PHENICIA NT1
Palm country

Paul and his companions sailed to this land north of Israel, on the coast of the Mediterranean Sea, as they traveled to Jerusalem. Same as Phenice 1.

ONLY REFERENCE
ACTS 21:2

PHILADELPHIA NT2
Fraternal affection

A city where one of the seven churches of Asia Minor met. In the book of Revelation, Jesus commended and encouraged this church, which had kept His word and avoided denying His name. As a result, God would protect them from the trials that lay ahead. But the Lord also warned the church to hold on to what they already had so they would not lose their crown.

FIRST REFERENCE
REVELATION 1:11
LAST REFERENCE
REVELATION 3:7

PHILIPPI NT6
Fond of horses

1) Also known as Caesarea Philippi, this city northeast of Lake Huleh was built by Herod the Great. Near here Jesus asked His disciples who people were saying the Son of man was. Same as Caesarea 1.

FIRST REFERENCE
MATTHEW 16:13
LAST REFERENCE
MARK 8:27

2) A chief city of northeastern Macedonia that Paul and his fellow laborers visited to preach the Gospel. Here Lydia became a convert, and a slave girl with a spirit of divination was healed. But the slave's owners dragged Paul and Silas before the magistrates, and the two men were imprisoned. Their jailor was converted before these prisoners were released by the magistrates.

From this city Paul wrote the books of 1 and 2 Corinthians. Paul wrote an epistle to the believers of Philippi while he was in Rome.

FIRST REFERENCE
ACTS 16:12
LAST REFERENCE
1 THESSALONIANS 2:2

PHILISTIA OT3
Rolling (that is, migratory)

The country of the Philistines that hugged the coast of the Mediterranean Sea, south of Mount Carmel and west of Judah. Though there are frequent references to the Philistines in scripture, the name Philistia only appears in the psalms, where the psalmist describes God's triumph over that nation and speaks of people of Philistia coming to know God.

FIRST REFERENCE
PSALM 60:8
LAST REFERENCE
PSALM 108:9

PHRYGIA NT3

People from this area of western central Asia Minor witnessed the coming of the Holy Spirit at Pentecost. Paul and Silas preached in Phrygia, and the apostle returned to this area after he preached in Antioch. From Laodicea, a city in Phrygia, Paul wrote the book of 1 Timothy.

FIRST REFERENCE
ACTS 2:10
LAST REFERENCE
ACTS 18:23

PHUT OT1

The land belonging to a descendant of Ham of the same name. The men of Phut were in Tyre's army.

ONLY REFERENCE
EZEKIEL 27:10

PI-BESETH OT1

An Egyptian city whose young men would be killed and whose remaining population would be taken captive, according to Ezekiel's prophecy.

ONLY REFERENCE
EZEKIEL 30:17

PI-HAHIROTH OT4
Mouth of the gorges

A place where the Israelites camped before they crossed the Red Sea.

FIRST REFERENCE
EXODUS 14:2
LAST REFERENCE
NUMBERS 33:8

PIRATHON OT1
Chieftancy

Home and burial place of the judge Abdon.

ONLY REFERENCE
JUDGES 12:15

PISGAH — OT5
A cleft

A Moabite mountain northeast of the Dead Sea where the Israelites stopped while Moses asked the Amorite king Sihon if they could travel through his land. King Balak of Moab brought Balaam here to make sacrifices when he wanted Balaam to curse the Israelites as Joshua led them to the Promised Land. Before entering Canaan, Israel conquered the Amorite land "even unto the sea of the plain, under the springs of Pisgah" (Deuteronomy 4:49).

On Pisgah, Moses climbed to a vantage point from which he could view the Promised Land just before he died.

FIRST REFERENCE
NUMBERS 21:20
LAST REFERENCE
DEUTERONOMY 34:1

PISIDIA — NT2

An area of Asia Minor that lay directly north of Pamphylia. Paul and Barnabas visited Pisidia's synagogue, where Paul preached to the congregation. They later returned to Antioch of Pisidia, where they ordained church leaders and encouraged believers.

FIRST REFERENCE
ACTS 13:14
LAST REFERENCE
ACTS 14:24

PISON — OT1
Dispersive

One of the four rivers fed by Eden's river. The Pison flowed in the land of Havilah, which was known for its gold.

ONLY REFERENCE
GENESIS 2:11

PITHOM — OT1

During their enslavement, the Israelites built this store city in northeastern Egypt.

ONLY REFERENCE
EXODUS 1:11

PONTUS — NT3
A sea

People from this Roman province of Asia Minor witnessed the coming of the Holy Spirit at Pentecost. Pontus was the birthplace of Paul's fellow laborer Aquila. The apostle Peter wrote his first epistle to the Christians in Pontus and other provinces of Asia Minor.

FIRST REFERENCE
ACTS 2:9
LAST REFERENCE
1 PETER 1:1

PRAETORIUM — NT1
Governor's courtroom

The hall where Pilate's soldiers humiliated Jesus with a purple robe, crown of thorns, mockery, and beatings before His crucifixion. It is also translated "judgment hall" (John 18:28) and "the common hall" (Matthew 27:27).

ONLY REFERENCE
MARK 15:16

PTOLEMAIS   NT1
Ptolemy

A Phoenician seacoast town south of Tyre. On his way to Jerusalem, Paul stopped here for a day. Same as Accho.

ONLY REFERENCE
ACTS 21:7

PUL   OT1

A north African nation to which God promises to send survivors of persecution. They will declare God's glory when He executes His final judgment of the world.

ONLY REFERENCE
ISAIAH 66:19

PUNON   OT2
Perplexity

A campsite of the Israelites on their way to the Promised Land.

FIRST REFERENCE
NUMBERS 33:42
LAST REFERENCE
NUMBERS 33:43

PUTEOLI   NT1
Little wells (that is, mineral springs)

An Italian port where the apostle Paul ended his sea voyage and began his journey by land to Rome.

ONLY REFERENCE
ACTS 28:13

-R-

RAAMAH   OT1
Name of a grandson of Ham

A nation of traders on the Persian Gulf who brought precious goods to Tyre.

ONLY REFERENCE
EZEKIEL 27:22

RAAMSES   OT1

During their enslavement, the Israelites built this store city in northeastern Egypt.

ONLY REFERENCE
EXODUS 1:11

RABBAH   OT13
Great

1) A royal Ammonite city on the border of the tribe of Reuben's territory. Joab besieged Rabbah while King David stayed behind in Jerusalem and fell into sin with Bathsheba. Joab won the city and called on David to encamp against it, so that the king, not the battle commander, would receive praise. David received the crown of Rabbah's king and took great spoils from the city.

The prophet Jeremiah foretold that war would come to Rabbah, and it would become a desolate heap. He called on the city's women to mourn for the loss of their leaders (Jeremiah 49:2–3). Ezekiel prophesied that Ammon would be attacked and delivered over to men from the east. He foresaw Rabbah turned into a stable for camels under God's judging hand (Ezekiel 25:5). Amos saw God kindling a fire in the walls of the city and its leaders going into captivity. Same as Rabbath.

FIRST REFERENCE
JOSHUA 13:25
LAST REFERENCE
AMOS 1:14
KEY REFERENCE
2 SAMUEL 12:26–29

2) A city that became part of the inheritance of the tribe of Judah following the conquest of the Promised Land.

ONLY REFERENCE
JOSHUA 15:60

RABBATH   OT2
Great

An Ammonite city where Og, king of Bashan, had his nine-cubit-long bedstead. The prophet Ezekiel foretold Babylon's attack on Rabbath and Judah. Same as Rabbah 1.

FIRST REFERENCE
DEUTERONOMY 3:11
LAST REFERENCE
EZEKIEL 21:20

RABBITH   OT1
Multitude

A city that became part of the inheritance of Issachar when Joshua cast lots in Shiloh to provide territory for the seven tribes that had yet to receive their land.

ONLY REFERENCE
JOSHUA 19:20

RACHAL   OT1
Merchant

A city of Judah to which David sent some of the spoils from his warfare with the Amalekites.

ONLY REFERENCE
I SAMUEL 30:29

RAHAB   OT3
Boaster

A name for Egypt that reflects that nation's pride. Psalm 87 looks forward to a day when Rahab will worship the Lord. Psalm 89:10 and Isaiah 51:9 speak of Rahab being broken and cut.

FIRST REFERENCE
PSALM 87:4
LAST REFERENCE
ISAIAH 51:9

RAKKATH   OT1
A beach (as with an expanded stony area)

A fortified or walled city that became part of the inheritance of Naphtali when Joshua cast lots in Shiloh to provide territory for the seven tribes that had yet to receive their land.

ONLY REFERENCE
JOSHUA 19:35

RAKKON   OT1
Thinness

A city that became part of the inheritance of Dan when Joshua cast lots in Shiloh to provide territory for the seven tribes that had yet to receive their land.

ONLY REFERENCE
JOSHUA 19:46

RAMA   NT1

A city of the tribe of Ephraim spoken of in a prophecy in Jeremiah 31:15 that describes Rachel weeping for her children. Matthew compares it to the mourning after Herod killed the children of Bethlehem and the surrounding area. Same as Ramah 3.

ONLY REFERENCE
MATTHEW 2:18

RAMAH   OT36
Height (as a seat of idolatry)

1) A city that became part of the inheritance of Benjamin when Joshua cast lots in Shiloh to provide territory for the seven tribes that had yet to receive their land. The prophet Deborah lived near Ramah. When King Baasha of Israel began to fortify the city to control who went in and out of Israel, King Asa of Judah arranged with Ben-hadad, king of Syria, to attack cities of Israel. As Baasha left to fight Ben-hadad, Asa brought his people to Ramah. They carried away the building materials and fortified their own cities with them. After the Babylonian exile, the people of Ramah returned and resettled their city. The Babylonians imprisoned the prophet Jeremiah in Ramah.

FIRST REFERENCE
JOSHUA 18:25
LAST REFERENCE
HOSEA 5:8
KEY REFERENCES
2 CHRONICLES 16:1–6; JEREMIAH 40:1

2) A fortified or walled city that became part of the inheritance of Naphtali when Joshua cast lots in Shiloh to provide territory for the seven tribes that had yet to receive their land.

FIRST REFERENCE
JOSHUA 19:29
LAST REFERENCE
JOSHUA 19:36

3) Hometown of Elkanah and Hannah, the prophet Samuel's parents. As a child, Samuel lived in Shiloh with Eli the priest, but when the prophet was an adult, Ramah became his home. When Saul sought to kill him, David came to Samuel at his home. Saul tried to send men to take David, but the messengers could not do the deed, but began to prophesy instead. When Saul went himself, he also prophesied. Samuel was buried in his home at Ramah.

A prophecy in Jeremiah 31:15 poetically speaks of Rachel weeping for her children in Ramah. Matthew 2:18 compares it to the mourning after Herod killed the children of Bethlehem and the surrounding area. Same as Rama and Ramathaim-Zophim.

FIRST REFERENCE
1 SAMUEL 1:19
LAST REFERENCE
JEREMIAH 31:15
KEY REFERENCES
1 SAMUEL 19:18–24; 25:1

4) A shortened form of Ramoth-gilead, where King Joram of Israel went to be healed of battle wounds. Same as Ramoth-gilead.

FIRST REFERENCE
2 KINGS 8:29
LAST REFERENCE
2 CHRONICLES 22:6

RAMATH OT1
Height (as a seat of idolatry)

A city that became part of the inheritance of Simeon when Joshua cast lots in Shiloh to provide territory for the seven tribes that had yet to receive their land.

ONLY REFERENCE
JOSHUA 19:8

RAMATHAIM-ZOPHIM OT1
Double height of watchers

Hometown of Elkanah, the prophet Samuel's father. Same as Ramah 3.

ONLY REFERENCE
I SAMUEL 1:1

RAMATH-LEHI OT1
Height of a jawbone

After Samson was captured by the Philistines and brought to Lehi, he killed a thousand of them with the jawbone of a donkey. Then he named the place where he threw the bone Ramath-lehi.

ONLY REFERENCE
JUDGES 15:17

RAMATH-MIZPEH OT1
Height of the watchtower

A city east of the Jordan River that Moses made part of the inheritance of Gad.

ONLY REFERENCE
JOSHUA 13:26

RAMESES OT4

Joseph established his father, his brothers, and their families in this area of Lower Egypt. Four hundred years later, the Israelites left Rameses to begin their exodus to the Promised Land.

FIRST REFERENCE
GENESIS 47:11
LAST REFERENCE
NUMBERS 33:5

RAMOTH OT7
Heights

1) One of the six cities of refuge established in Israel for those who had committed accidental murder. Ramoth was given to the Levites by the tribe of Gad.

FIRST REFERENCE
DEUTERONOMY 4:43
LAST REFERENCE
I CHRONICLES 6:80

2) One of the forty-eight cities given to the Levites as God had commanded. Ramoth was given to them by the tribe of Issachar.

ONLY REFERENCE
I CHRONICLES 6:73

3) A city of Judah to which David sent some of the spoils from his warfare with the Amalekites.

ONLY REFERENCE
I SAMUEL 30:27

4) A city that King Jehoshaphat of Judah wanted to win back from the Syrians. Same as Ramoth-gilead.

ONLY REFERENCE
I KINGS 22:3

RAMOTH-GILEAD
OT19

Heights of Gilad

One of the six cities of refuge established in Israel for those who had committed accidental murder. Ramoth-gilead was given to the Levites by the tribe of Gad.

Under King Solomon's governmental organization, the son of Geber was the officer in charge of providing the king with provisions from this city. King Ahab of Israel joined with Judah's king Jehoshaphat to free Ramoth-gilead from Syria's power. Despite his going into battle in disguise, Ahab was killed by an archer. At Ramoth-gilead, Ahab's son, King Joram, and King Ahaziah of Judah battled the Syrian king Hazael. Joram was wounded in the battle.

Elisha secretly anointed Jehu king of Israel at Ramoth-gilead and told him to fight the house of Ahab. Same as Ramah 4 and Ramoth 4.

FIRST REFERENCE
I KINGS 4:13
LAST REFERENCE
2 CHRONICLES 22:5
KEY REFERENCES
I KINGS 22:4–29; 2 KINGS 9:1–14;
2 CHRONICLES 18

RED SEA OT26/NT2

A reed

This sea east of Egypt and west of Arabia is first mentioned in scripture when God relented and drove the locusts of the eighth plague against Egypt into the Red Sea. Though scholars have debated what body of water Red (or Reed) Sea refers to and have argued about the route of the Exodus, the miracles the scriptures describe concerning it are no less amazing.

God led Moses and the Israelites to the Red Sea after Pharaoh allowed them to leave Egypt following the tenth plague God sent against the Egyptians. Pharaoh then changed his mind, and he and his troops pursued the Israelites. Moses called on his people to stand still and see God's salvation. As Moses lifted up his rod, the sea parted before them and the Israelites crossed it on dry ground. But when the Egyptians followed, God commanded Moses to stretch his hand over the sea, and Israel's enemies were swallowed up in the water. Then God led His people to "journey into the wilderness by the way of the Red sea" (Deuteronomy 1:40).

God promised His people that He would "set thy bounds from the Red sea even unto the sea of the Philistines" (Exodus 23:31).

Throughout scripture, the crossing of the Red Sea is a picture of God's salvation of Israel. Joshua reminds his nation of God's faithfulness and might as shown in this action. In the book of Nehemiah, the Levites led the people in worship and reminded them that God had heard their cry when their backs were to the Red Sea and they saw Egypt's warriors before them. The psalms use the Red Sea crossing as an example of God's mercy toward Israel. Hebrews reminds the Jewish Christians that Israel passed through the sea by faith.

FIRST REFERENCE
EXODUS 10:19
LAST REFERENCE
HEBREWS 11:29
KEY REFERENCE
EXODUS 13:17–14:31

REHOB   OT7
Width (that is, avenue or area)

When Moses sent spies into Canaan, he told them to explore the area from the Desert of Zin to Rehob. The city of Rehob became part of the inheritance of Asher when Joshua cast lots in Shiloh to provide territory for the seven tribes that had yet to receive their land. Later this city became one of the forty-eight cities given to the Levites as God had commanded. The tribe of Asher did not drive out the Canaanites who lived here when they conquered the Promised Land; instead they lived under the Rehobites' pagan influence.

FIRST REFERENCE
NUMBERS 13:21
LAST REFERENCE
1 CHRONICLES 6:75

REHOBOTH   OT4
Streets

1) An ancient Assyrian city built by Asshur. Saul (or Shaul) of Rehoboth ruled over Edom before Israel had kings.

FIRST REFERENCE
GENESIS 10:11
LAST REFERENCE
1 CHRONICLES 1:48

2) A well dug by Isaac. It was the first one the local people did not take from him.

ONLY REFERENCE
GENESIS 26:22

REKEM   OT1
Variegated color

A city that became part of the inheritance of Benjamin when Joshua cast lots in Shiloh to provide territory for the seven tribes that had yet to receive their land.

ONLY REFERENCE
JOSHUA 18:27

REMETH   OT1
Height

A city that became part of the inheritance of Issachar when Joshua cast lots in Shiloh to provide territory for the seven tribes that had yet to receive their land.

ONLY REFERENCE
JOSHUA 19:21

REMMON · OT1
Name of a Syrian deity

A city that became part of the inheritance of Simeon when Joshua cast lots in Shiloh to provide territory for the seven tribes that had yet to receive their land.

ONLY REFERENCE
JOSHUA 19:7

REMMON-METHOAR · OT1
Remmon (a Syrian deity), the one marked off (that is, which pertains to)

A city that became part of the inheritance of Zebulun when Joshua cast lots in Shiloh to provide territory for the seven tribes that had yet to receive their land.

ONLY REFERENCE
JOSHUA 19:13

REPHAIM · OT6
A giant

A valley southwest of Jerusalem that the Philistines raided shortly after David was anointed king of Israel. Twice David fought and defeated them. First, he went to Baal-perazin, and God handed the Philistines over to Israel. The second time, David and his men fought the Philistines from Gibeon to Gezer. During harvesttime, the Philistines again camped in the valley, making Bethlehem their garrison. David assembled his forces at the cave of Adullam.

When David longed for some water from Bethlehem, three of his brave warriors broke through the lines and got it for him. When they brought it to him, he refused to drink and poured it out before God. "Is it not the blood of men who went at the risk of their lives?" he asked (2 Samuel 23:17 NIV).

FIRST REFERENCE
2 SAMUEL 5:18
LAST REFERENCE
ISAIAH 17:5

REPHIDIM · OT5
Balusters

A campsite of the Israelites on their way to the Promised Land. There was no water to drink at Rephidim, so God moved Israel to the rock of Horeb. While the Israelites were at Rephidim, they were attacked by the Amalekites. Moses stood on top of the hill, and as long as his arms were raised, Israel prevailed. When he grew tired, Aaron and Hur stood beside him and held up his hands until Joshua won the battle. Moses built an altar here and called it Jehovah-nissi, "God is my banner."

FIRST REFERENCE
EXODUS 17:1
LAST REFERENCE
NUMBERS 33:15

RESEN · OT1
To curb; a halter (as restraining)

An ancient Assyrian city built by Asshur.

ONLY REFERENCE
GENESIS 10:12

REZEPH OT2
A red-hot stone for baking

When Rabshekeh brought King Hezekiah of Judah an intimidating message from King Sennacherib of Assyria, he used Rezeph as an example of a fortress that had not withstood Assyria's might.

FIRST REFERENCE
2 KINGS 19:12
LAST REFERENCE
ISAIAH 37:12

RHEGIUM NT1

A port in southern Italy that Paul passed through on his way to Rome.

ONLY REFERENCE
ACTS 28:13

RHODES NT1

Luke mentions this Aegean island, which also had a city by the same name, as a point on Paul's voyage to Jerusalem.

ONLY REFERENCE
ACTS 21:1

RIBLAH OT11
Fruitful; fertile

A city on the border of the Promised Land, in the land of Hamath, where Pharaoh Necho imprisoned King Jehoahaz of Judah. When King Nebuchadnezzar of Babylon captured Jerusalem, King Zedekiah of Judah was brought to Riblah for judgment by his captor. Nebuchadnezzar's men slew Zedekiah's sons as he watched; then they put out Zedekiah's eyes and carried him to Babylon. At Riblah the Babylonians also killed Judah's chief spiritual and temple leaders. Same as Diblath.

FIRST REFERENCE
NUMBERS 34:11
LAST REFERENCE
JEREMIAH 52:27

RIMMON OT8
Name of a Syrian deity

1) One of the forty-eight cities given to the Levites as God had commanded. Rimmon was given to them by the tribe of Zebulun. Zechariah foresaw that in the day of the Lord, Rimmon would be part of a lifted-up plain where people would live.

FIRST REFERENCE
1 CHRONICLES 6:77
LAST REFERENCE
ZECHARIAH 14:10

2) A rock near Gibeah to which six hundred Benjaminites fled when the Israelites burned their city because they had abused and killed the concubine of a visiting Levite. Later Israel made peace with this errant tribe at the rock.

FIRST REFERENCE
JUDGES 20:45
LAST REFERENCE
JUDGES 21:13

3) A city that became part of the inheritance of the tribe of Judah following the conquest of the Promised Land. Later it became part of Simeon's territory.

RIMMON-PAREZ OT2

Pomegranate of the breach

A campsite of the Israelites on their way to the Promised Land.

FIRST REFERENCE
NUMBERS 33:19
LAST REFERENCE
NUMBERS 33:20

RISSAH OT2

A ruin (as dripping to pieces)

A campsite of the Israelites on their way to the Promised Land.

FIRST REFERENCE
NUMBERS 33:21
LAST REFERENCE
NUMBERS 33:22

RITHMAH OT2

The Spanish broom

A campsite of the Israelites on their way to the Promised Land.

FIRST REFERENCE
NUMBERS 33:18
LAST REFERENCE
NUMBERS 33:19

FIRST REFERENCE
JOSHUA 15:32
LAST REFERENCE
I CHRONICLES 4:32

ROGELIM OT2

Fullers (as tramping the cloth in washing)

Hometown of Barzillai, who brought food and other goods to King David as he fled from Absalom's rebellion.

FIRST REFERENCE
2 SAMUEL 17:27
LAST REFERENCE
2 SAMUEL 19:31

ROME NT13

Strength

This city was the center of the New Testament world and the capital of the Roman Empire. Though Rome's political influence dominated New Testament believers, the city of Rome is not frequently mentioned in scripture. "Strangers of Rome" witnessed the coming of the Holy Spirit to believers at Pentecost and heard them speak their own tongue. The Roman emperor Claudius commanded Jews to depart from Rome, so Aquila and his wife, Priscilla, moved to Corinth, where they met the apostle Paul. The apostle longed to visit Rome and wrote to the Christians there, probably while he was in Corinth. He remarked to the fledgling church that the whole world spoke of their faith (Romans 1:8) and that he was ready to preach the Gospel in their city (Romans 1:15).

After Paul's appearance in the temple in Jerusalem enflamed some Jews, a peacekeeping Roman guard stepped in. When the soldiers planned to scourge him, Paul demanded the treatment due a Roman citizen (Acts 22:25). Though he was not freed, God told Paul he would testify about Him in Rome. Before Festus, the Roman procurator of Judea, Paul appealed to Caesar Augustus for judgment. But not until his case was heard by King Herod Agrippa II was Paul sent to Rome under a Roman guard.

From Rome Paul wrote the epistles of Galatians, Ephesians, Philippians, Colossians, 2 Timothy, and Philemon.

FIRST REFERENCE
ACTS 2:10
LAST REFERENCE
2 TIMOTHY 1:17
KEY REFERENCES
ACTS 18:2; 23:11

RUMAH   OT1
Height

Hometown of Zebudah, mother of King Jehoiakim of Judah.

ONLY REFERENCE
2 KINGS 23:36

-S-

SALAMIS   NT1
Vibration (that is, billow)

A city on the east coast of the island of Cyrus where Barnabas and Saul preached the Word of God in the Jewish synagogues.

ONLY REFERENCE
ACTS 13:5

SALCAH   OT2
Walking

A city ruled by Og, king of Bashan. After the conquest of the Promised Land, it became part of the inheritance of the tribe of Gad. Same as Salchah.

FIRST REFERENCE
JOSHUA 12:5
LAST REFERENCE
JOSHUA 13:11

SALCHAH   OT2
Walking

A city of King Og of Bashan that became part of the inheritance of the tribe of Gad. Same as Salcah.

FIRST REFERENCE
DEUTERONOMY 3:10
LAST REFERENCE
1 CHRONICLES 5:11

SALEM   OT2/NT2
Peaceful

The city ruled by King Mechizedek, a priest of God who blessed

Abraham. Melchizedek also received a tithe of Abraham's spoils of war from the city of Sodom. Same as Jebus, Jebusi, Jerusalem, and Zion.

FIRST REFERENCE
GENESIS 14:18
LAST REFERENCE
HEBREWS 7:2

SALIM NT1

To agitate; to rock; to topple; or by implication, to destroy

A place near Aenon, the site where John the Baptist baptized believers. Both Salim and Aenon were probably on the west bank of the Jordan River.

ONLY REFERENCE
JOHN 3:23

SALMON OT1

A phantom (that is, an illusion or resemblance)

A mountain, perhaps near Shechem. The psalmist David compares the snow on this mountain with the way God scattered the kings who opposed him. Same as Zalmon.

ONLY REFERENCE
PSALM 68:14

SALMONE NT1

A high place that forms the northeastern point of the island of Crete. Paul passed by here on his voyage to Rome.

ONLY REFERENCE
ACTS 27:7

SAMARIA
OT111/NT13
Watch station

1) The third capital of the northern kingdom of Israel. Sometimes the name is also used to describe the nation (see Samaria 2). King Omri of Israel bought the hill of Samaria for two talents and built his capital city there, moving the capital from Tirzah.

In Samaria, Omri's son, King Ahab, built an altar to the pagan god Baal, leading his people into pagan worship. When Ben-hadad, king of Syria, put together an alliance of nations and attacked Samaria, an unnamed prophet came to Ahab, calling him to battle. Though Israel won the battle with the Syrians, the prophet warned that Syria would return. Again God promised Israel victory. The second time, Syria was routed, but Ahab made a covenant with Ben-hadad. God told Ahab that because he did not kill Ben-hadad, Ahab's life would be taken in his place. In a battle at Ramoth-gilead, Ahab was killed by a Syrian archer.

Syria again attacked Israel in an attempt to take the prophet Elisha captive. The prophet asked God to blind the enemy. Elisha then led them into the city of Samaria. When their eyes were opened by the Lord, Elisha made peace between the king and Syria. But Syria again attacked, besieging the city of Samaria and starving the people. Four fearful lepers discovered that in the night the Lord made the Syrians hear the sound of chariots and they fled.

In Samaria, Jehu killed all of Ahab's line, as God had commanded him to do. Jehu called the people of Israel to worship Baal and then had his guard kill all the idolaters. Jehu had all the idols destroyed. But idolatry was not dead in Samaria, for its kings, including Jehu, still did not follow the Lord.

During the reign of King Hosea of Israel, Shalmaneser, king of Assyria, attacked Samaria, besieging it for three years. Finally, as Isaiah had predicted, Assyria took the city and carried away its people as captives.

The prophet Ezekiel compared Samaria's sin to that of Sodom, and the prophet Hosea clearly states that its rebellion against God caused it to become desolate (Hosea 13:16).

The apostle Philip preached Christ to the city of Samaria, and the people began to listen. But a sorcerer, Simon, bewitched them, so many turned to him instead. Peter and John were sent to the city to pray that the Christians there would receive the Holy Spirit. When Simon tried to buy the Holy Spirit, Peter called on him to repent.

FIRST REFERENCE
I KINGS 16:24
LAST REFERENCE
ACTS 8:14
KEY REFERENCES
I KINGS 20; 2 KINGS 6:11–23; 7:1–16; 10:11–29;
EZEKIEL 16:46–55

2) Another name for the northern kingdom of Israel, taken from the name of its capital. Following Assyria's conquest of the kingdom and deportation of the Jews, people from other lands were settled in Samaria. Though they eventually learned something about the Lord, the Samaritans developed a syncretistic religion, combining their pagan religious practices with Judaism. This impure worship was despised by the people of Judah.

King Josiah of Judah broke down the pagan altars that King Jeroboam of Israel had established in Samaria, and he burned human bones on the altars to pollute them.

When Rabshakeh wanted to convince the people of Jerusalem to support the Assyrians, he used Samaria as an example of the mighty conquests of King Sennacherib.

God spoke against the false prophets of Samaria through the prophet Jeremiah, but He held out hope for that nation. The prophet Hosea spoke of the destruction of Samaria's idols and its king.

FIRST REFERENCE
I KINGS 13:32
LAST REFERENCE
OBADIAH 1:19
KEY REFERENCES
2 KINGS 23:15–19; JEREMIAH 23:13; 31:5

3) During the New Testament era, Samaria was the central Roman province of western Palestine. Knowing the Jews' hatred for the Samaritans' theological error, Jesus used the example of the Good Samaritan to teach spiritual truth to the Jews (Luke 10:30–37). On the

border between Samaria and Galilee, He healed ten leprous men, of whom only one gave thanks. At Sychar He spoke to a Samaritan woman about living water and declared Himself as the Messiah (John 4:4–26).

At His ascension into heaven, Jesus foretold that His disciples would be His witnesses in Samaria. After the death of Stephen, when the church was scattered, some believers fled to Samaria. Later, Paul and Barnabas traveled through the province and reported on the conversion of Gentiles there.

FIRST REFERENCE
LUKE 17:11
LAST REFERENCE
ACTS 15:3

SAMOS NT1

An island in the Aegean Sea, southwest of Ephesus. Paul stopped in Samos on his way to Jerusalem.

ONLY REFERENCE
ACTS 20:15

SAMOTHRACIA NT1

Samos of Thrace

An island of the northeastern Aegean Sea. Paul stopped in Samothracia briefly on his way to Philippi.

ONLY REFERENCE
ACTS 16:11

SANSANNAH OT1

A bough

A city that became part of the inheritance of the tribe of Judah following the conquest of the Promised Land.

ONLY REFERENCE
JOSHUA 15:31

SAPHIR OT1

Beautiful

A city of Judah whose shameful behavior, the prophet Micah declared, would cause them to go into exile.

ONLY REFERENCE
MICAH 1:11

SARDIS NT3

A city northeast of Ephesus, in Asia Minor's district of Lydia. It is only mentioned in Revelation, in the letter to the seven churches of Asia Minor. Though the church at Sardis had a reputation for being alive in Christ, Jesus said they were dead and needed to repent. Only a few believers there were not defiled.

FIRST REFERENCE
REVELATION 1:11
LAST REFERENCE
REVELATION 3:4

SAREPTA NT1

A Sidonian city to which God sent the prophet Elijah after he fled from Jezebel and a drought began in Israel. In Sarepta, a widow cared for the prophet until the drought ended. Same as Zarephath.

ONLY REFERENCE
LUKE 4:26

SARID · OT2
A survivor

A city that became part of the inheritance of Zebulun when Joshua cast lots in Shiloh to provide territory for the seven tribes that had yet to receive their land.

FIRST REFERENCE
JOSHUA 19:10
LAST REFERENCE
JOSHUA 19:12

SARON · NT1
Sharon

A plain in western Palestine that parallels the eastern coast of the Mediterranean Sea. When Peter healed Aeneas in Lydda, on this plain's eastern edge, many people from Saron believed in Christ. Same as Sharon 1.

ONLY REFERENCE
ACTS 9:35

SEBA · OT2

A kingdom on the west coast of the Red Sea, possibly near Cush, that the psalmist says will bring gifts to Solomon. The prophet Isaiah says God gave Seba for His people's redemption.

FIRST REFERENCE
PSALM 72:10
LAST REFERENCE
ISAIAH 43:3

SECACAH · OT1
Enclosure

A city that became part of the inheritance of the tribe of Judah following the conquest of the Promised Land.

ONLY REFERENCE
JOSHUA 15:61

SECHU · OT1
An observatory

A place probably near Ramah. Here King Saul, wanting to capture David, questioned people regarding the whereabouts of David and the prophet Samuel.

ONLY REFERENCE
I SAMUEL 19:22

SEIR · OT37
Rough

1) A mountainous area originally inhabited by the Horites, Seir lay east of the Arabah Valley. Jacob sent a message to his brother, Esau, at his home in Mount Seir before they were reunited. Esau's descendants, the Edomites, conquered Seir.

Balaam foresaw that Seir would be a possession of the Israelites. But on their way to the Promised Land, God told the Israelites to treat the land carefully and not provoke the Edomites because He would not give Israel the land. Not until the rule of King David did Israel conquer Edom (2 Samuel 8:11–14).

When the Moabites, Ammonites, and inhabitants of Mount Seir came against Judah, King Jehoshaphat called on God to protect Judah from these people whom God had not allowed the nation of Israel to conquer when it entered the Promised Land. God protected His people from their enemies by ambushing them Himself, causing the Ammonites and Moabites to rise up against the people of Mount Seir and slaughter them.

The people of Seir claimed that Judah was like all pagan nations and rejoiced at its desolation. The prophet Ezekiel promised that God would make the Edomite nation desolate.

FIRST REFERENCE
GENESIS 14:6
LAST REFERENCE
EZEKIEL 35:15
KEY REFERENCES
GENESIS 33:14–16; NUMBERS 24:18;
2 CHRONICLES 20:5–23; EZEKIEL 35:2–15

2) A mountain that formed part of the border of the tribe of Judah's territory.

ONLY REFERENCE
JOSHUA 15:10

SEIRATH OT1
Roughness

A place in Mount Ephraim to which Ehud escaped after he killed Eglon, king of Moab.

ONLY REFERENCE
JUDGES 3:26

SELA OT1
To be lofty

Edom's capital city, from which the prophet Isaiah declared that some escaped Moabites would send a lamb to Jerusalem, indicating submission to Israel. Same as Joktheel and Selah.

ONLY REFERENCE
ISAIAH 16:1

SELAH OT1
To be lofty

Edom's capital city, which King Amaziah of Judah captured and renamed Joktheel. Same as Joktheel and Sela.

ONLY REFERENCE
2 KINGS 14:7

SELA-HAMMAHLEKOTH OT1
Rock of the divisions

A gorge in the wilderness of Maon where David and Saul met. When Saul heard that the Philistines had attacked Israel, he left David there.

ONLY REFERENCE
1 SAMUEL 23:28

SELEUCIA NT1
From Seleucus (a Syrian king)

A Syrian city that Barnabas and Saul visited on their first missionary journey before they sailed for Cyprus.

ONLY REFERENCE
ACTS 13:4

SENAAH OT2
Thorny

A city in Judah to which captives returned after the Babylonian exile.

FIRST REFERENCE
EZRA 2:35
LAST REFERENCE
NEHEMIAH 7:38

SENEH OT1
Thorn

A cliff on one side of a pass that Jonathan and his armor bearer had to cross to get to the Philistines' garrison before their heated battle at Michmash.

ONLY REFERENCE
I SAMUEL 14:4

SENIR OT2
Peak

The name the Amorites gave Mount Hermon (Deuteronomy 3:9). Same as Hermon, Shenir, Sion 1, and Sirion.

FIRST REFERENCE
I CHRONICLES 5:23
LAST REFERENCE
EZEKIEL 27:5

SEPHAR OT1
Census

A mountain in Arabia on the eastern border of the area where Shem's descendants settled.

ONLY REFERENCE
GENESIS 10:30

SEPHARAD OT1

A place of uncertain location where the prophet Obadiah reported that exiles from Jerusalem lived. Obadiah foretold that one day they would possess the cities of the Negeb.

ONLY REFERENCE
OBADIAH 1:20

SEPHARVAIM OT6

A Mesopotamian city whose people Shalmaneser, king of Assyria, brought to the conquered northern kingdom of Israel (Samaria) to repopulate it. The new settlers brought their pagan worship with them. When Rabshakeh tried to intimidate Judah, he used the gods of Sepharvaim as examples of deities who had not saved their people and pointed out that Sepharvaim's king had not stopped Assyria.

FIRST REFERENCE
2 KINGS 17:24
LAST REFERENCE
ISAIAH 37:13

SHAALABBIN OT1
Foxholes

A town that became part of the inheritance of Dan when Joshua cast lots in Shiloh to provide territory for the seven tribes that had yet to receive their land. Same as Shaalbim.

ONLY REFERENCE
JOSHUA 19:42

SHAALBIM OT2
Foxholes

A town of Dan that was taken by the Amorites. The Ephraimites took up arms in favor of their fellow Jews and made the Amorites subject to Dan. Under King Solomon's governmental organization, the son of Dekar was the officer in charge of supplying the king with provisions from this place. Same as Shaalabbin.

FIRST REFERENCE
JUDGES 1:35
LAST REFERENCE
I KINGS 4:9

SHAARAIM OT2
Double gates

David pursued the Philistines to this city that was part of the inheritance of the tribe of Simeon.

FIRST REFERENCE
I SAMUEL 17:52
LAST REFERENCE
I CHRONICLES 4:31

SHAHAZIMAH OT1
Proudly

A city that became part of the inheritance of Issachar when Joshua cast lots in Shiloh to provide territory for the seven tribes that had yet to receive their land.

ONLY REFERENCE
JOSHUA 19:22

SHALEM OT1
Complete (figuratively, friendly)

A city of Shechem where Jacob bought land and erected an altar called El-elohe-Israel.

ONLY REFERENCE
GENESIS 33:18

SHALIM OT1
Foxes

A district that the future King Saul passed through as he searched for his father's missing donkeys.

ONLY REFERENCE
I SAMUEL 9:4

SHALISHA OT1
Trebled land

A district that the future King Saul passed through as he searched for his father's missing donkeys.

ONLY REFERENCE
I SAMUEL 9:4

SHALLECHETH OT1
A felling of trees

A gate at the temple in Jerusalem, "by the causeway of the going up," or "on the road that goes up" (ESV).

ONLY REFERENCE
I CHRONICLES 26:16

SHAMIR OT3
A thorn

1) A city that became part of the inheritance of the tribe of Judah following the conquest of the Promised Land.

ONLY REFERENCE
JOSHUA 15:48

2) A city on Mount Ephraim where the judge Tola lived and was buried.

FIRST REFERENCE
JUDGES 10:1
LAST REFERENCE
JUDGES 10:2

SHAPHER OT2
Beauty

A mountain where the Israelites camped on their way to the Promised Land.

FIRST REFERENCE
NUMBERS 33:23
LAST REFERENCE
NUMBERS 33:24

SHARAIM OT1
Double gates

A city that became part of the inheritance of the tribe of Judah following the conquest of the Promised Land.

ONLY REFERENCE
JOSHUA 15:36

SHARON OT6

1) A plain of western Palestine that parallels the eastern part of the Mediterranean Sea. The "rose of Sharon" (Song of Solomon 2:1) was a flowering bulb that grew on this plain. Isaiah predicted that the plain will be like a wilderness when God fills "Zion with judgment and righteousness" (Isaiah 33:5), and Sharon will see God's glory. Flocks will be kept there for God's people. Same as Saron.

FIRST REFERENCE
1 CHRONICLES 27:29
LAST REFERENCE
ISAIAH 65:10

2) An area of "pasturelands" (ESV and NIV) in the land of the tribe of Gad. Scripture gives no clear description of Sharon's location.

ONLY REFERENCE
1 CHRONICLES 5:16

SHARUHEN OT1
Abode of pleasure

A city that became part of the inheritance of Simeon when Joshua cast lots in Shiloh to provide territory for the seven tribes that had yet to receive their land.

ONLY REFERENCE
JOSHUA 19:6

SHAVEH OT2
Plain

A valley, also called the King's Dale, where Chedorlaomer, king of Elam, and his Mesopotamian allies overcame the Emims.

FIRST REFERENCE
GENESIS 14:5
LAST REFERENCE
GENESIS 14:17

SHEBA OT17
Seven (2)

1) The land of the queen of Sheba who visited King Solomon of Israel to test his wisdom. Sheba's queen brought him gifts of spices, gold, and precious stones, part of the lucrative trade conducted by the caravans of her country. The prophet Isaiah predicted that one day, when the Redeemer comes to Zion, Sheba will bring gold and incense and praises to the Lord. In his prophecy foretelling the judgment of Tyre, Ezekiel spoke of Sheba as Tyre's merchants.

FIRST REFERENCE
I KINGS 10:1
LAST REFERENCE
EZEKIEL 38:13
KEY REFERENCES
I KINGS 10:1–10; 2 CHRONICLES 9:1–12;
ISAIAH 60:6

2) A city that became part of the inheritance of Simeon when Joshua cast lots in Shiloh to provide territory for the seven tribes that had yet to receive their land.

ONLY REFERENCE
JOSHUA 19:2

SHEBAH OT1
Seven or seventh

A well dug by Isaac's servants at the site that became the city of Beersheba. This city took its name from the well.

ONLY REFERENCE
GENESIS 26:33

SHEBAM OT1
Spice

A city east of the Jordan River that the Reubenites and Gadites requested as part of their inheritance because it had good grazing land for cattle.

ONLY REFERENCE
NUMBERS 32:3

SHEBARIM OT1
Ruins

A place to which the men of Ai chased the three thousand Israelite troops who attacked their city.

ONLY REFERENCE
JOSHUA 7:5

SHECHEM OT45
Ridge

A place in the land of Canaan where Jacob bought some land and built an altar called El-elohe-Israel. At the oak tree near Shechem, the patriarch buried all the idols in his household; then he built the altar at Bethel. Following Israel's conquest of the Promised Land, Shechem became one of the six cities of refuge established for those who had committed accidental murder. It was given to the Levites by the tribe of Ephraim. At Shechem Joshua gave his last address to the people of Israel, reminding them of their history and the faithfulness of God. He warned them of the dangers of idolatry and encouraged them to serve God.

Shechem was the home of Gideon's son Abimelech. The men of Shechem made him their king. But three years later he had to put down a rebellion there. Though the ruler of the city pushed the rebels out of Shechem, Abimelech conquered the city and sowed it with salt. The men in the tower of Shechem were killed when Abimelech led his supporters to burn the tower.

Rehoboam was supposed to be crowned king of Israel at Shechem. But Jeroboam, son of Nebat, and the people of Israel confronted the new king, asking him to lighten their burdens. When Rehoboam refused, the nation split into two kingdoms: Judah, which consisted of the tribes of Judah, Simeon, and part of Benjamin and was ruled by Rehoboam, and the northern kingdom of Israel. Jeroboam was crowned king of Israel and rebuilt Shechem. Same as Sichem and Sychem.

FIRST REFERENCE
GENESIS 33:18
LAST REFERENCE
JEREMIAH 41:5
KEY REFERENCES
JOSHUA 24; JUDGES 9; I KINGS 12:1–20, 25

SHEMA OT1
A sound; a rumor; an announcement

A city that became part of the inheritance of the tribe of Judah following the conquest of the Promised Land.

ONLY REFERENCE
JOSHUA 15:26

SHEN OT1
Crag

A place near the spot where Samuel set up a stone named Eben-ezer to commemorate a victory of Israel over the Philistines.

ONLY REFERENCE
I SAMUEL 7:12

SHENIR OT2
Peak

The Amorites' name for Mount Hermon. Same as Hermon, Senir, Sion 1, and Sirion.

FIRST REFERENCE
DEUTERONOMY 3:9
LAST REFERENCE
SONG OF SOLOMON 4:8

SHEPHAM OT2
Bare spot

A place God used to identify the borders of Israel when He first gave the land to His people.

FIRST REFERENCE
NUMBERS 34:10
LAST REFERENCE
NUMBERS 34:11

SHESHACH OT2

A symbolic name for Babylon used by the prophet Jeremiah.

FIRST REFERENCE
JEREMIAH 25:26
LAST REFERENCE
JEREMIAH 51:41

SHIBMAH OT1
Spice

A city built by the tribe of Reuben.

ONLY REFERENCE
NUMBERS 32:38

SHICRON OT1
Drunkenness

A city that formed part of the border of the tribe of Judah's territory.

ONLY REFERENCE
JOSHUA 15:11

SHIHON OT1
Ruin

A city that became part of the inheritance of Issachar when Joshua cast lots in Shiloh to provide territory for the seven tribes that had yet to receive their land.

ONLY REFERENCE
JOSHUA 19:19

SHIHOR OT1
Dark (that is, turbid)

A river, perhaps the Nile or the River of Egypt (Genesis 15:18). When King David prepared to bring the ark of the covenant to Jerusalem, he called together all of Israel, from "Shihor of Egypt" to "the entering of Hemath." Same as Sihor.

ONLY REFERENCE
1 CHRONICLES 13:5

SHIHOR-LIBNATH OT1
Darkish whiteness

A landmark, probably a stream, that indicated the border of the inheritance of Asher. This landmark was mentioned when Joshua cast lots in Shiloh to provide territory for the seven tribes that had yet to receive an inheritance.

ONLY REFERENCE
JOSHUA 19:26

SHILHIM OT1
Javelins or sprouts

A city that became part of the inheritance of the tribe of Judah following the conquest of the Promised Land.

ONLY REFERENCE
JOSHUA 15:32

SHILOAH   OT1
Rill

A stream or spring in Jerusalem that was considered sacred by the Jews. Because the people of Judah rejected the stream's gentle waters and rejoiced in the Syrian king Rezin, the Lord promised to bring the king of Assyria against Judah. Same as Siloah and Siloam.

ONLY REFERENCE
ISAIAH 8:6

SHILOH   OT32
Tranquil

A town in the territory of Ephraim where the Israelites assembled after the battles to conquer the Promised Land. They set up the tabernacle, and at its door Joshua cast lots to give land to the seven tribes that had yet to receive any. Here, too, the Levites were allotted cities and their suburbs as God had commanded (Numbers 35:2). The tabernacle, Israel's worship center, remained at Shiloh until the time of Samuel.

When the tribes of Reuben, Gad, and Manasseh built an altar by the Jordan River, the rest of Israel met at Shiloh to go to war against these eastern tribes. The three tribes explained that they built this altar as a witness to their faith, not as a place of worship, and war was averted.

Israel fought the tribe of Benjamin over its abuse and murder of a Levite's concubine and vowed not to give their daughters as wives to the Benjaminites. When they realized that the people from Jabesh-gilead had not joined in the battle, the Israelite army attacked that town and killed all but four hundred virgins, whom they brought to Shiloh. The Israelites agreed that the remaining Benjaminites should be given these women. Because there were not enough women for the tribe, the nation decided that during a festival in Shiloh the men who needed brides should catch the young women of Shiloh.

When Hannah, mother of the prophet Samuel, asked the Lord for a child, she went to Shiloh to pray. God answered her prayer, and she gave her son, Samuel, to the priest Eli to raise and train in the priesthood. Later God revealed himself to Samuel in Shiloh. When the Philistines attacked Israel and the battle went badly, Israel removed the ark from Shiloh; it was captured by the Philistines and never returned to Shiloh.

At Shiloh, the wife of King Jeroboam heard the prophet Ahijah's prediction of their son's death and the destruction of the northern kingdom of Israel. The prophet Jeremiah used Shiloh as an example of God's punishment of the unfaithful.

FIRST REFERENCE
JOSHUA 18:1
LAST REFERENCE
JEREMIAH 41:5
KEY REFERENCES
JOSHUA 18:1–10; JUDGES 21:1–23; I SAMUEL
I; I KINGS 14:1–18

SHIMRON-MERON
OT1

Guard of lashing

A city on the western side of the Jordan River conquered by Joshua and the Israelites.

ONLY REFERENCE
JOSHUA 12:20

SHINAR
OT7

The ancient land of Babel where Nimrod ruled, where the tower of Babel was built, and where the cities of Erech, Akkad, and Calneh were located. Shinar became one of the allies of Chedorlaomer, king of Elam, who made war with Sodom and Gomorrah. Later the land of Shinar was called Babylon (Daniel 1:2).

The prophet Isaiah promised that when Christ returns, His people of Shinar will be recovered.

FIRST REFERENCE
GENESIS 10:10
LAST REFERENCE
ZECHARIAH 5:11

SHOCHO
OT1

During the reign of King Ahaz, Shocho was one of the cities of the southern low country of Judah that was invaded and occupied by the Philistines. Same as Shochoh and Shoco.

ONLY REFERENCE
2 CHRONICLES 28:18

SHOCHOH
OT1

A city of Judah near the spot where the Philistines camped before David fought Goliath. Same as Shocho and Shoco.

ONLY REFERENCE
1 SAMUEL 17:1

SHOCO
OT1

A city of Judah that King Rehoboam fortified to defend his nation. Same as Shocho and Shochoh.

ONLY REFERENCE
2 CHRONICLES 11:7

SHOPHAN
OT1

A city built by the tribe of Gad.

ONLY REFERENCE
NUMBERS 32:35

SHUAL
OT1

A jackal (as a burrower)

A land near Ophrah. During King Saul's reign, the Philistine army camped near Michmash and sent out a company in this direction.

ONLY REFERENCE
1 SAMUEL 13:17

SHUNEM   OT3
Quietly

A city that became part of the inheritance of Issachar when Joshua cast lots in Shiloh to provide territory for the seven tribes that had yet to receive their land. The Philistine army camped at Shunem when it opposed King Saul's army at Gilboa. A woman of Shunem provided the prophet Elisha with food and lodging when he passed through the city. In return for her help, the prophet told her that she would bear a son. When the boy became ill and died, the prophet brought him back to life.

FIRST REFERENCE
JOSHUA 19:18
LAST REFERENCE
2 KINGS 4:8

SHUR   OT6
A wall (as going about)

A wilderness area of the northern Sinai Peninsula. Following Hagar's expulsion from Abraham's camp, the angel of the Lord found her "by the fountain in the way to Shur" (Genesis 16:7). The people of Ishmael, Hagar's son, would live "from Havilah unto Shur" (Genesis 25:18). After the destruction of Sodom and Gomorrah, Abraham lived between Kadesh and Shur.

King Saul fought the Amalekites from Havilah to Shur. When David served King Achish of Gath, he battled the Geshurites, Gezrites, and Amalekites. These people lived in the land from Shur to Egypt.

FIRST REFERENCE
GENESIS 16:7
LAST REFERENCE
1 SAMUEL 27:8

SHUSHAN   OT21
A lily or a straight trumpet

The Persian capital, in the province of Elam. King Ahasuerus (also called Xerxes) reigned in Shushan. Here he held the feast at which Queen Vashti refused to appear. Esther was brought to the palace in Shushan, along with the other women from whom Ahasuerus planned to chose a wife. Esther's cousin Mordecai came to her at the palace to tell her of Haman's plan to destroy the Jews. The brave queen confronted Ahasuerus while all the Jews of the city prayed for her. She succeeded in her case with the king, and a commandment was made in the city that the Jews could protect themselves from the attack Haman had planned against them. In Shusan, the Jews killed eight hundred men and Haman's ten sons, whose bodies were hanged.

After Ahasuerus, King Artaxerxes ruled at the palace of Shushan; Nehemiah served this king. Daniel also was in this palace when he had a vision of a ram and a goat.

FIRST REFERENCE
NEHEMIAH 1:1
LAST REFERENCE
DANIEL 8:2
KEY REFERENCES
ESTHER 4:8; 9:6–15

SIBMAH
OT4
Spice

A Moabite town that became part of the inheritance of the tribe of Reuben. In his oracle about Moab, Isaiah foretold that the harvest of Sibmah's vineyards would fail.

FIRST REFERENCE
JOSHUA 13:19
LAST REFERENCE
JEREMIAH 48:32

SIBRAIM
OT1
Double hope

A landmark mentioned in the book of Ezekiel as the northern boundary of Palestine. It lay between Hamath and Damascus.

ONLY REFERENCE
EZEKIEL 47:16

SICHEM
OT1
Ridge

The place to which Abram first went when he traveled to Canaan at God's command. Here God promised He would give the land to Abram's heirs. Abram built an altar to God at Sichem. Same as Shechem and Sychem.

ONLY REFERENCE
GENESIS 12:6

SIDDIM
OT3
Flats

A vale near the Dead Sea where Chedorlaomer, king of Elam, and his Mesopotamian allies fought with the kings of Sodom and Gomorrah and their allies. The vale was full of slime pits.

FIRST REFERENCE
GENESIS 14:3
LAST REFERENCE
GENESIS 14:10

SIDON
OT1/NT12
Fishery

An ancient city of the Phoenicians that lay north of Tyre and sometimes gave its name to the people of this land (see Luke 4:26).

People from the area of Sidon followed Jesus when they heard of the things He had done. When Jesus received little response from people in the cities of Israel where He had done many miracles, He cried out that Tyre and Sidon would have humbly repented had they seen these things. When Jesus visited the area of Tyre and Sidon, the Syro-Phoenician woman called on Him to cast a devil from her daughter.

The apostle Paul stopped briefly in Sidon on his way to · Rome. Same as Zidon.

FIRST REFERENCE
GENESIS 10:19
LAST REFERENCE
ACTS 27:3
KEY REFERENCES
MATTHEW 11:21–22; MARK 7:24–31

SIHOR — OT3
Dark (that is, turbid)

A river that some have identified as the Nile, others as the Brook (or River) of Egypt. It was identified as yet-unconquered land at the end of Joshua's life. Same as Shihor.

FIRST REFERENCE
JOSHUA 13:3
LAST REFERENCE
JEREMIAH 2:18

SILLA — OT1
An embankment

An unidentifiable place near Beth-millo where King Joash of Judah was murdered by his servants.

ONLY REFERENCE
2 KINGS 12:20

SILOAH — OT1
Rill

A pool in Jerusalem that was restored by Shallum during Nehemiah's repairs to the city. Same as Shiloah and Siloam.

ONLY REFERENCE
NEHEMIAH 3:15

SILOAM — NT3
Rill

Jesus spoke of a tower of Siloam that fell, killing eighteen people. Though there is no clear identification of the tower's location, the pool of Siloam was in the southern part of King David's Jerusalem.

Same as Shiloah and Siloah.

FIRST REFERENCE
LUKE 13:4
LAST REFERENCE
JOHN 9:11

SIN — OT6

1) An Egyptian city on which the prophet Ezekiel predicted God would pour out His wrath.

FIRST REFERENCE
EZEKIEL 30:15
LAST REFERENCE
EZEKIEL 30:16

2) A wilderness south of the Negev that the Israelites crossed and camped in during the Exodus.

FIRST REFERENCE
EXODUS 16:1
LAST REFERENCE
NUMBERS 33:12

SINA — NT2
Greek form of Sinai

The mountain where God appeared to Moses in a burning bush. Same as Sinai.

FIRST REFERENCE
ACTS 7:30
LAST REFERENCE
ACTS 7:38

SINAI — OT33/NT4

The wilderness peninsula that lies between Egypt and the Promised Land through which the Israelites traveled during the Exodus. The mountain that bears this name is in the south-central part of the peninsula, in a range of mountains often called Horeb in the scriptures. God called Moses to Mount Sinai and told him to sanctify the people. At the base of the mountain, God spoke to Moses and called him up, alone, to receive the Law. Because Moses was gone for many days, his people became impatient and pressured Aaron to build them an idol in the shape of a calf. Enraged at their unfaithfulness, Moses broke the first covenant tablets when he returned. After the idol was destroyed, God called Moses back to Mount Sinai to receive a new copy.

In Sinai's wilderness Moses arranged a census of the Israelites. Then God had Moses take a census of the Levites and established their role in worship. Finally God established the celebration of Passover, and the Israelites left the Sinai wilderness.

In the book of Galatians, Paul compares the bondage of the covenant of law made at Sinai with the freedom of the law of Jerusalem. Same as Sina.

FIRST REFERENCE
EXODUS 16:1
LAST REFERENCE
GALATIANS 4:25
KEY REFERENCES
EXODUS 19; 32:1–6; 34:1–2;
GALATIANS 4:24–25

SION   OT2/NT7
Peak

1) Another name for Mount Hermon. Same as Hermon, Senir, Shenir, and Sirion.

ONLY REFERENCE
DEUTERONOMY 4:48

2) A Greek word for the name Zion. It refers to Jerusalem, especially the temple area, focusing on it as a holy city. In the book of Revelation, John sees the Lamb on Mount Sion with 144,000 saints.

FIRST REFERENCE
PSALM 65:1
LAST REFERENCE
REVELATION 14:1

SIPHMOTH   OT1
Bare spots

A city of Judah to which David sent some of the spoils from his warfare with the Amalekites.

ONLY REFERENCE
1 SAMUEL 30:28

SIRAH   OT1
Departure

A well near Hebron. Joab called Abner back from Sirah to Hebron, where Joab killed him.

ONLY REFERENCE
2 SAMUEL 3:26

SIRION   OT2
God has prevailed

The Sidonian name for Mount Hermon. Same as Hermon, Senir, Sion 1, and Shenir.

FIRST REFERENCE
DEUTERONOMY 3:9
LAST REFERENCE
PSALM 29:6

SITNAH OT1
Opposition

A well dug by Isaac's servants that they had to defend against the local people, who laid claim to it. Eventually Isaac left the well to them.

ONLY REFERENCE
GENESIS 26:21

SMYRNA NT2
Myrrh

A city of Asia Minor north of Ephesus. It is only mentioned in Revelation, in the letter to the seven churches of Asia Minor. Christ assured these believers that He knew their works and tribulations and encouraged them to remain faithful to Him.

FIRST REFERENCE
REVELATION 1:11
LAST REFERENCE
REVELATION 2:8

SOCHOH OT1
To entwine (that is, to shut in)

Under King Solomon's governmental organization, a place responsible for supplying provisions for the king. Same as Socoh.

ONLY REFERENCE
I KINGS 4:10

SOCOH OT1
To entwine (that is, to shut in)

A city that became part of the inheritance of the tribe of Judah following the conquest of the Promised Land. Same as Sochoh.

ONLY REFERENCE
JOSHUA 15:35

SODOM OT39/NT9
Burnt

One of five Canaanite "cities of the plain" that may have been at the southern end of the Dead Sea. Abram's nephew Lot chose this land when Abram offered him whatever area he preferred. Though the men of Sodom "were wicked and sinners before the LORD" (Genesis 13:13), Lot pitched his tents near the city. When the king of Sodom fought King Chedorlaomer of Elam and his Mesopotamian allies, Sodom lost. The city was plundered, and Lot, his goods, and some of his household were taken. Abram rescued Lot, his people, and his goods. Abram refused to take anything from Sodom's king in return for his effective raid.

When Abram learned that God planned to destroy Sodom and the other plain cities, he bargained with Him. The Lord agreed that if ten righteous people could be found within Sodom's walls, He would not destroy the city. When Abram's part of the bargain could not be fulfilled, and Sodom's men wanted to have sex with the angels who warned Lot to leave the city, the Lord took Lot's family out of Sodom and destroyed it with fire and brimstone.

The major prophets repeatedly

point to Sodom and Gomorrah's extreme wickedness and God's destruction of these cities as warnings to God's people of the punishment that follows ungodliness.

Jesus told His disciples that it would be more tolerable for Sodom and Gomorrah than for a city that would not receive them. He also warned Capernaum that if His deeds had been done in Sodom, that city would have been saved. Jesus warned that the day in which He returns will be as unexpected as the day when Sodom was destroyed. Same as Sodoma.

FIRST REFERENCE
GENESIS 10:19
LAST REFERENCE
REVELATION 11:8
KEY REFERENCES
GENESIS 13:12–13; 14; 18:16–33; 19:1–29

SODOMA NT1
Greek form of Sodom

Paul quotes Isaiah ("Esaias" in the KJV), saying that unless the Lord of hosts had left the Israelites descendants, they would have been like Sodoma. Same as Sodom.

ONLY REFERENCE
ROMANS 9:29

SOREK OT1
A vine

The valley in which Samson's beloved, Delilah, lived.

ONLY REFERENCE
JUDGES 16:4

SPAIN NT2

Although there is no record of his making the trip, Paul told the Romans that he planned to go to Spain after he visited them.

FIRST REFERENCE
ROMANS 15:24
LAST REFERENCE
ROMANS 15:28

SUCCOTH OT18
Booths

1) A city where Jacob built a house and booths for his cattle. Moses made Succoth part of the inheritance of Gad. When the princes of Succoth refused to feed Gideon's men, he promised a harsh retribution. He returned there and tore the flesh of the elders of the city with thorns and briers. In the valley of Succoth, Solomon established a foundry to make the brass fittings of the temple.

FIRST REFERENCE
GENESIS 33:17
LAST REFERENCE
PSALM 108:7

2) A campsite of the Israelites on their way to the Promised Land.

FIRST REFERENCE
EXODUS 12:37
LAST REFERENCE
NUMBERS 33:6

SUR OT1
Turned off (that is, deteriorated)

A gate in Jerusalem's temple where Jehoiada stationed a guard of soldiers for protection when he crowned Joash king of Israel. Also called "the gate of the foundation" (2 Chronicles 23:5).

ONLY REFERENCE
2 KINGS 11:6

SYCHAR NT1

A place in Samaria where Jacob dug a well. In the first-century city of Sychar, Jesus met the Samaritan woman, discussed spiritual issues with her, and told her that He was the Messiah she was looking for.

ONLY REFERENCE
JOHN 4:5

SYCHEM NT1
Shechem

Defending himself before the Sanhedrin, Stephen spoke of Abraham's burial place in Sychem at the cave of Machpelah. Same as Shechem and Sichem.

ONLY REFERENCE
ACTS 7:16

SYENE OT2

A town of southern Egypt, on the Nile's first cataract, at modern-day Aswan. Both references to it in scripture refer to Syene's tower and Egypt's destruction.

FIRST REFERENCE
EZEKIEL 29:10
LAST REFERENCE
EZEKIEL 30:6

SYRACUSE NT1

A Sicilian city where Paul stayed for three days on his way to Rome.

ONLY REFERENCE
ACTS 28:12

SYRIA OT67/NT8
The highland

A nation northeast of Israel that included the biblical cities of Antioch and Damascus. During the era of the judges, Israel began to follow the gods of Syria, so God allowed His people to be oppressed by their enemies.

When the Syrians of Damascus supported Hadadezer, king of Zobah, King David conquered them and made them his tributaries. Geshur, a Syrian city that David ruled, became Absalom's home when he fled from Israel after killing his half brother Amnon. During Solomon's rule, Rezon became king of Syria and a persistent enemy of Israel.

Asa, king of Judah, paid the Syrian king Ben-hadad to break his alliance with Baasha, king of Israel, and attack Israel's cities. But Hanai the seer told Asa that because he relied on Syria, not God, he would have wars with that nation throughout his reign.

Another king named Ben-hadad brought his troops against Israel's king Ahab at Samaria. But when Israel's troops went out against Syria, the Syrians fled. However, the prophet who had foretold the victory warned Ahab that the Syrians would return in the spring. Ahab followed the prophet's plans for defense of Israel. Though Israel won the battle with the Syrians, Ahab made a covenant with Ben-hadad and let him go. Because Ahab did not obey the Lord in destroying his enemy, the prophet predicted that Ahab would die in Ben-hadad's place. Though Ahab disguised himself, he died in battle with Syria at Ramoth-gilead (2 Chronicles 18:28–34).

Naaman, commander of the Syrian army, came to the prophet Elisha to be healed of leprosy. Though he objected to washing in the Jordan River, preferring the rivers of his own nation, Naaman's servants convinced him to follow the prophet's directions, and he was healed. When Syria again fought with Israel, Elisha repeatedly warned Israel's king where the Syrians would be. Hearing that Elisha did this, the king of Syria sent an army to Dothan to capture the prophet. But instead, at Elisha's prayer, God struck the enemy with blindness, and Elisha led them to the city of Samaria, where the prophet made a temporary peace between the two nations. But King Ben-hadad (probably Ben-hadad II) besieged Samaria until there was famine in the city. When the situation became desperate, God made Israel's enemy hear the sound of a great army's chariots and horses, and the Syrians fled.

The prophet Elisha foretold the death of King Ben-hadad and the accession to the throne by King Hazael, who would make war on Israel. Jehoash, king of Judah, paid Hazael not to attack Jerusalem (2 Kings 12:17–18). Instead, Hazael and his son Ben-hadad opposed King Jehoahaz of Israel. Just before he died, the prophet Elisha foretold that Israel would strike down Syria three times (2 Kings 13:19).

King Ahaz of Judah was besieged by King Rezin of Syria and King Pekah of Israel, who captured many of the people of Judah. So Ahaz called on King Tiglath-pileser of Assyria and paid him tribute to rescue his nation. As a result, Judah became subservient to Assyria.

The prophet Amos foretold that Syria would go into captivity in Kir.

Jesus' fame went "throughout all Syria" (Matthew 4:24). When the council of Jerusalem wrote a letter declaring that Gentiles need not be circumcised, they addressed it to the believers of Syria. Paul, Barnabas, Judas, and Silas visited Antioch and delivered the letter. Then Paul and Silas visited the churches of Syria to encourage them in their faith. After leaving Corinth, Paul brought Priscilla and Aquila with him to Syria. On his final visit to Jerusalem, Paul landed in the Syrian city of Tyre and visited the church there for a week. Same as Aram.

FIRST REFERENCE
JUDGES 10:6
LAST REFERENCE
GALATIANS 1:21
KEY REFERENCES
2 SAMUEL 15:7–10; 1 KINGS 20;
2 KINGS 5:1–14; 6:8–7:20

SYRIA-DAMASCUS
OT1

A Syrian city that King David garrisoned after he had overthrown Hadar-ezer, king of Zobah. Same as Damascus.

ONLY REFERENCE
1 CHRONICLES 18:6

SYRIA-MAACHAH
OT1

Aram of the two rivers

A Syrian kingdom that provided troops to the Ammonites when they had offended King David and prepared to fight with Israel.

ONLY REFERENCE
1 CHRONICLES 19:6

-T-

TAANACH OT6

A city on the western side of the Jordan River that was conquered by Joshua and the Israelites. This city southeast of Megiddo became a Levitical city of Manasseh, but the tribe did not drive the original inhabitants out of the city. Deborah and Barak's song, following the victory over Sisera, mentions fighting that went on between Taanach and the waters of Megiddo (Judges 5:19). Under King Solomon's governmental organization, Baana was the officer in charge of supplying the king with provisions from Taanach. Same as Tanach.

FIRST REFERENCE
JOSHUA 12:21
LAST REFERENCE
1 CHRONICLES 7:29

TAANATH-SHILOH OT1

Approach of Shiloh

A city on the border of the tribe of Ephraim's territory.

ONLY REFERENCE
JOSHUA 16:6

TABBATH OT1

A place to which the Midianites and their allies fled after Gideon and his men overcame them.

ONLY REFERENCE
JUDGES 7:22

TABERAH OT2
Burning

A place in the wilderness of Paran where the Israelites complained and the fire of the Lord burned the edges of the campground. When Moses prayed, the fire died down.

FIRST REFERENCE
NUMBERS 11:3
LAST REFERENCE
DEUTERONOMY 9:22

TABOR OT10
Broken region

1) A mountain that became a landmark on the border of the tribe of Issachar's territory. This landmark was mentioned when Joshua cast lots in Shiloh to provide territory for the seven tribes that had yet to receive an inheritance. Through Deborah, God commanded Barak to draw up to Mount Tabor before engaging in battle with Sisera, commander of the Canaanites.

FIRST REFERENCE
JOSHUA 19:22
LAST REFERENCE
HOSEA 5:1

2) A plain (also translated "the oak of Tabor" [ESV] or the "great tree of Tabor" [NIV]) where Samuel told Saul he would meet three men who would give him two loaves of bread following Saul's anointing as king of Israel.

ONLY REFERENCE
1 SAMUEL 10:3

3) One of the forty-eight cities given to the Levites as God had commanded. Tabor was given to them by the tribe of Zebulun.

ONLY REFERENCE
1 CHRONICLES 6:77

TADMOR OT2
Palm city

A city in the wilderness, called Tamar in some translations, that King Solomon fortified.

FIRST REFERENCE
1 KINGS 9:18
LAST REFERENCE
2 CHRONICLES 8:4

TAHAPANES OT1

An Egyptian city that, according to Jeremiah, had "shaved the crown of [Israel's] head" because Israel had forsaken the Lord. By this, God meant that Egypt had humbled the Israelites. Same as Tahpanhes and Tehaphnehes.

ONLY REFERENCE
JEREMIAH 2:16

TAHATH OT2
The bottom (as depressed)

A campsite of the Israelites on their way to the Promised Land.

FIRST REFERENCE
NUMBERS 33:26
LAST REFERENCE
NUMBERS 33:27

TAHPANHES OT5

An Egyptian city to which the Jews of Judah fled to escape the rule of the Chaldean (Babylonian) Empire. Jeremiah foretold that his people would not escape Babylon by their flight to Tahpanhes, because the Babylonian king Nebuchadnezzar would also attack and destroy Egypt. Same as Tahapanes and Tehaphnehes.

FIRST REFERENCE
JEREMIAH 43:7
LAST REFERENCE
JEREMIAH 46:14

TAHTIM-HODSHI OT1

Lower ones monthly

After he went to Gilead, Joab, King David's battle commander, visited this land when he took a census of the Israelites.

ONLY REFERENCE
2 SAMUEL 24:6

TAMAR OT2

A palm tree

A city identifying the boundary of the tribe of Gad in Ezekiel's vision of the land of Israel.

FIRST REFERENCE
EZEKIEL 47:19
LAST REFERENCE
EZEKIEL 48:28

TANACH OT1

One of the forty-eight cities given to the Levites as God had commanded. Tanach was given to them by the tribe of Manasseh. Same as Taanach.

ONLY REFERENCE
JOSHUA 21:25

TAPPUAH OT5

An apple

1) A kingdom on the western side of the Jordan River that Joshua and his troops conquered. This city became part of the inheritance of the tribe of Judah following the conquest of the Promised Land.

FIRST REFERENCE
JOSHUA 12:17
LAST REFERENCE
JOSHUA 15:34

2) A land on the border of the territory of the tribes of Manasseh and Ephraim. Though the land of Tappuah belonged to Manasseh, the town of the same name belonged to Ephraim.

FIRST REFERENCE
JOSHUA 16:8
LAST REFERENCE
JOSHUA 17:8

TARAH OT2

A campsite of the Israelites on their way to the Promised Land.

FIRST REFERENCE
NUMBERS 33:27
LAST REFERENCE
NUMBERS 33:28

TARALAH OT1

A reeling

A city that was part of the inheritance of the tribe of Benjamin.

ONLY REFERENCE
JOSHUA 18:27

TARSHISH OT21
A gem, perhaps the topaz (as the region of the stone)

A Phoenician seaport in southern Spain that traded in silver, iron, tin, and lead and formed the western limit of the world with which the Jews were familiar. The phrase "ships of Tarshish" became synonymous with large trading vessels such as those Solomon used in his trade with King Hiram of Tyre. The psalmist envisioned the kings of Tarshish bringing King Solomon gifts (Psalm 72:10).

Jehoshaphat, king of Judah, joined with the wicked King Ahaziah of Israel to trade with Tarshish, but the ships they built in Ezion-gaber were broken and never made the voyage.

In the psalms and the prophecy of Isaiah, the power of these vessels bows down before God. Their impressive strength cannot compare to His. Isaiah promises that when God gathers people of "all nations and tongues" to see His glory, the ships of Tarshish will bring God's people from afar (Isaiah 66:18).

When Jonah tried to flee from God's command to preach to Nineveh, he headed for Tarshish. But as the ship he boarded at Joppa was about to be shipwrecked, the sailors threw the prophet overboard at his own command. Same as Tharshish.

FIRST REFERENCE
2 CHRONICLES 9:21
LAST REFERENCE
JONAH 4:2
KEY REFERENCES
2 CHRONICLES 9:21; 20:35–37;
ISAIAH 66:19; JONAH 1:3

TARSUS NT5
A flat basket

The main city of the Roman province of Cilicia, Tarsus was the hometown of Saul (later Paul). It was also one of the first places the apostle visited with Barnabas. When Barnabas was sent to Antioch following Peter's vision about God's acceptance of Gentiles, he stopped in Tarsus to collect Saul and bring him along. When Paul was accused of bringing a Gentile into the temple, he spoke to the crowd and proudly declared that he was born in Tarsus.

FIRST REFERENCE
ACTS 9:11
LAST REFERENCE
ACTS 22:3

TEHAPHNEHES OT1

An Egyptian city that the prophet Ezekiel said would see God "break. . .the yokes of Egypt" as its people went into captivity. Same as Tahpanhes and Tahapanes.

ONLY REFERENCE
EZEKIEL 30:18

TEKOA OT4
A trumpet

A city of Judah that King Rehoboam fortified in order to defend his nation. King Jehoshaphat of Judah led his troops into the wilderness of Tekoa. The day before they set out, all Judah had participated in a prayer meeting to praise and petition God because the nation was about to be attacked by the Ammonites, the Moabites, and the people of Mount Seir. Following Jehoshaphat's public prayer, Jahaziel foretold that God would deliver the nation of Judah. The next morning, singers praised God while the army set out, and God turned Judah's enemies upon each other and destroyed them.

The prophet Amos was a herder of Tekoa. Same as Tekoah.

FIRST REFERENCE
2 CHRONICLES 11:6
LAST REFERENCE
AMOS 1:1

TEKOAH — OT3
A trumpet

King David's battle commander Joab called on a wise woman from Tekoah to show the mourning king that he should allow his son Absalom to come back to Jerusalem. Absalom had murdered his half brother Amnon for raping their sister Tamar; then he had fled Israel. Same as Tekoa.

FIRST REFERENCE
2 SAMUEL 14:2
LAST REFERENCE
2 SAMUEL 14:9

TEL-ABIB — OT1
Mound of green growth

A town on the Chebar River where the prophet Ezekiel visited some exiles from Judah. After he had been there seven days, the Lord told him he was a watchman for Israel.

ONLY REFERENCE
EZEKIEL 3:15

TELAIM — OT1
Lambs

A place where King Saul numbered his troops before a battle with the Amalekites.

ONLY REFERENCE
1 SAMUEL 15:4

TELASSAR — OT1

When Rabshakeh threatened the people of Judah with destruction, he used the Mesopotamian city of Telassar as an example of a city that had been destroyed by his nation. Same as Thelasar.

ONLY REFERENCE
ISAIAH 37:12

TELEM — OT1
Oppression

A city that became part of the inheritance of the tribe of Judah following the conquest of the Promised Land.

ONLY REFERENCE
JOSHUA 15:24

TEL-HARESHA — OT1

Mound of workmanship

A city in Judah to which captives returned after the Babylonian exile. These people could not prove they were Israelites. Same as Tel-harsa.

ONLY REFERENCE
NEHEMIAH 7:61

TEL-HARSA — OT1

Mound of workmanship

A city in Judah to which captives returned after the Babylonian exile. These people could not prove they were Israelites. Same as Tel-haresha.

ONLY REFERENCE
EZRA 2:59

TEL-MELAH — OT2

Mound of salt

A city in Judah to which captives returned after the Babylonian exile. These people could not prove they were Israelites.

FIRST REFERENCE
EZRA 2:59
LAST REFERENCE
NEHEMIAH 7:61

TEMA — OT1

A place in Arabia named for one of Ishmael's sons who settled there. Job compares his grief over the lack of support he received from friends to a caravan from Tema that searched for water but did not find it.

ONLY REFERENCE
JOB 6:19

TEMAN — OT5

The south (as being on the right hand of a person facing east)

An area of Edom that the prophets foresaw being destroyed. Ezekiel said it would be made desolate, and Amos declared God would send a fire that would "devour the palaces of Bozrah" (Amos 1:12). Habakkuk saw God coming from Teman in all His glory.

FIRST REFERENCE
JEREMIAH 49:7
LAST REFERENCE
HABAKKUK 3:3

THARSHISH — OT3

A gem, perhaps a topaz (as the region of the stone)

A Phoenician seaport in southern Spain that traded in silver, iron, tin, and lead and formed the western limit of the world with which the Jews were familiar. Its ships were large trading vessels such as those Solomon used in his trade with King Hiram of Tyre. Same as Tarshish.

FIRST REFERENCE
I KINGS 10:22
LAST REFERENCE
I KINGS 22:48

THEBEZ   OT3
Whiteness

Gideon's son Abimelech conquered this city, but the people of Thebez continued to defend a tower. When Abimelech began to burn the tower, a woman dropped a piece of a millstone on his head, breaking his skull. He called his armor bearer to kill him so it would not be said that he was killed by a woman.

FIRST REFERENCE
JUDGES 9:50
LAST REFERENCE
2 SAMUEL 11:21

THELASAR   OT1

When Rabshakeh threatened the people of Judah with destruction, he used the Mesopotamian city of Thelasar as an example of a city that had been destroyed by his nation. Same as Telassar.

ONLY REFERENCE
2 KINGS 19:12

THESSALONICA
NT6
Thessalos conquest

A Macedonian city where Paul preached in the synagogue. Though some people of the city believed, others accused Christians of believing in a king other than Caesar. The Christians of the city sent Paul and Silas away to Berea. Thessalonica was the hometown of Aristarchus, who sailed with Paul as he was on his way to Rome. While Paul was

in Thessalonica, the Colossians helped to meet his ministry needs.

FIRST REFERENCE
ACTS 17:1
LAST REFERENCE
2 TIMOTHY 4:10

THIMNATHAH
OT1
A portion assigned

A town that became part of the inheritance of Dan when Joshua cast lots in Shiloh to provide territory for the seven tribes that had yet to receive their land.

ONLY REFERENCE
JOSHUA 19:43

THREE TAVERNS
NT1

A place between the Forum of Appius and Rome where some Christians met Paul as he traveled to Rome.

ONLY REFERENCE
ACTS 28:15

THYATIRA   NT4

A city of Asia Minor, in the Roman province of Asia, where Lydia was converted to Christ. Here Paul was followed by a slave girl possessed with a spirit of divination. After Paul cast out the spirit, her owners brought him and Silas in front of the magistrates. Paul and Silas were beaten and imprisoned, but an earthquake opened the prison doors for them. They remained in their cell and preached to their jailor, who was converted.

Thyatira was one of the seven churches of Asia Minor addressed in the book of Revelation. Though the church in that city was faithful in many ways, it did not restrain a false prophet. She misled believers into practicing fornication and eating meat that had been sacrificed to idols. The Lord called the Christians of Thyatira to repent.

FIRST REFERENCE
ACTS 16:14
LAST REFERENCE
REVELATION 2:24

TIBERIAS NT3
Pertaining to the river Tiberis or Tiber

The Sea of Tiberias is another name for the Sea of Galilee. The city of Tiberias, on the west shore of the sea, was named to honor the emperor Tiberius.

FIRST REFERENCE
JOHN 6:1
LAST REFERENCE
JOHN 21:1

TIBHATH OT1
Slaughter

A city of Hadadezer, king of Zobah. After defeating Hadadezer in battle, King David brought bronze from Tibhath to Israel. When Solomon built the temple, he made various bronze temple implements from the metal his father, David, had collected there.

ONLY REFERENCE
1 CHRONICLES 18:8

TIMNAH OT3
A portion assigned

1) A city that became part of the inheritance of the tribe of Judah following the conquest of the Promised Land. Same as Timnath 1.

ONLY REFERENCE
JOSHUA 15:57

2) A town that formed part of the border of the tribe of Judah's territory. During the reign of King Ahaz, it was one of the cities of the southern low country of Judah that was invaded and occupied by the Philistines. The invasion caused Ahaz to call on the Assyrians for help. Same as Timnath 2.

FIRST REFERENCE
JOSHUA 15:10
LAST REFERENCE
2 CHRONICLES 28:18

TIMNATH OT8
A portion assigned

1) A city where Tamar lay in wait for her father-in-law, Judah, and seduced him, because he had not given his son Shelah to her as a husband. Same as Timnah 1.

FIRST REFERENCE
GENESIS 38:12
LAST REFERENCE
GENESIS 38:14

2) Hometown of Samson's Philistine wife. Here Samson also tore apart a lion. When he returned later, there was a swarm of bees and honey in the carcass. Same as Timnah 2.

FIRST REFERENCE
JUDGES 14:1
LAST REFERENCE
JUDGES 14:5

TIMNATH-HERES
OT1
Portion of the sun

A city in Mount Ephraim, on the north side of the hill Gaash, Timnath-heres was part of Joshua's inheritance and was the place where he was buried. Same as Timnath-serah.

ONLY REFERENCE
JUDGES 2:9

TIMNATH-SERAH
OT2
Portion of the sun

A city in Mount Ephraim that Israel gave as an inheritance to Joshua. Same as Timnath-heres.

FIRST REFERENCE
JOSHUA 19:50
LAST REFERENCE
JOSHUA 24:30

TIPHSAH
OT1
Ford

1) A ford on the Euphrates River that marked a boundary of Solomon's kingdom.

ONLY REFERENCE
1 KINGS 4:24

2) A town of Israel that refused to support Menahem as king. Menahem attacked Tiphsah and slaughtered all its pregnant women when he won the city.

ONLY REFERENCE
2 KINGS 15:16

TIRZAH
OT14
Delightsomeness

A Canaanite city on the western side of the Jordan River that was conquered by Joshua and the Israelites. During the divided kingdom, Tirzah became the capital of Israel.

When Jeroboam's son became sick, his wife went to the prophet Ahijah to ask if he would be healed. The prophet told her that as soon as she entered Tirzah, her son would die. Though Baasha, king of Israel, began to build Ramah, when King Ben-hadad of Syria attacked his nation, Baasha returned to Tirzah, which remained the capital for the rest of his reign. Omri besieged the city, and King Zimri burned his own palace and died in it. Omri became king of Israel and kept the capital in Tirzah for six years, then moved it to Samaria.

FIRST REFERENCE
JOSHUA 12:24
LAST REFERENCE
SONG OF SOLOMON 6:4
KEY REFERENCES
1 KINGS 15:20–21; 16:15–18

TISHBE OT6
Recourse

Referred to only in the description of "Elijah the Tishbite," this town in Gilead was the prophet's home.

FIRST REFERENCE
1 KINGS 17:1
LAST REFERENCE
2 KINGS 9:36

TOB OT2
Good

The land to which Jephthah fled after his half brothers pushed him out of Gilead. He gathered adventurers around him in Tob and ended up becoming Gilead's battle commander.

FIRST REFERENCE
JUDGES 11:3
LAST REFERENCE
JUDGES 11:5

TOCHEN OT1
A fixed quantity

A city that was part of the land of the tribe of Simeon.

ONLY REFERENCE
1 CHRONICLES 4:32

TOLAD OT1
Posterity

A city that was part of the land of the tribe of Simeon.

ONLY REFERENCE
1 CHRONICLES 4:29

TOPHEL OT1
Quagmire

A place in the wilderness through which the Israelites traveled on their way to the Promised Land. Near here Moses spoke the teachings of the book of Deuteronomy to Israel.

ONLY REFERENCE
DEUTERONOMY 1:1

TOPHET OT9
A smiting (figuratively, contempt)

A place in the Valley of Hinnom, southwest of Jerusalem, where children were sacrificed to the Ammonite god Moloch. Jeremiah foretold that because of the evil Judah had done, the valley would be filled with the dead and Judah would become desolate. Same as Topheth.

FIRST REFERENCE
ISAIAH 30:33
LAST REFERENCE
JEREMIAH 19:14

TOPHETH OT1
A smiting (figuratively, contempt)

When Josiah was king of Judah, he desecrated this place in the Valley of Hinnom where children had been sacrificed to the Ammonite god Moloch. Same as Tophet.

ONLY REFERENCE
2 KINGS 23:10

TRACHONITIS
NT1

Rough district

A Roman province ruled by Philip, brother of Herod Antipas.

ONLY REFERENCE
LUKE 3:1

TROAS
NT6

A Trojan or the plain of Troy

A Roman colony and seaport that lay ten miles from ancient Troy. Here Paul received the vision of a man of Macedonia who asked the apostle to come there and help. Immediately Paul and his companions left Troas and set out for Macedonia. As Paul headed toward Jerusalem, he and seven companions traveled to Troas and stayed there for a week. The night before their departure, Paul preached until midnight. Eutychus, a young man who was seated in a window, fell asleep and tumbled to the ground. The believers took him up, dead, but through a miracle, Paul brought him back to life.

FIRST REFERENCE
ACTS 16:8
LAST REFERENCE
2 TIMOTHY 4:13

TROGYLLIUM
NT1

A town of Asia Minor, opposite the island of Samos, where Paul stayed as he headed toward Jerusalem. Here he stayed for a while during his journey between Samos and Miletus.

ONLY REFERENCE
ACTS 20:15

TYRE
OT25/NT12

A stone (by implication, a knife)

A fortified Phoenician port and center of trade, Tyre had two harbors and consisted of both an island and a city on the mainland. King Hiram of Tyre built a causeway to connect the two parts of the city. Tyre became part of the inheritance of Asher when Joshua cast lots in Shiloh to provide territory for the seven tribes that had yet to receive their land. But it remained in the hands of the Phoenicians, whose trade in valuable goods such as gold, precious stones, and almug wood extended throughout the Mediterranean and as far as Ophir (1 Kings 9:28; 10:11). A joint trading venture between Israel and Tyre brought King Solomon "gold, and silver, ivory, and apes, and peacocks" (1 Kings 10:22).

King David developed a trade relationship with Tyre and its king, Hiram (Huram), who provided trees, carpenters, and masons to build David's palace. Before his death, David had begun to gather cedar logs through trade with Tyre; they were to be used by his son Solomon to build the temple in Jerusalem. When Solomon took the throne, he expanded the trade and labor relationship between the countries, sending to Hiram for cedar and fir trees, gold, and skilled carpenters to build the temple. In return, Solomon gave Hiram food for his royal household. The two kings made a peace treaty with each other.

After Israel built a fleet of ships, Hiram sent Solomon sailors. From Tyre Solomon also hired the workman Huram (Huram-abi) to do metalwork, carpentry, and stonework for the temple (2 Chronicles 2:13–14). After twenty years, Solomon gave Hiram twenty towns in Galilee as thanks for his help, but the king of Tyre was not pleased with them.

When Nehemiah rebuked the Israelites for trading on the sabbath, men of Tyre who lived in Jerusalem were bringing in fish and other goods to sell on the day of worship.

In his oracle about Tyre, the prophet Isaiah foresaw the city's destruction because of its pride. Joel rebuked Tyre for sending the people of Judah into slavery with the Greeks (Joel 3:4–6).

People in Tyre heard of the miracles of Jesus and came to follow Him. Because a huge crowd gathered around Him, Jesus preached to them from a boat. When Jesus took to task Israel's cities of Chorazin and Bethsaida, where He had done many miracles, He told them that if these works had been done in Tyre and its sister city, Sidon, the people would have repented. On judgment day, He declared, it would be more bearable for those Gentile cities than for the cities of Israel that denied Him.

When Jesus traveled to Tyre and Sidon, a Syro-Phoenician woman insisted that He help her daughter, who had an unclean spirit. Jesus pointed out that He was sent to Israel and compared the woman to a dog. Instead of taking offense, she reminded Him that crumbs fell from the master's table to the dogs. Commending her great faith, Jesus healed her daughter.

King Herod Agrippa, who ruled Judea, had a dispute with Tyre and its sister city, Sidon. The cities relied on food from Judea. Because their need was great, they gained the support of the king's chamberlain (an official who cared for his sleeping quarters) and tried to make peace with Herod (Acts 12:20). When they met with the king, he made a speech. "This is the voice of a god, not of a man" they declared. Because Herod Agrippa did not correct them, an angel of God struck the king down; he was eaten by worms and died (Acts 12:22–23 NIV).

On his way to Jerusalem, Paul stayed in Tyre for a week with the believers in the city, who warned him not to go to Jerusalem. Same as Tyrus.

FIRST REFERENCE
JOSHUA 19:29
LAST REFERENCE
ACTS 21:7
KEY REFERENCES
I KINGS 5:1–12; 9:10–13; I CHRONICLES 22:4; MATTHEW 11:21–24

TYRUS   OT22
A rock

Another name for Tyre, used in the King James Version exclusively in the Prophets. Jeremiah listed Tyrus with the kingdoms on which God would bring disaster through the expansion of the Chaldean (Babylonian) Empire under Nebuchadnezzar. God told the prophet to send this message to Tyrus through the envoys who came to Jerusalem.

Ezekiel foretold Tyrus's complete destruction with God's words: "Therefore thus saith the Lord GOD; Behold, I am against thee, O Tyrus, and will cause many nations to come up against thee, as the sea causeth his waves to come up. And they shall destroy the walls of Tyrus, and break down her towers: I will also scrape her dust from her, and make her like the top of a rock. It shall be a place for the spreading of nets in the midst of the sea" (Ezekiel 26:3–5).

Despite its trade that spanned much of the known world and the ships that carried diverse goods, mourning would fall upon the nations Tyrus traded with. The city's destruction came because her heart grew proud (Ezekiel 28:5).

Though Nebuchadnezzar, king of Babylon, besieged Tyrus for thirteen years, he could not conquer the island portion of the city. Instead of Tyrus, God gave Egypt to Babylon.

The prophet Amos declared that God would not turn back His wrath because Tyrus broke a treaty and delivered captives to Edom. For this God would bring down fire on Tyrus's walls (Amos 1:9–10).

Zechariah foretold that though Tyrus had built a stronghold and achieved power on the sea, neither would avail. She would lose her possessions and power. Under the attack of Alexander the Great, all this came true. Same as Tyre.

FIRST REFERENCE
JEREMIAH 25:22
LAST REFERENCE
ZECHARIAH 9:3
KEY REFERENCE
EZEKIEL 26:2–28:19

-U-

ULAI
OT2

A river (or canal) near Susa, in the Elam province. Here Daniel had his vision of the ram and the goat, which symbolized the Median, Persian, and Greek empires. After he had seen the vision, a man's voice came from between the riverbanks, telling Gabriel to make the meaning of the vision clear to Daniel. The prophet saw a man who explained that the vision had to do with the "time of the end" (Daniel 8:19 NIV) and identified the vision with each of those empires.

FIRST REFERENCE
DANIEL 8:2
LAST REFERENCE
DANIEL 8:16

UMMAH
OT1
Association

A city that became part of the inheritance of Asher when Joshua cast lots in Shiloh to provide territory for the seven tribes that had yet to receive their land.

ONLY REFERENCE
JOSHUA 19:30

UPHAZ
OT2

A place from which gold was brought to create idols. In Daniel's vision, a man wore a belt of gold from Uphaz. Possibly the same as Ophir.

FIRST REFERENCE
JEREMIAH 10:9
LAST REFERENCE
DANIEL 10:5

UR
OT4
Flame; hence the east (being the region of light)

A Mesopotamian place, probably a city, where Abram's father, Terah, and his family lived. Terah's third son, Haran, died in Ur. Then the family left Ur to travel to Canaan. Genesis 15:7 and Nehemiah 9:7 identify God as the force behind their move and the One who called them to found a new nation.

FIRST REFERENCE
GENESIS 11:28
LAST REFERENCE
NEHEMIAH 9:7

UZ
OT3
Consultation

A land east of Judah where Job lived. In Jeremiah's prophecies, Uz is listed among the lands on which God's wrath would fall through the conquest of the Chaldean king Nebuchadnezzar.

FIRST REFERENCE
JOB 1:1
LAST REFERENCE
LAMENTATIONS 4:21

UZZA — OT2
Strength

A garden where King Amon of Israel was buried after he was murdered by his own servants.

FIRST REFERENCE
2 KINGS 21:18
LAST REFERENCE
2 KINGS 21:26

UZZEN-SHERAH — OT1
Plat of Sheerah

A town built by Sherah, the daughter of Ephraim.

ONLY REFERENCE
1 CHRONICLES 7:24

-Z-

ZAANAIM — OT1
Removals

Though translated "the plain of Zaanaim" in the King James Version, modern translations seem agreed that it is some kind of tree: for example, "the great tree" (NIV), "the terebinth tree" (NKJV), or "the oak" (ESV) in Zaanaim (or Zaananim). Here Heber the Kenite pitched his tent before the battle between Sisera and Barak. Sisera came to the tent of Heber's wife, Jael, and was killed by her. Same as Zaanannim.

ONLY REFERENCE
JUDGES 4:11

ZAANAN — OT1
Sheep pasture

A town of Judah that Micah foresaw would cower behind its doors when the Assyrians attacked.

ONLY REFERENCE
MICAH 1:11

ZAANANNIM — OT1
Removals

A town that became part of the inheritance of Naphtali when Joshua cast lots in Shiloh to provide territory for the seven tribes that had yet to receive their land. Same as Zaanaim.

ONLY REFERENCE
JOSHUA 19:33

ZABULON — NT3
Greek form of Zebulun

The land inherited by the tribe of Zebulun. Matthew places the city of Capernaum within its borders and points out that by living there, Jesus fulfilled the prophecy in Isaiah 9:1–2 that this tribe would see a great light.

FIRST REFERENCE
MATTHEW 4:13
LAST REFERENCE
REVELATION 7:8

ZAIR — OT1
Little; few; young; ignoble

When Edom revolted against Judah's rule, Joram (Jehoram), king of Judah, attacked this place in Edom then fled without fully subduing the Edomites.

ONLY REFERENCE
2 KINGS 8:21

ZALMON — OT1
Shady

After Abimelech and his men razed the city of Shechem, they went to Mount Zalmon to get wood to burn its remaining tower. Same as Salmon.

ONLY REFERENCE
JUDGES 9:48

ZALMONAH — OT2
Shadiness

A campsite of the Israelites on their way to the Promised Land.

FIRST REFERENCE
NUMBERS 33:41
LAST REFERENCE
NUMBERS 33:42

ZANOAH — OT4
Rejected

1) A city that became part of the inheritance of the tribe of Judah following the conquest of the Promised Land. Hanun and the inhabitants of Zanoah worked on Jerusalem's Valley Gate during the repairs under Nehemiah. Zanoah was resettled by the Jews after the Babylonian exile.

FIRST REFERENCE
JOSHUA 15:34
LAST REFERENCE
NEHEMIAH 11:30

2) Another city that became part of the inheritance of the tribe of Judah following the conquest of the Promised Land.

ONLY REFERENCE
JOSHUA 15:56

ZAPHON — OT1
Boreal

A city east of the Jordan River that Moses made part of the inheritance of Gad.

ONLY REFERENCE
JOSHUA 13:27

ZAREAH — OT1
A wasp (as stinging)

A city of Judah resettled by the Jews after the Babylonian exile.

ONLY REFERENCE
NEHEMIAH 11:29

ZARED OT1
Lined with shrubbery

A valley between Moab and Edom where the Israelites camped before they fought with the Amorite king Sihon. Same as Zered.

ONLY REFERENCE
NUMBERS 21:12

ZAREPHATH OT3
Refinement

A Phoenician city north of Tyre. During a drought he had predicted, the prophet Elijah hid from King Ahab of Israel in the Cerith ravine. When the Cerith Brook dried up, God sent Elijah to Zarephath. He asked a widow there for water and food, and she told him she was making a last meal for herself and her son. Through the prophet, God promised that her meager provisions would not run out until the Lord sent rain on the land. Later Elijah brought the son back to life, proving to the woman that he was a man of God and that the word of the Lord was true.

Obadiah foretold that Israelite exiles would possess the land as far north as Zarephath. Same as Sarepta.

FIRST REFERENCE
I KINGS 17:9
LAST REFERENCE
OBADIAH 1:20

ZARETAN OT1
To pierce; to puncture

This town was near Adam, where the Israelites crossed the Jordan River on their way to the Promised Land and the water stood up in a heap so they could cross on dry ground. Called Zarethan in some translations. Same as Zarthan.

ONLY REFERENCE
JOSHUA 3:16

ZARETH-SHAHAR OT1
Splendor of the dawn

A city east of the Jordan River that was part of the inheritance of the tribe of Reuben. Zareth-shahar was "in the mount of the valley."

ONLY REFERENCE
JOSHUA 13:19

ZARTANAH OT1
To pierce; to puncture

Under King Solomon's governmental organization, a place responsible for supplying provisions for the king.

ONLY REFERENCE
I KINGS 4:12

ZARTHAN OT1
To pierce; to puncture

In the plain of the Jordan River, between Succoth and Zarthan, workers cast the brass pieces for

King Solomon's temple. Same as Zaretan.

ONLY REFERENCE
I KINGS 7:46

ZEBAIM — OT2
Gazelles

A city in Judah to which captives returned after the Babylonian exile.

FIRST REFERENCE
EZRA 2:57
LAST REFERENCE
NEHEMIAH 7:59

ZEBOIIM — OT2
Gazelles

A Canaanite kingdom that, along with some Canaanite allies, made war with Chedorlaomer, king of Elam, and his Mesopotamian allies. After serving Chedorlaomer for twelve years, Zeboiim and the other Canaanites rebelled without success against the Mesopotamians. Same as Zeboim 1.

FIRST REFERENCE
GENESIS 14:2
LAST REFERENCE
GENESIS 14:8

ZEBOIM — OT5
Gazelles

1) One of the five Canaanite cities of the plain that probably lay south of the Dead Sea. Along with Sodom and Gomorrah, Zeboim was destroyed by fire and brimstone. In the book of Hosea, God considers overthrowing Ephraim as he did Zeboim, but His heart changes and He doesn't do it. Same as Zeboiim.

FIRST REFERENCE
GENESIS 10:19
LAST REFERENCE
HOSEA 11:8

2) A valley in the land of the tribe of Benjamin. When the Philistines camped at Michmash, they sent raiding parties "toward the borderland overlooking the Valley of Zeboim facing the desert" (1 Samuel 13:18 NIV). The Benjaminites resettled Zeboim after the Babylonian exile.

FIRST REFERENCE
I SAMUEL 13:18
LAST REFERENCE
NEHEMIAH 11:34

ZEBULUN — OT17
Habitation

Of the forty-four references in scripture to the word Zebulun, fewer than half refer specifically to the land of that name. More often, details about this territory are connected to references to the tribe.

In his blessing on Zebulun, Jacob declared, "Zebulun shall dwell at the haven of the sea; and he shall be for an haven of ships; and his border shall be unto Zidon" (Genesis 49:13). Though Zebulun received a landlocked territory, after the conquest of the Promised Land, it was just east of the coastal lands of Asher, ten miles from the sea (Joshua 19:10–16). Zebulun never extended as far as Zidon, but it did encompass land of the Phoenicians, for whom Zidon was an important city.

Zebulun gave four towns to the Levites: Jokneam, Kartah, Dimnah, and Nahalal (Joshua 21:34–35). First Chronicles 6:77 adds Rimmon 1 and Tabor 3 to the tally, but it's possible Rimmon and Dimnah were the same town.

The judge Elon the Zebulonite died and was buried in Aijalon 2, a city of Zebulun.

The tribe of Zebulun never drove the Canaanites out of Kitron and Nahalon. Instead these pagan people lived with the tribe. Their influence undoubtedly led the tribe into idolatry. When King Hezekiah of Judah sent letters to Zebulun, inviting the people to celebrate Passover in Jerusalem, many scorned his message, but a few humbled themselves and came. However, the king noticed that many of these well-meaning people failed to follow the law by not purifying themselves beforehand.

Though Isaiah spoke of the gloom brought to Zebulun and Naphtali when those lands were invaded by the Assyrians, he also promised they would see a great light, and joy would be their harvest (Isaiah 9:1–3). The prophecy was fulfilled in Matthew 4:13–15 when Jesus moved to Capernaum and began preaching His Gospel message. Same as Zabulon.

FIRST REFERENCE
GENESIS 49:13
LAST REFERENCE
EZEKIEL 48:33

ZEDAD   OT2
A siding

A landmark of Israel's northern border between Lebo-hamath and Ziphron. Zedad appears in God's description of the boundaries that He gave to Moses and the vision of the restored Israel that He gave to Ezekiel.

FIRST REFERENCE
NUMBERS 34:8
LAST REFERENCE
EZEKIEL 47:15

ZELAH   OT2
A limping or full

A city that became part of the inheritance of Benjamin when Joshua cast lots in Shiloh to provide territory for the seven tribes that had yet to receive their land. Here the bones of King Saul and his son Jonathan were buried in the tomb of Saul's father, Kish. After the Philistines had recovered their bodies from the battlefield and hanged them in Beth-shan, the men of Jabesh-gilead stole back their bones. King David took the bones from the men of Jabesh-gilead and saw that they were interred in Kish's tomb.

FIRST REFERENCE
JOSHUA 18:28
LAST REFERENCE
2 SAMUEL 21:14

ZELZAH OT1
Clear shade

A city of Benjamin where Samuel foretold that Saul would meet two men who would tell him the donkeys he was searching for had been found.

ONLY REFERENCE
1 SAMUEL 10:2

ZEMARAIM OT2
Double fleece

1) A city that became part of the inheritance of Benjamin when Joshua cast lots in Shiloh to provide territory for the seven tribes that had yet to receive their land.

ONLY REFERENCE
JOSHUA 18:22

2) A mountain in Ephraim's hill country where Abijah, king of Judah, spoke to King Jeroboam of Israel and his men. Abijah told Jeroboam that their golden idols and multitude of warriors did not guarantee they would win the battle. He begged them not to fight against the Lord. Though Jeroboam surrounded the troops of Judah, God defeated Israel when His people cried out to Him and gave a battle shout.

ONLY REFERENCE
2 CHRONICLES 13:4

ZENAN OT1
Sheep pasture

A city that became part of the inheritance of the tribe of Judah following the conquest of the Promised Land.

ONLY REFERENCE
JOSHUA 15:37

ZEPHATH OT1
Watchtower

A city taken by the tribes of Judah and Simeon. They killed the people of the town, destroyed it, and renamed it Hormah. Same as Hormah.

ONLY REFERENCE
JUDGES 1:17

ZEPHATHAH OT1
Watchtower

Asa, king of Judah, fought Zerah the Ethiopian at this valley in Judah. God struck the enemy before Asa, and the Ethiopians were overthrown.

ONLY REFERENCE
2 CHRONICLES 14:10

ZER OT1
Rock

A fortified or walled city that became part of the inheritance of Naphtali when Joshua cast lots in Shiloh to provide territory for the seven tribes that had yet to receive their land.

ONLY REFERENCE
JOSHUA 19:35

ZERED OT2
Lined with shrubbery

A brook running into the southwest corner of the Dead Sea, Zered lay between Edom and Moab. God commanded Israel to cross this brook, thus ending their years of wandering in the desert. Same as Zared.

FIRST REFERENCE
DEUTERONOMY 2:13
LAST REFERENCE
DEUTERONOMY 2:14

ZEREDA OT1
Puncture

Hometown of Jeroboam, son of Nebat, who became king of Israel when King Rehoboam offended his people.

ONLY REFERENCE
I KINGS 11:26

ZEREDATHAH OT1
Puncture

A place in the plain of the Jordan River near which the brass implements for the temple were cast.

ONLY REFERENCE
2 CHRONICLES 4:17

ZERERATH OT1
Puncture

A place to which the Midianite army fled when Gideon and his three hundred troops attacked them at Phurah.

ONLY REFERENCE
JUDGES 7:22

ZIDON OT20
Lie alongside (as in catching fish)

A Phoenician seaport north of Tyre, sometimes called "great Zidon" because of its power and influence. Though the tribe of Asher received Zidon as part of its territory, they never drove out the Zidonians. Instead the pagan worship of Zidon began to influence Israel and led to Israel's oppression by pagan peoples.

To Zarephath, a town belonging to Zidon, God sent the prophet Elijah after he prophesied a time of drought. Under Ezra's direction, men of Zidon brought cedar trees to Jerusalem for the rebuilding of the temple.

Against Tyre and Zidon, Phoenicia's major cities—whose names are often connected in the Prophets—Isaiah spoke an oracle of Tyre's destruction. With Tyre's destruction, Zidon, too, would be brought low. Jeremiah included Zidon in the list of places that would drink the cup of God's wrath, and the prophet warned the people of Zidon that God had given their lands into the hands of the Chaldean king Nebuchadnezzar. Before Pharaoh attacked and overwhelmed Gaza, Jeremiah foresaw that Zidon and Tyre would be cut off from all help. He foretold that God's glory would be made clear in Zidon, and His judgments would be executed there.

Through the prophet Joel, God accused Zidon of taking His silver and gold and other treasures into its temples. Zidon's inhabitants had sold the people of Judah and Jerusalem to the Greeks. God would pay them back, selling their children into Judah's hands, and they, too, would be sold to the Sabeans. Same as Sidon.

FIRST REFERENCE
GENESIS 49:13
LAST REFERENCE
ZECHARIAH 9:2
KEY REFERENCES
JUDGES 1:31; ISAIAH 23:1–4, 12; EZEKIEL 28:21–23

ZIKLAG   OT15

A town that became part of the inheritance of the tribe of Judah following the conquest of the Promised Land. Ziklag became part of the inheritance of Simeon when Joshua cast lots in Shiloh to provide territory for the seven tribes that had yet to receive their land. But it did not remain in Israel's control. When David served Achish, king of Gath, the king gave him Ziklag to live in. There many mighty men of valor came to David from Saul's own tribe of Benjamin and from Gad, Judah, and Manasseh.

The Amalekites invaded Ziklag and carried off the Israelites' wives and children, including David's wives Ahinoam and Abigail. A deserted Egyptian servant of an Amalekite brought David and his men to the Amalekites so they could rescue their families. In Ziklag David heard the news that Saul was dead, and he killed the messenger, who thought he had brought good news and expected a reward. Even after David's death, Ziklag remained in Judah's hands.

Ziklag was resettled by the Jews after the Babylonian exile.

FIRST REFERENCE
JOSHUA 15:31
LAST REFERENCE
NEHEMIAH 11:28
KEY REFERENCES
I SAMUEL 27:3–6; 30; I CHRONICLES 12:1–22

ZIMRI   OT1
Musical

One of many nations that would drink the cup of God's wrath, according to the Lord's revelation to Jeremiah. Though Zimri is listed with Elam and Media, nothing is known about this country.

ONLY REFERENCE
JEREMIAH 25:25

ZIN   OT10
A crag

A desert explored by the twelve spies whom Joshua sent to view the Promised Land. Kadesh, where Moses' sister, Miriam, died and the Israelites quarreled with God, was in the wilderness (or desert) of Zin. The Israelites camped here after they left Ezion-geber and made their way toward Mount Hor. When the Promised Land was divided between the tribes, the desert of Zin was on the southern border of the tribe of Judah's territory.

FIRST REFERENCE
NUMBERS 13:21
LAST REFERENCE
JOSHUA 15:3

Conspicuousness

Originally the name for a fortified mound on one of Jerusalem's southern hills, Zion, or Mount Zion, became the name for the temple mount, then the city of Jerusalem, and was even sometimes applied to the whole nation of Israel. It is often used in a poetic sense that glorifies God and Israel's role in bringing about His purposes.

Though the tribe of Judah had previously conquered Jerusalem, David reconquered the city, which was then held by the Jebusites. The new king promised that whoever first struck the Jebusites would be his battle commander, a position that Joab won. David lived in the fortress at first; then he built the city's fortifications while Joab restored the rest of the city.

Solomon brought the ark of the covenant to Zion, where it was placed in the temple on the spot claimed by tradition as Mount Moriah. The temple was dedicated with sacrifices and a prayer by King Solomon (2 Chronicles 5–6).

The psalms speak of Zion in connection with God's glory and salvation, and the "daughter of Zion" personifies Jerusalem and its people. God is spoken of as living in Zion (Psalms 76:2; 135:21) and having chosen Zion as His dwelling place (Psalm 132:13). During the Babylonian exile, the people of Judah wept when they thought of their destroyed city (Psalm 137:1).

Isaiah made frequent use of the word Zion. Though Judah faced destruction, the prophet foresaw a day when all nations would flow to Zion, and the law would go out of the city as God judged the nations and swords were beaten into plowshares. The prophet also encouraged the people of Zion to take heart, for God's anger would turn from them and He would punish the Assyrians, who threatened their safety. Though Judah stubbornly sought protection in Egypt, against God's command, the prophet foresaw a day when the people of Judah would again live in Zion and no longer weep. God's ransomed people would return to the city singing and would experience everlasting joy.

Because Assyria despised Jerusalem, God promised King Hezekiah of Judah that He would turn the enemy back and Assyria would never enter Jerusalem. This took place when God killed 185,000 Assyrians in their camp overnight. The rest returned home. Repeatedly Isaiah's prophecy encouraged God's people to trust in His salvation. Though Zion doubted, He could no more forget His people than a mother could forget her child, and He would comfort them. A day would come when unbelievers would not enter the city and God would return to Zion. A Redeemer would come there and Israel would turn from sin.

Jeremiah also called the people of Judah to return to God, who would bring them to Zion even as the Chaldeans (Babylonians) came from the north. When Zion would seek to repent, God would not relent for a time. But as others called her an outcast, God's compassion would turn again to Zion. Again His people would sing on Zion's heights. The prophet promised the destruction of Babylon for its mistreatment of Zion.

The prophet Joel foretold a day of the Lord in which God's wrath would fall first on His own people in Zion, then on their enemies. Obadiah added that during this day, some in Mount Zion would escape, and it would be made holy. "Deliverers will go up on Mount Zion to govern the mountains of Esau. And the kingdom will be the LORD's" (Obadiah 1:21 NIV).

Micah took the leaders of Israel to task for their dishonest rule and promised that Zion would be destroyed. He repeated Isaiah's promise that the law would go forth from Zion, swords would be beaten into plowshares, and all people would live in peace. Though Zion left the city and was sent to Babylon, she would be rescued by God.

Zephaniah encouraged Zion, telling the city she would rejoice when the Lord took away His judgments against her and came into Zion's midst and rejoiced over her. Zechariah promised that the Lord's cities would "overflow with prosperity" (Zechariah 1:17 ESV), and Zion would be comforted. Again, Zion would be the apple of God's eye, and He would make the nations that plundered her become plunder. Zion, he declared, would

rejoice when her king came to her, mounted on a donkey. This prophecy was fulfilled in Jesus' earthly ministry and will again be fulfilled in His messianic kingdom. Same as Jebus, Jebusi, Jerusalem, and Salem.

FIRST REFERENCE
2 SAMUEL 5:7
LAST REFERENCE
ZECHARIAH 9:13
KEY REFERENCES
2 SAMUEL 5:7–9; 1 CHRONICLES 11:4–9;
ISAIAH 2:1–4; MICAH 4; ZECHARIAH 9:9

ZIOR   OT1
Small

A city that became part of the inheritance of the tribe of Judah following the conquest of the Promised Land.

ONLY REFERENCE
JOSHUA 15:54

ZIPH   OT8
Flowing

1) A city that became part of the inheritance of the tribe of Judah following the conquest of the Promised Land.

When King Saul pursued him, David stayed in the wilderness of Ziph. At Horesh, in this wilderness, David made a covenant with Saul's son Jonathan. When the people of Ziph planned to hand David over to Saul, David heard about it and remained in the wilderness of Maon. Later the Ziphites came to Saul at Gibeah and told him where David was hiding. Saul brought his warriors to the wilderness of Ziph.

David slipped into their camp at night and took a spear and water jug from beside the king. In the morning, he stood a distance away and confronted Saul's battle commander Abner with his failure to protect the king. David spoke with Saul and showed him the spear, proving that he would not take advantage of the king's vulnerability and kill him during the night.

King Rehoboam of Judah fortified Ziph to defend his nation.

FIRST REFERENCE
JOSHUA 15:24
LAST REFERENCE
2 CHRONICLES 11:8

2) A city that became part of the inheritance of the tribe of Judah following the conquest of the Promised Land.

ONLY REFERENCE
JOSHUA 15:55

ZIPHRON   OT1
To be fragrant

A place that God used to identify the borders of Israel when He first gave it to His people.

ONLY REFERENCE
NUMBERS 34:9

ZIZ   OT1
Bloom

A cliff near which the Moabites and Ammonites camped when they planned to attack King Jehoshaphat of Judah. God told the king to go to Ziz, and "at the end of the brook, before the wilderness of Jeruel," he would find his enemies. The Lord promised to fight for Judah. When Judah obeyed God, the Ammonites, the Moabites, and the inhabitants of Seir fought among themselves, and Judah picked up the spoil.

ONLY REFERENCE
2 CHRONICLES 20:16

ZOAN   OT7

An Egyptian city in the northeastern portion of the Nile River delta, Zoan became the capital of northern Egypt during that nation's twenty-fifth dynasty. Taking the unfaithful northern kingdom to task, the psalmist Asaph pointed out that when Israel was in Egypt, at Zoan, God did miracles before the people of Ephraim. Despite Egypt's reputation for its wise men, in his oracle concerning that nation, Isaiah called the officials of Zoan fools. Ezekiel prophesied that God would set Zoan on fire.

FIRST REFERENCE
NUMBERS 13:22
LAST REFERENCE
EZEKIEL 30:14

ZOAR   OT10
Little

A Canaanite city of the plain that Lot looked toward when he chose the plain of the Jordan River as his land. Zoar joined in the Canaanite war against King Chedorlaomer of Elam and his Mesopotamian allies. When destruction was about to fall on Sodom, Lot asked the angels who came to warn him if instead of fleeing to the mountains, he could go to Zoar. The city was not destroyed as a result of Lot's request. He and his family left at dawn, and all except his wife, who was turned into a pillar of salt for looking back, reached the city after sunrise. Afraid to stay in Zoar, Lot and his daughters fled to a cave in the mountains.

When God showed Moses the Promised Land from Mount Nebo, he could see as far as Zoar. The prophet Isaiah foretold that Moab's fugitives would go as far as Zoar when they tried to escape their own nation's destruction. Same as Bela.

FIRST REFERENCE
GENESIS 13:10
LAST REFERENCE
JEREMIAH 48:34

ZOBA OT2
A station

After their king, Hanun, offended King David, the Ammonites hired men from Zoba to fight against Israel. Same as Zobah.

FIRST REFERENCE
2 SAMUEL 10:6
LAST REFERENCE
2 SAMUEL 10:8

ZOBAH OT11
A station

A Syrian kingdom with which King Saul battled as he fought the enemies surrounding Israel. When King David sought to control land by the Euphrates River, he fought Hadadezer, son of Zobah's king Rehob, as far as Hamath. David dedicated the plunder from his conflict with Zobah to the Lord. Later Zobah supported the Ammonites as, having offended David, they went to battle with him. Nevertheless, one man of Zobah came to serve David; one of his brave warriors was "Igal the son of Nathan of Zobah" (2 Samuel 23:36).

When David conquered Zobah, Rezon gathered rebels around him and took control of Damascus. During Solomon's lifetime, Rezon was his enemy. Same as Zoba.

FIRST REFERENCE
1 SAMUEL 14:47
LAST REFERENCE
1 CHRONICLES 19:6

ZOHELETH OT1
Crawling (that is, serpent)

A stone south of Jerusalem, near the spring of En-rogel, where King David's son Adonijah sacrificed sheep, oxen, and cattle. Adonijah also invited to this place the royal officials and his brothers—except Solomon—as he attempted to become king of Israel.

ONLY REFERENCE
1 KINGS 1:9

ZOPHIM OT1
Watchers

A field near the top of Mount Pisgah where King Balak of Moab built seven altars and burned a bull and a ram on each. He tried to convince Balaam to curse the Israelites, who were about to invade the Promised Land.

ONLY REFERENCE
NUMBERS 23:14

ZORAH OT8
Wasp (as stinging)

A town that became part of the inheritance of Dan when Joshua cast lots in Shiloh to provide territory for the seven tribes that had yet to receive their land. Samson's parents lived in Zorah when the angel of the Lord came to them to tell them they would have a son. Samson was buried between Zoar and Eshtaol in the tomb of his father, Manoah. When the Danites were seeking their own land, they sent spies from Zoar and Eshtaol to scout out the land.

FIRST REFERENCE
JOSHUA 19:41
LAST REFERENCE
2 CHRONICLES 11:10

ZOREAH OT1
A wasp (as stinging)

A city that became part of the inheritance of the tribe of Judah following the conquest of the Promised Land.

ONLY REFERENCE
JOSHUA 15:33

ZUPH OT1
Honeycomb

A district through which Saul passed as he searched for his father's lost donkeys. Saul's servant advised him to seek out Samuel the prophet and ask where they should search. Samuel told them the donkeys had been found and then anointed Saul king of Israel.

ONLY REFERENCE
1 SAMUEL 9:5

MAPS

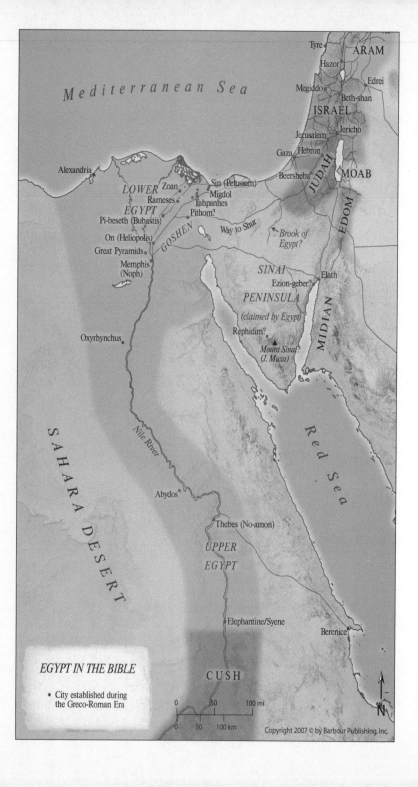

Tyre

ARAM

Hazor

Edrei

Megiddo

Beth-shan

ISRAEL

Mediterranean Sea

Jerusalem

Jericho

Gaza

Hebron

Alexandria

Beersheba

JUDAH

MOAB

LOWER Zoan

Sin (Pelusium)

Rameses

Migdol

EGYPT Tahpanhes

EDOM

Pi-beseth (Bubastis)

Pithom?

On (Heliopolis)

GOSHEN

Way to Shur

Brook of Egypt?

Great Pyramids

Memphis
(Noph)

SINAI

Ezion-geber?

Elath

PENINSULA

(claimed by Egypt)

MIDIAN

Oxyrhynchus

Rephidim?

Mount Sinai?
(J. Musa)

SAHARA

Nile River

Red Sea

Abydos

DESERT

Thebes (No-amon)

UPPER

EGYPT

Elephantine/Syene

Berenice

EGYPT IN THE BIBLE

CUSH

• City established during
the Greco-Roman Era

0   50   100 mi

0   50   100 km

N

Copyright 2007 © by Barbour Publishing, Inc.

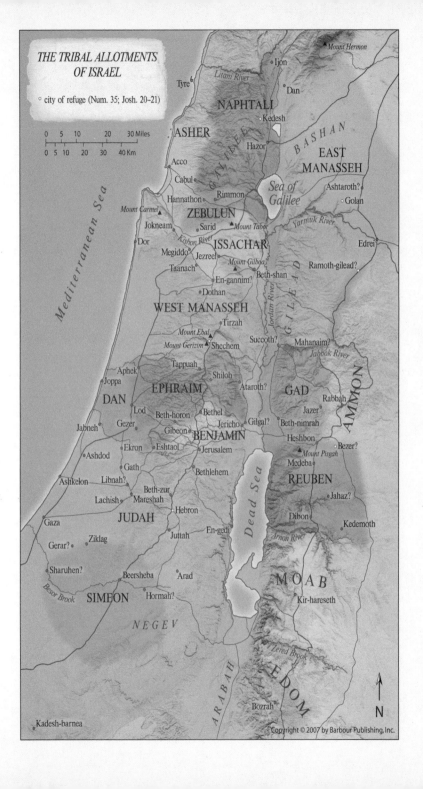

THE TRIBAL ALLOTMENTS
OF ISRAEL

○ city of refuge (Num. 35; Josh. 20–21)

0   5   10   20   30 Miles
0 5 10   20   30   40 Km

Mount Hermon

Ijon

Tyre

Litani River

Dan

NAPHTALI

ASHER

Kedesh

BASHAN

Hazor

EAST
MANASSEH

Acco

Cabul

Hannathon   Rimmon

Sea of
Galilee

Ashtaroth?

Golan

Mount Carmel

ZEBULUN

Mediterranean Sea

Jokneam

Sarid   Mount Tabor

Yarmuk River

Dor

Kishon River

ISSACHAR

Megiddo   Jezreel

Edrei

Taanach   Mount Gilboa

En-gannim?   Beth-shan

Ramoth-gilead?

Dothan

WEST MANASSEH

GILEAD

Tirzah

Mount Ebal

Jordan River

Mahanaim?

Mount Gerizim   Shechem   Succoth?

Jabbok River

Tappuah

AMMON

Aphek   Shiloh

Joppa   Ataroth?   GAD

DAN   EPHRAIM   Rabbah

Lod   Jazer

Beth-horon   Bethel   Beth-nimrah

Jabneh   Gezer   Gibeon   Jericho   Gilgal?

Ekron   Eshtaol BENJAMIN   Heshbon   Bezer?

Ashdod   Jerusalem   Mount Pisgah

Gath   Medeba

Ashkelon Libnah?   Bethlehem   REUBEN

Beth-zur

Lachish Mareshah   Jahaz?

Gaza   Hebron   Dibon

JUDAH   En-gedi   Kedemoth

Gerar? Ziklag   Juttah

Dead Sea

Arnon River

Sharuhen?   Beersheba   Arad

Besor Brook   SIMEON   Hormah?

MOAB

NEGEV   Kir-haresheth

ARABAH

Zered Brook

EDOM

Kadesh-barnea

Bozrah

N

Copyright © 2007 by Barbour Publishing, Inc.

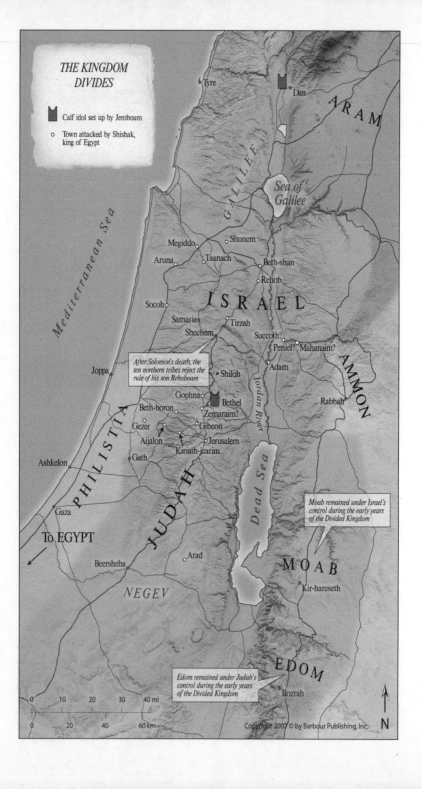

THE KINGDOM DIVIDES

◼ Calf idol set up by Jeroboam

○ Town attacked by Shishak, king of Egypt

After Solomon's death, the ten northern tribes reject the rule of his son Rehoboam

Moab remained under Israel's control during the early years of the Divided Kingdom

Edom remained under Judah's control during the early years of the Divided Kingdom

ARAM

Tyre

Dan

GALILEE

Sea of Galilee

Mediterranean Sea

Megiddo
Shunem
Aruna
Taanach
Beth-shan
Rehob
Socoh

ISRAEL

Samaria
Tirzah
Shechem
Succoth?
Peniel? Mahanaim?
Adam

AMMON

Rabbah

Joppa

Shiloh

Gophna
Bethel
Zemaraim?
Beth-horon
Gibeon
Gezer
Aijalon
Kiriath-jearim
Jerusalem
Gath

JUDAH

Ashkelon

Gaza

To EGYPT

Beersheba
Arad

NEGEV

Dead Sea

MOAB

Kir-hareseth

EDOM

Bozrah

PHILISTIA

Jordan River

0 10 20 30 40 mi

0 20 40 60 km

Copyright 2007 © by Barbour Publishing, Inc.

N

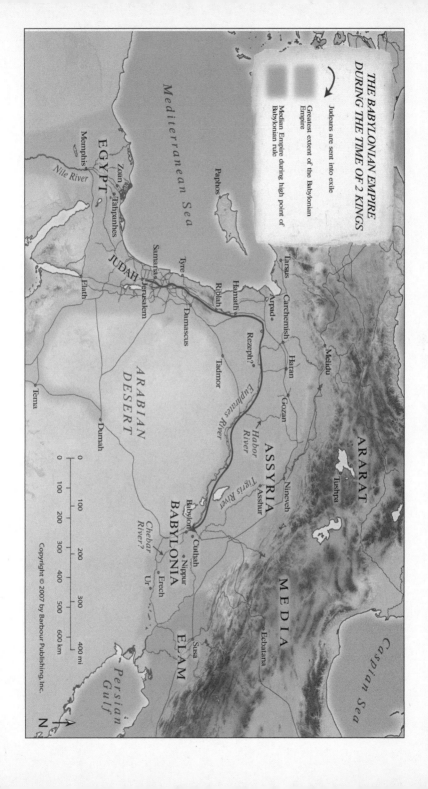

THE BABYLONIAN EMPIRE
DURING THE TIME OF 2 KINGS

Judeans are sent into exile

Greatest extent of the Babylonian
Empire

Median Empire during high point of
Babylonian rule

Mediterranean Sea

EGYPT

Memphis
Zoan
Tahpanhes
Nile River
Elath

Paphos

JUDAH
Samaria
Tyre
Jerusalem
Hamath
Riblah
Arpad
Damascus
Rezeph?
Tadmor
Tema

ARABIAN
DESERT

Dumah

Euphrates River

Tarsus
Carchemish
Haran
Gozan
Meliku

Habor River

ASSYRIA

Nineveh
Asshur
Tigris River

ARARAT

Tushpa

Caspian Sea

BABYLONIA
Babylon
Cuthah
Chebar River?
Nippur
Erech
Ur

MEDIA

Ecbatana

ELAM
Susa

Persian Gulf

0 100 200 300 400 500 600 km
0   100   200   300   400 mi

Copyright © 2007 by Barbour Publishing, Inc.

N

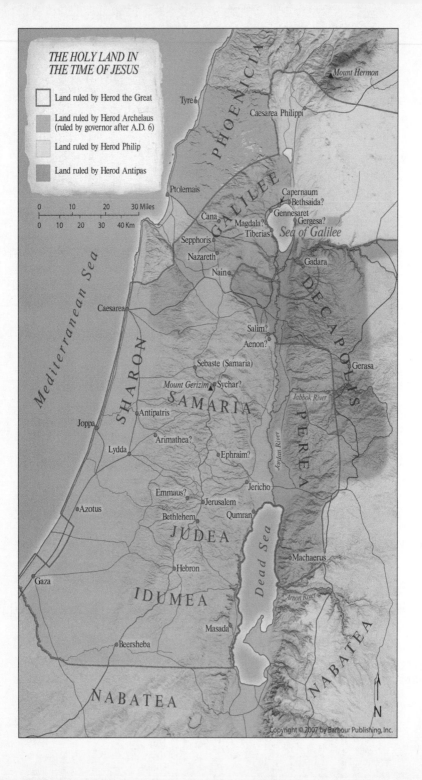

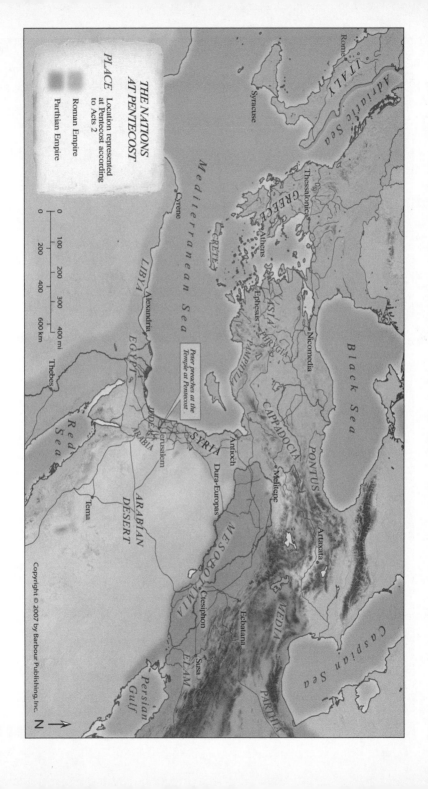

THE NATIONS
AT PENTECOST

PLACE Location represented
at Pentecost according
to Acts 2

Roman Empire
Parthian Empire

0   100   200   300   400 mi
0   200   400   600 km

Peter preaches at the
Temple at Pentecost

Copyright © 2007 by Barbour Publishing, Inc.

N →

Mediterranean Sea

Rome

ITALY

Adriatic Sea

Syracuse

GREECE

Thessalonica

Athens

CRETE

ASIA

Ephesus

PHRYGIA

PAMPHYLIA

Nicomedia

PONTUS

Black Sea

CAPPADOCIA

Cyrene

LIBYA

Alexandria

EGYPT

Thebes

Red Sea

JUDEA

Jerusalem

ARABIA

SYRIA

Antioch

Dura-Europas

Melitene

Artaxata

Caspian Sea

*ARABIAN
DESERT*

Tema

MESOPOTAMIA

Ctesiphon

Ecbatana

MEDIA

Susa

ELAM

*Persian
Gulf*

PARTHIA

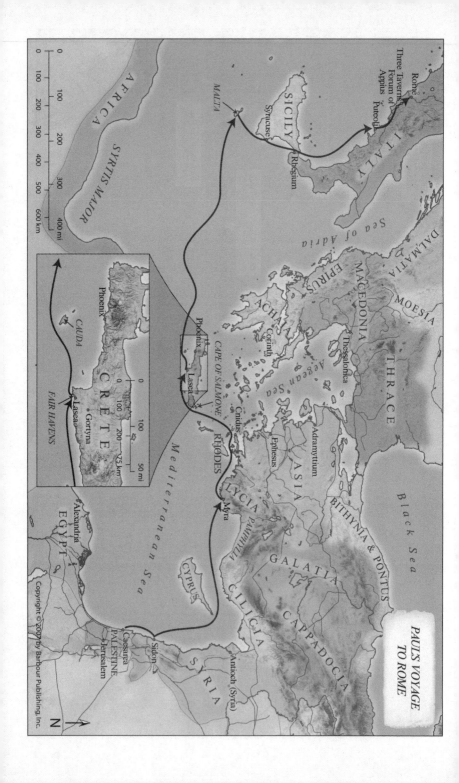

PAUL'S VOYAGE TO ROME

THE
DICTIONARY
OF
BIBLE PLACES

then look for

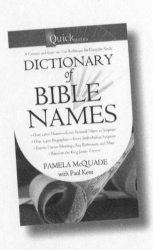

THE
DICTIONARY
OF
BIBLE NAMES

Get more from your personal Bible time by understanding the meaning and story behind some 2,000 Bible names. Covering more than 3,400 individuals in scripture, the *Dictionary of Bible Names* describes the number of times each name is mentioned, the number of individuals—male or female—who had that name, the meaning of the name, a biography of the person(s), and the first, last, and key references, chapter-and-verse, for further study. The *Dictionary of Bible Names* is perfect for personal Bible study, Sunday school or small group preparation, pleasure reading. . .even as a baby book!

Paperback • 5.25" x 8.25" • 400 pages • $9.99 • ISBN 978-1-60260-480-3

Available wherever Christian books are sold.